HIGH-INVOLVEMENT INNOVATION

HIGH-INVOLVEMENT INNOVATION

BUILDING AND SUSTAINING COMPETITIVE ADVANTAGE THROUGH CONTINUOUS CHANGE

John Bessant

School of Management
Cranfield University

WILEY

Copyright © 2003   John Wiley & Sons Ltd, The Atrium, Southern Gate, Chichester, West Sussex PO19 8SQ, England

Telephone (+44) 1243 779777

Email (for orders and customer service enquiries): cs-books@wiley.co.uk
Visit our Home Page on www.wileyeurope.com or www.wiley.com

This publication is designed to provide accurate and authoritative information in regard to the subject matter covered. It is sold on the understanding that the Publisher is not engaged in rendering professional services. If professional advice or other expert assistance is required, the services of a competent professional should be sought.

Other Wiley Editorial Offices

John Wiley & Sons Inc., 111 River Street, Hoboken, NJ 07030, USA

Jossey-Bass, 989 Market Street, San Francisco, CA 94103-1741, USA

Wiley-VCH Verlag GmbH, Boschstr. 12, D-69469 Weinheim, Germany

John Wiley & Sons Australia Ltd, 33 Park Road, Milton, Queensland 4064, Australia

John Wiley & Sons (Asia) Pte Ltd, 2 Clementi Loop #02-01, Jin Xing Distripark, Singapore 129809

John Wiley & Sons Canada Ltd, 22 Worcester Road, Etobicoke, Ontario, Canada M9W 1L1

Wiley also publishes its books in a variety of electronic formats. Some content that appears in print may not be available in electronic books.

Library of Congress Cataloging-in-Publication Data

Bessant, J. R.
    High involvement innovation : building and sustaining competitive advantage through continuous change / John Bessant.
      p. cm.
    Includes bibliographical references and index.
    ISBN 0-470-84707-7 (pbk. : alk. paper)
     1. Competition. 2. Organizational change. I. Title.

HD41.B378 2003
658.4'06—dc21

2003041083

British Library Cataloguing in Publication Data

A catalogue record for this book is available from the British Library

ISBN 0-470-84707-7

Typeset in 10/12pt Palatino by Laserwords Private Limited, Chennai, India
Printed and bound in Great Britain by TJ International, Padstow, Cornwall
This book is printed on acid-free paper responsibly manufactured from sustainable forestry in which at least two trees are planted for each one used for paper production.

CONTENTS

ACKNOWLEDGEMENTS

This book is an excellent demonstration of the principles of high-involvement innovation—quite simply, without the help of a great many people it would not have been possible to produce it! I am grateful to many friends and colleagues for their help and encouragement and would like to take this opportunity to say a large 'thank you' to all of them.

In particular I would like to mention the various members of the CIRCA team at the University of Brighton—Steve Webb, John Gilbert, Jane Burnell, Sarah Caffyn, Maeve Gallagher, Sarah Austin, Jeff Readman, Michael Vaag and, of course, Pauline Nissen, who held the whole project together, ran the Network and was always around to ensure that the project stayed on a continuously improving trajectory. In the same vein, I owe a debt to the many members of the CIRCA and CENTRIM networks who shared the company perspective on high-involvement innovation and who taught me a great deal about how the problems of implementation emerge and are handled in practice.

I would also like to thank many colleagues in the Euro—and now global—CINet for all their helpful comments and heroic efforts to put CI on the map—especially Harry Boer, Jens Riis, Frank Gertsen, Ritta Smeds, Ross Chapman, Mariano Corso, Paul Hyland, Jose Gieskes and Paul Coughlan. Thanks too are due to Kristian Stokbro and colleagues at the Confederation of Danish Industries for their long-standing interest in and support of our work on continuous improvement.

I am very grateful to several friends who patiently read the manuscript and gave me some helpful suggestions to improve it—especially Dave Francis, Raphie Kaplinsky, Carlota Perez and Howard Rush. In similar vein, my thanks go to the anonymous reviewers who provided some clear guidance on the overall shape and direction of the book, as well as encouragement to go ahead. And to the team at John Wiley—especially Steve Hardman and Sarah Booth—for steering the book through to eventual publication.

In the final stages of putting this book together in late 2002 we learned of the sudden and tragic death of Keith Pavitt, a friend and colleague at Sussex and co-author, with Joe Tidd and myself, of the textbook *Managing Innovation*. Keith had a deep understanding of the challenges in innovation and had a major influence on many of us around the world, not just through his personal insights but also in his concern that we take our own ideas further. I'd like to acknowledge the big debt I owe him and hope that this book helps throw a little more light onto questions that he helped us learn how to ask.

Finally I'd like to thank my family for putting up with my 'disappearing into my study' act on too many occasions—without their understanding and support this book would never have happened.

John Bessant
Cranfield

Chapter 1

'MANY HANDS MAKE LIGHT WORK!'

1.1 Innovation — A Survival Imperative

Change is a pre-requisite for survival amongst individual human beings and even more so in the organizations which they create and in which they work. Put simply, if an organization does not change what it offers the world—its products or services—and the ways in which it creates and delivers those offerings, it may not survive. In a competitive environment this implies a continuous race, well captured by the character of the Red Queen in Lewis Carroll's *Through the Looking Glass*, as she explained to Alice: ' "A slow sort of country!" said the Queen. "Now, here, you see, it takes all the running you can do, to keep in the same place. If you want to get somewhere else, you must run at least twice as fast as that!" '

The pressure for such constant innovation means that creativity is a key resource. But the image we often have of the creative act is one involving artists or composers, working alone and inspired by the desire to create something to leave to posterity. Whilst 'creative arts' of this kind have their cast of determined and individualistic characters, they only represent the tip of an iceberg. We may not all be a Leonardo or a Beethoven but there is a strong drive in human beings, which finds expression in all sorts of creative ways—we want to make and do new things and we want to improve the things we already have and do.

In organizational terms there is a second powerful force at work, which puts innovation centre stage. In a competitive environment there is a kind of simple Darwinian process at work—from the earliest days in the caves it was the people who worked out better ways of hunting, foraging and fire-making who stood the best chance of survival. Sad though it is to reflect upon, it was those who were most innovative in warfare—in, for example, weapons and tactics—who won battles and wars and came to dominate. On a more positive note, it was the drive to innovate in fields like health care and social welfare which meant that the species grew.

In particular, in the economic field this pattern emerged strongly. Societies that were open and exploring grew and prospered through developments in what they traded and how they carried that trade out—for example, new ships, new methods of navigation, new products and new financial mechanisms to handle transactions. Similar patterns underpin the periods of high growth that accompanied moves like that from an increasingly efficient agricultural sector towards city life and the 'Industrial Revolution' in Europe.

1.2 The Range of Innovation

Sometimes change needs to be radical. In the year 2000 a German company achieved its best ever financial performance and came to dominate the European tourism industry via a string of airlines, travel agencies, currency and insurance service businesses. Yet Preussag began life less than a century earlier as the Prussian state mining and smelting company, a public sector body set up to manage the lead mines in north-east Germany! Its journey from lead ore to leisure has been tortuous, a mixture of luck and strategy, which has taken it through such unlikely places as steel manufacturing and mouthwash sales and distribution! One constant theme though is that of *change*—if this giant had not found ways to shift its offerings and its delivery processes it would not have survived.

Alternatively, take the case of the Mannesmann brothers working in the small German town of Solingen in the late nineteenth century. Their invention of the seamless steel tube was to revolutionize the way in which pipes and tubes of all shapes and sizes were made—instead of their being welded together along a seam with the risks of bursting or leakage, pipes could now be produced that were perfect. The development of their business took the Mannesmann brothers into steel and metals manufacturing and into various applications of pipes and tubes—in construction, in distribution, in boiler making and in other fields. From the 1960s, after a strategic review of the business, they concentrated more on the higher value applications and on making engineering equipment to help use and work with tubes and other metal products. Their interests in control and instrumentation led them to learn about communications and from this they were able to make a bid—successful as it turned out—for one of the German licences for mobile telephony. By the late 1990s they had built up a large operation in mobile telephones, but their progress was eventually halted by a hostile takeover—at the time the biggest in history—by Vodafone–Airtouch.

Once again this is a story of luck and strategic judgement. There were times when the future of the company was very much in doubt and times when its fortunes shone. But the company's long-term survival depended on the ability of the organization to change and to keep changing itself in a highly turbulent and competitive world.

Not all organizations need to make such radical changes to survive. For many it is a case of continuing to do what they are good at and supporting this with a steady stream of changes and improvements. Rather than a 'great leap forward', most innovation is gradual, moving incrementally forward with a sequence of little, cumulative improvements. For example, although the invention of the electric light bulb was a dramatic breakthrough, little improvements in the design of the bulb and in the process for manufacturing it led to a fall in price of over 80% between 1880 and 1896 (Bright 1949). In recent times the dramatic growth and success of the Japanese car manufacturing industry are primarily the result of a 40 year programme of systematic and continuous improvement of product and process design (Womack *et al.* 1991). Even the Internet, which appears to be driven by fast and radical change, is actually the convergence of many incremental developments, which go back to networking amongst scientists in the nuclear physics community in the 1980s (Berners-Lee 2000).

Most innovation falls into this pattern of occasional breakthroughs followed by long periods of improvement and development within the space created by the breakthrough (Utterback 1994). 3M—a company that recently celebrated its 100th birthday and so is clearly a long-term survivor—illustrates this well. Although we can point to many famous breakthrough innovations—for example, 'Scotch tape', 'Post-It notes' and 'Scotchgard'—most of 3M's business success comes from being able to exploit these breakthroughs through extended incremental innovation. It sets itself the ambitious goal of achieving up to 50% of its sales from products that it has developed during the previous three years—a stretching target when we consider that the product range extends to over 50 000 items! Feeding this is the ability to manage innovation, not only in product development, but also in creating and refining the processes underpinning those products (Gundling 2000).

In similar fashion many other long-term survivor firms can point to a pattern of careful innovation management covering both breakthrough and incremental improvement within the envelope of those breakthroughs—examples include Corning Glass, Philips and General Electric (Graham and Shuldiner 2001; Welch 2001).

1.3 'But That's Not Really Innovation. . .'

One of the difficulties we face in trying to manage innovation is that we make assumptions about its nature. For example, we focus on the 'breakthrough nature' and discount the value of small increments of change whose impact only appears in cumulative form. Or else we confuse 'invention'—coming up with a bright idea—with 'innovation'—the whole process of taking that idea into successful implementation and use. We often assume that, once a breakthrough has been made, innovation stops and imitation begins—and in doing so we neglect the fact that adoption of something new in a particular context can still have a marked effect, even if the original innovation took place decades ago. For example, the impact of medical techniques in the developing world is still significant even though many of them date back a long time.

Throughout this book we will try and adopt an approach to innovation that sees it as a spectrum of activity. At one end of this continuum are radical and even breakthrough innovations of the dramatic kind that we see as headlines in the media. But at the other end are those tiny incremental improvements that often fall off the radar screen but whose effect over time and in cumulative form can still be significant. We will also look at innovation not in terms of absolute novelty—newness to the world—but rather in relative terms; is it an innovation that makes a difference in a particular situation? For example, the adoption of a simple shop-floor layout approach like the 5-S programme (described in Chapter 5) might appear to most people to be trivial, but its impact on a factory where there is a chaotic layout, where people work without basic discipline or standard operating procedures and where there is regard only for output rather than quality can be dramatic.

Much of the thrust of this book is about involving people who have not normally been considered part of the creative resources available to the organization. In this respect their ability to contribute to breakthrough innovation is likely to be limited, at least in the short term. But they are, nonetheless, capable of making a contribution via such incremental improvements and these can, over time, have a major impact on the fortunes of the firm.

1.4 Managing the Innovation Agenda

The risk is that, even if firms recognize and accept the need for continuous innovation, they may find difficulties in framing an appropriate innovation agenda. With limited resources they may find themselves putting scarce eggs into too few or the wrong baskets. Innovation can take many forms—from simple, incremental development of what is already there to radical development of totally new options. It can range from changes in what is offered—product or service—through to the ways in which that offering is created and delivered (process innovation). It can reflect the positioning of a particular offering; for example putting a well-established product into a new market represents a powerful source of innovation. And it can involve rethinking the underlying mental models associated with a particular product or service (Francis 2001). (This distinction has similarities with the 'value chain' approach, which sees upgrading via product and process change, change in position within the value chain and moving to a different value chain (Kaplinsky and Morris 2001).)

TABLE 1.1   The innovation agenda.

	'Do better' innovation	*'Do different' innovation*
Product/service innovation—change in what is offered	This is incremental product development. For example, the Bic ballpoint was originally developed in 1957 but remains a strong product with daily sales of 16 million units. Although superficially the same shape, closer inspection reveals a host of incremental changes that have taken place in materials, inks, ball technology, safety features, etc.	Radical shift to new product concept for the firm, perhaps for the industry as well. An emerging example of this could be the replacement of the incandescent light bulb, originally developed in the late 19th century by Edison and Swan (amongst others). This may be replaced by the solid state white light emitting diode technology patented by Nichia Chemical. This technology is 85% more energy efficient, has 16 times the life of a conventional bulb, is brighter, more flexible in application and is likely to be subject to the scale economies associated with electronic component production

TABLE 1.1   (*continued*)

	'Do better' innovation	*'Do different' innovation*
Process innovation—change in the ways in which it is created and delivered	These are incremental improvements in key performance parameters, for example, cost reduction, quality enhancement, time reduction, etc. A good example of incremental process innovation can be found in the 'lean production' field, where intra- and inter-firm efforts to drive out waste have led to sometimes spectacular performance improvements—but achieved within the same envelope established by the original processes (Womack and Jones 1997)	These are radical shifts to new process routes for the firm and, perhaps, for the industry as well. Examples are the Bessemer process for steelmaking replacing conventional charcoal smelting, the Pilkington float-glass process replacing grinding and polishing, the Solvay continuous process for alkali production replacing the batch mode Leblanc process, etc.
Position innovation—change in the context in which it is applied	This includes the launching of a product or deployment of a process in familiar context and redefining the perception of a product for customers. For example, in mobile telephones a shift has taken place from a business tool to a leisure and recreation aid, with considerable associated incremental product and process development (ring tones, cartoon displays, text messaging) emerging as a result of such positional innovation	This requires creating completely new markets rather than extending and deepening existing segments or incremental brand identity changes (Moore 1999). For example, satellite navigation was originally developed for military use, but is now used by sailors, motorists, surveyors and even postmen. Christensen's study of the rapid evolution of the hard-disk drive industry highlights the ways in which unimagined markets can quickly become the key segment (Christensen 1997)
Paradigm innovation—change in the underlying mental models surrounding it	These are evolutionary changes in the way that business activities are undertaken that provide the opportunity for incremental innovation in paradigm or business model. An example might be rethinking the Rolls-Royce motor car business as that of supplying luxury experience, competing with expensive watches, holidays, clothes, etc., rather than as a transportation mechanism	These are new business or industry models, for example, 'mass production' vs. 'craft production' (Freeman and Perez 1989). An example of a recent transformational innovation in paradigm was the development of Internet solutions to many business areas such as banking, insurance, travel, etc. (Evans and Wurster 2000)

The challenge is for firms to be aware of the extensive space within which innovation possibilities exist and to try and develop a strategic portfolio that covers this territory effectively, balancing risks and resources. Table 1.1 maps out some options.

1.5 Learning, Knowledge Management and Innovation

'Innovation has nothing to do with how many R&D dollars you have. . . it's not about money. It's about the people you have, how you're led, and how much you get it.'
(Steve Jobs, interview with *Fortune Magazine*, cited in Kirkpatrick (1998))

What an organization knows at any moment in time is deployed in the products or services that it offers and the processes whereby it produces that offering. As Figure 1.1 shows, knowledge provides the fuel for innovations—the changes that help it catch up and sometimes move ahead. This is the heart of the 'core competence' argument, which suggests that organizations need to work at building and managing their knowledge resources (Kay 1993; Prahalad and Hamel 1994; Coombs and Metcalfe 2002).

Knowledge

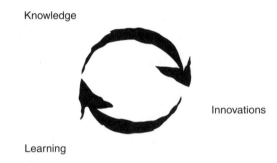

Innovations

Learning

FIGURE 1.1   Learning, knowledge and innovation.

This puts a premium on the processes that it has in place for learning and knowledge management. Not for nothing do people speak of 'the knowledge economy' or of 'competing on knowledge' (Teece 1998). In a world where access to information is fast and widespread, those organizations that can create and use their own knowledge are likely to be able to build and sustain competitive advantage. So organizations need to become good at learning—and occasionally forgetting (letting go of knowledge that they no longer need).

If learning and knowledge management are so important, then we should look at who is involved in this core renewal process. And here we reach an interesting conclusion. Organizations themselves don't learn—it is the people within them that do that (Hedberg 1981). This does not mean that managing learning at the level of the organization is unimportant; organizations provide the stage on which individual learning can take place and some stages are more supportive than others. In the end learning is essentially a human process involving individuals and groups in different configurations.

Whether people are skilled and competent at learning or not is a variable, as are the conditions under which they operate within the firm. Those organizations that invest in developing the specific knowledge and skills of their employees and the general capability to learn, those that provide opportunities and space for interaction and shared learning, those that emphasize effective communication and sharing of information, those that recognize and reward learning behaviour—these are likely to be the organizations that succeed in developing into the kind of learning organization that is much talked about but hard to achieve.

So in this sense people really *are* the organization's most valuable assets—not because this phrase makes good publicity in the annual report or mission statement, but because people actually do represent the powerhouse for learning. Without actively committed and focused learning, any organization is likely to stagnate and will struggle to create the steady stream of change it needs to survive. Investments in assets like buildings, equipment or IT systems may help the business, but without a core learning capability the long-term future must be in doubt.

1.6 The Innovation Paradox

The paradox that this raises is simple to express but hard to understand. Organizations need creativity and active learning in order to survive in a hostile environment. In today's turbulent times with challenges coming from all directions—uncertainty in competing in a global market, unpredictability in political and social stability, technological frontiers being pushed back at a dizzying pace—the one certainty is that we need all the creativity and learning capacity that we can get.

Yet the majority of our organizations still throttle back their capabilities in this direction by only looking to a relatively small group of specialists to provide this. Individuals and groups are 'licensed' by virtue of their specialist training or position in the organization—as 'R&D', 'engineering', 'market research', 'systems design', etc. Although more extreme forms of hierarchical management have begun to fall away, there is still a sense in which many organizations assume that innovation comes from these special zones in the organization.

What we are seeing is the working through of an old—but not immutable—model of how to organize. Looking back, we can see that managing agricultural production was the dominant challenge for all countries until comparatively recently. And, whilst the forms of management were often less than enlightened (including a sizeable element of slavery), there was a clear relationship between what people did and what they produced. The vast majority of work was as direct labour rather than involved in indirect activity, and the challenges faced were relatively simple tasks. Where specialized skills were needed—craftsmen working as wheelwrights, as blacksmiths, as masons, as carpenters, etc.—there was the Guild system to regulate and professionalize. Here strong emphasis was placed on a learning process, from apprenticeship, through journeyman to master craftsman, and this process established clear standards of performance and what might be termed 'professional' values. Again there was a close link between what a craftsman produced and the man himself (who often had a strong sense of pride in the quality of his work).

The Agricultural and Industrial Revolutions changed all of this. The gradual drift towards the cities and the increasing use of machinery led to a rethink of how operations were managed. Its origins can be traced back to Adam Smith and his famous observations of the pin-making process, which marked the emergence of the concept of the division of labour. By breaking up the task into smaller, specialized tasks performed by a skilled worker or special machine, productivity could be maximized. During the next hundred years or so, considerable emphasis was placed on trying to extend this further, by splitting tasks up and then mechanizing the resulting smaller tasks wherever possible to eliminate variation and enhance overall managerial control (Piore and Sabel 1982; Kaplinsky 1984; Best 1990).

The resulting model saw people increasingly involved as only one of several 'factors of production'—and in a rapidly mechanizing world, often in a marginal 'machine-minding' role. At the same time the need to co-ordinate different operations in the emerging factories led to a rise in indirect activity and a separation between doing and thinking/deciding. This process accelerated with the increasing demand for manufactured goods throughout the 19th century, and much work was done to devise ways of producing high volumes in reproducible quality and at low prices.

Developments in these ideas took place in a number of locations, each adding elements to the emerging model. As Jaikumar (1988) puts it:

'Whereas the English system saw in work the combination of skill in machinists and versatility in machines, the American system introduced to mechanisms the modern scientific principles of reductionism and reproducibility. It examined the processes involved in the manufacture of a product, broke them up into sequences of simple operations, and mechanized the simple operations by constraining the motions of a cutting tool with jigs and fixtures. Verification of performance through the use of simple gauges insured reproducibility. Each operation could now be studied and optimized.'

With the rise of industrial society came the increasing pressure to separate out hand and brain—so that by the turn of the twentieth century it was possible for people to speak of 'thinkers' and 'doers'. Developments in manufacturing organization and technology moved rapidly and the emergence of a 'scientific management' approach meant that skilled specialists were able to analyse and devise 'the one best way' to accomplish a wide range of tasks. It is hard to argue with the results they were able to achieve—for example, in a series of famous experiments Frederick Taylor was able to increase dramatically the productivity of businesses as diverse as steelmaking, dock handling and engineering (Taylor 1947).

The most famous example of this 'scientific' approach was probably in the emerging models for automobile manufacturing, which were pioneered by Henry Ford and his team of engineers. Faced with the challenge of a widely differing workforce, many of whom lacked manufacturing skills and in a lot of cases spoke poor English as a second language, they developed an approach to making cars that had profound impacts. From a highly variable activity with low productivity and variable quality, the 'mass production' system changed car manufacturing dramatically. The dramatic impact of this pattern on productivity can be seen in the case of the first assembly line, installed in 1913 for flywheel assembly, where the assembly time fell from 20 man minutes to 5. By 1914 three lines were being used in the chassis department to reduce assembly time from around 12 hours to less than 2 hours.

This approach extended beyond the actual assembly operations to embrace raw-material supply (such as steelmaking) and transport and distribution. At its height a factory operating on this principle was able to turn out high volumes (8000 cars/day) with short lead times—for example, as a consequence of the smooth flow that could be achieved, it took only 81 hours to produce a finished car from raw iron ore—and this included 48 hours for the raw materials to be transported from the mine to the factory! In the heyday of the integrated plants such as at River Rouge, productivity, quality, inventory and other measures of manufacturing performance were at levels that would still be the envy even of the best organized Japanese plants today. Table 1.2 highlights some of the key features of this blueprint for manufacturing, typified in the car plants of Henry Ford but applied to many other industries throughout the 1930s and beyond.

TABLE 1.2 Characteristics of the Ford/Taylor system for manufacturing, circa 1920.

- Standardization of products and components, of manufacturing process equipment, of tasks in the manufacturing process, and of control over the process
- Time and work study, to identify the optimum conditions for carrying out a particular operation and job analysis, to break up the task into small, highly controllable and reproducible steps
- Specialization of functions and tasks within all areas of operation. Once job-analysis and work-study information was available, it became possible to decide which activities were central to a particular task and to train an operator to perform those smoothly and efficiently. Those activities that detracted from this smooth performance were separated out and became, in turn, the task of another worker. So, for example, in a machine shop the activities of obtaining materials and tools, or maintenance of machines, or of progressing the part to the next stage in manufacture, or quality control and inspection were all outside the core task of actually operating the machine to cut metal. Thus, there was considerable narrowing and routinization of individual tasks and an extension of the division of labour. One other consequence was that training for such narrow tasks became simple and reproducible and thus new workers could quickly be brought on stream and slotted into new areas as and when needed
- Uniform output rates and systemization of the entire manufacturing process. The best example of this is probably the assembly line for motor cars, where the speed of the line determined all activity
- Payment and incentive schemes based on results—on output, on productivity, etc.
- Elimination of worker discretion and passing of control to specialists
- Concentration of control of work into the hands of management within a bureaucratic hierarchy with extensive reliance on rules and procedures—doing things by the book

There is little doubt that this was a 'better' way of making cars—at least in terms of the overall production figures (although the question of whether the conditions under which manufacturing took place were better is perhaps more open to question). But the trap it set was to help embed two powerful beliefs:

- That there is only one 'best' way and
- That this was something which only specialists could be involved in designing and refining

The belief in the one best way began to fade as others found different 'better ways' and the need for constant innovation asserted itself in this and the many other industries which began rapid growth in the early 20th century. Ford's dominance of the car industry fell away as the market began to demand more than the standard Model T in 'any colour as long as it's black!'. Innovation in manufacturing and services increasingly began to focus on meeting a number of different targets, involving non-price factors like speed of response, range of choice, degree of customization, quality, design, etc. as well as the consistently important one of price. Faced with a moving target like this the 'one best way' model began to show cracks, although the dominance of the 'Fordist' approach can still be seen as we move into the 21st century (Best 2001).

The underlying power of the second belief comes from a long history of marginalization of the potential contribution that much of a workforce could make. Clearly this is not the product of a conspiracy on the part of managers, but rather an unfortunate by-product of centuries of trying to make operations more efficient and effective.

1.7 From Doing to Thinking Organizations

'Microsoft's only factory asset is the human imagination.'

(Bill Gates)

It is easy to sit back as armchair critics of this view. Of course, we would agree that there is a nonsense about seeing people as either thinkers or doers. Any quick poll of a group of people in any organization about how they spend their spare time reveals an enormous palette of skills and experience—people are artists, musicians, teachers, organizers, accountants and many other things besides. In carrying out these roles they are all deploying huge reserves of creative problem finding and solving skills of the same kind as we need in organizational life. The statement 'with every pair of hands you get a free brain' has a resonance that it is pretty hard to ignore.

But creating the kind of organization in which everyone feels a sense of involvement and shared purpose and uses their individual and collective creative abilities to push forward the innovation frontiers is not simple. Not everyone wants to go in the same direction and people have different motivations for working, some of which do not include more than an instrumental relationship. Even if they do 'buy in' to the idea of contributing their ideas, they may lack formal skills and experience about how to make a contribution, or feel reluctant to offer what others might see as silly or simple ideas. Others might, reasonably, ask, 'what's in it for me?'—what share of the additional benefits arising from their ideas to the firm might they expect to receive? Organizing for higher involvement in the innovation process will need new structures and procedures if it is to be more than just another piece of wishful thinking.

It has proved hard enough to manage specialists in terms of enabling their creativity and innovation. The challenge of extending this to a much broader part of the workforce throws up real questions about how much management time and organizational resources it might consume—and whether these costs would outweigh any benefits.

Why should organizations bother with high-involvement innovation? There are two answers to this—the first is that there is increasing evidence from a wide range of sectors, geographical locations and firm sizes to suggest that it does make sense to mobilize people because of the direct financial benefits that they contribute. Chapter 2 explores this theme in more detail but it is worth noting some interesting data from the USA, which reviews several large-sample surveys and concludes that high-involvement human resource practices can be correlated with superior company performance in terms of sales revenue, shareholder value and profitability (Huselid 1995). This is matched by experience and research in countries as far afield as Finland, Australia and South Korea.

But the second reason is perhaps more compelling. In an environment where survival depends on change the organization needs the capacity to renew itself—and to do so on a continuing basis. Today's competitive conditions mean that the rate at which that needs to happen is accelerating and imitation and diffusion of ideas become facilitated by global communications, competition, etc. Particularly for high-income countries the solution to the problem becomes one of knowledge competition—maintaining a competitive edge through possession of knowledge assets, which are hard for others to copy, even if they have information about these assets.

The ability to maintain knowledge competition will depend on how capable the organization is at learning—and, since the process of learning is one which is people-based, the likely advantage will lie with those who have most active learners and the capacity to involve and co-ordinate them.

1.8 High-Involvement Innovation

This book looks at the theme of developing active involvement in the innovation process. It is not just about increasing participation from those who have been marginalized in the organization's thinking processes (although that is a big gap which most organizations need to close). It is also about how to get the best from highly skilled and creative staff who may feel equally frustrated and unable to express their creative capabilities—in some case to the point where they leave the organization and set up elsewhere.

There has been much recent interest in this topic of employee involvement and particularly in the experience of mobilizing what in Japan is called *kaizen*—the continuous stream of small improvement ideas that each worker is able to contribute. There is much that we can learn from this experience, and we will explore it in detail in the book. But such a view carries with it a risk, that innovation is seen as a binary task. No longer do we have the separation of thinkers and doers in the organization but instead the boundary is along lines of the novelty and impact of the innovations worked upon. Specialists do the clever things and the rest get on with the small improvements.

There is clear psychological evidence that different people have different preferred creative *styles*—the ways in which they like to deploy their creativity—with some feeling comfortable with high-risk projects and others preferring to work within clear and limited parameters (Kirton 1989). But everyone carries the basic creative capabilities for finding and solving problems and exploring new opportunities—and, given requisite skills, structures and support, can make a contribution right across the innovation spectrum (Rickards 1997; Cook 1999). For this reason we look in the book at the theme of high-involvement innovation, not just in terms of bringing into the process many people who have hitherto been excluded from it but also how they (and their working environment) can be developed to fulfil high-level innovation tasks.

The book draws on a variety of sources and much published research and documented experience in innovation management. It makes particular use of the findings from a ten-year research programme which has been running at the Centre for Research in Innovation Management (CENTRIM) at the University of Brighton, where a series of projects exploring issues in creating and sustaining high-involvement innovation have been carried out with a network of firms representing a wide range of size, sector and experience (Bessant *et al.* 1994).

1.9 What's in a Name?

The concept that the book explores is one of developing high involvement in innovation—something which is certainly not a new idea. Considerable work has gone on looking at it from outside organizations and trying to develop and sustain it within them. These explorations go back decades (and even centuries in some cases), so we should not be surprised to find the experience referred to by many different labels.

For example, we have already mentioned the term kaizen, which came to the attention of Western organizations in the late 1970s as they began to appreciate the significant performance gains that Japanese firms were able to make through mobilizing workforce participation in improvement innovation. The term was often translated as 'continuous improvement (CI)' and there is an extensive body of work that looks at high-involvement innovation under this banner (Robinson 1991; Schroeder and Robinson 1991; Boer *et al.* 1999).

Similarly the drive for quality improvement in products and services in the later part of the 20th century led to an interest in systematic approaches, which moved beyond the use of powerful statistical tools for quality control and into approaches that considered the role and contribution of the individual worker and the design of organizations that would facilitate it.

'Company-wide quality control' was a concept originating in the USA, but one which found successful adoption in Japan (Feigenbaum 1956). It re-emerged as the concept of 'total quality management (TQM)' and was adopted widely in the rest of the world, particularly as the drive to demonstrate conformance to quality assurance in processes using international standards (such as ISO 9000) was promoted by large companies and even governments. TQM covers a wide range of interpretations but a core theme is, once again, that of high involvement in improvement innovation (Kanji 1996).

Similar stories could be told around 'lean thinking' or 'learning organizations' and a host of other labels, but our concern is less with these labels than with the underlying principles of high-involvement innovation. For the sake of clarity the term 'high-involvement innovation' (sometimes shortened to HII) will be used throughout the book, but many of the illustrations make use of experiences with CI, TQM, lean etc. and are reported as such.

1.10 What's *Not* in the Book?

Innovation is a big topic and has been studied from a number of practical and research perspectives (Van de Ven *et al.* 1989). This book offers one perspective, taking as its core theme the need to extend involvement to people who have hitherto often been marginalized in the process. But 'high involvement' in its widest sense is more than just bringing more people into the process. It is, for example, about:

- Engaging cross-discipline knowledge sets and looking for ways to enable this to happen (Jassawalla and Sashittal 1999; Sapsed *et al.* 2002)
- Encouraging the formation and use of 'communities of practice', often forming at the boundaries of knowledge (Wenger 1999)
- Encouraging and enabling inter-functional and cross-process working within and between organizations (Davenport 1992; Cooper 1994; Swan 2003)
- Engaging in shared learning and development across organizational boundaries—and increasingly across regional and national ones (Dodgson 1993; Oliver and Blakeborough 1998; Coombs and Metcalfe 2002)

Although we will touch upon these themes during the book, their detailed exposition remains a task for future research and for other writing projects.

1.11 Structure of the Book

Building and sustaining high-involvement innovation is hard work. Why should organizations bother with this approach? Chapter 2 reports on case examples from a wide variety of countries, sectors and firm sizes to show the significant strategic benefits that come from paying attention to this theme. It covers continuous improvement ('doing what we do better'), where examples abound of success with kaizen, lean production, total quality management and other ways of mobilizing involvement and commitment to innovation. However, it also covers the challenge of radical innovation—'doing something different'—which is less frequent but more dramatic and which can also benefit from a high-involvement approach not only to creating such change but also to its successful implementation.

At first sight, high-involvement innovation is a 'no-brainer'. Faced with the idea that 'with every pair of hands you get a free brain', any organization would make a high priority of trying to motivate and mobilize that brain to help it achieve its goals. Not for nothing do many organizations make the explicit point in their mission statements, annual reports and other communications that 'people are our most valuable asset!'.

However, behind this apparently axiomatic point lies the real difficulty. In practice few organizations can claim to mobilize the full range of creativity and innovative capability that their employees have to offer. This arises not out of a conscious desire to marginalize them but as a result of the ways in which organizations have evolved—roots which go back hundreds of years and which shape the dominant beliefs about how organizations work. Chapter 3 looks at the blocks and barriers to high-involvement innovation and the need to change 'the way we do things around here'—to develop and sustain a fundamentally different organizational culture.

Without a framework against which to measure it, high-involvement innovation remains simply a worthy sentiment. Chapter 4 presents a model, based on ten years of research in innovation management, which allows organizations to position themselves and to think about how they might carry forward the development of an innovation culture. It is described in detail in an appendix, but this chapter will introduce the basic features.

The model has two dimensions—performance and practice. The former refers to the measurable indicators of innovation whilst the latter deals with the extent to which an innovation culture has been developed and implemented. Organizations can use this framework to position themselves and 'benchmark' themselves against others and/or against a model of good practice and performance.

The value of the model is that it recognizes that firms differ in a number of ways (including how far along the journey to high involvement they have already travelled) and that there is no single solution that will fit all of them. Instead it uses a series of 'archetypes' of organizations at different stages in their development and examines typical blocks and barriers associated with these stages and how they can be dealt with.

These archetypes and progress between them as stages on the journey towards a successful and sustainable innovation culture are described in the next five chapters.

Chapter 5 is about firms trying—sometimes for the first time—to make innovation a more widespread activity. This early stage is typified by organizations for which innovation is a fairly random or *ad hoc* activity and those that place high reliance on small 'licensed' groups of innovators. It looks at the limitations of such an approach and at ways of extending involvement in the innovation process to bring in more people.

Chapter 6 describes the next stage, which is typical of an organization that is trying in a formal and systematic way to extend participation in innovation. Many activities in the direction of 'kaizen', lean teams or quality circles would come under this banner. The strengths and benefits of such an approach are explored and ways to help embed and sustain such initiatives are described. At this level firms can expect to obtain benefits, but these will often be rather localized and limited in their impact; there is also a risk that activities at this level eventually run out of steam and fall away after the initial 'honeymoon' period.

The problem of fade-out mentioned above reflects a lack of connection between the bottom-up capability of high-involvement innovation and the top-down focus and direction of such activity. Chapter 7 describes the next stage, which involves providing a clear strategic focus linked to the needs of the business—and deploying it successfully throughout the organization. It also brings to the surface the importance of measurement as a key tool for ensuring progress is made on a continuing basis.

Firms that are able to build and sustain strategic innovation systems can point to significant 'bottom line' benefits on a sustained basis, for example year-on-year cost reductions or quality improvements. Whilst these are of considerable value, the limitation here is that innovation is by definition 'doing what we do better'—and, whilst there is enormous scope for driving out waste and for continuous improvement, the possibilities for doing different things are not well covered.

Chapter 8 looks at the very advanced stage in the development of high-involvement innovation where the organization is confident enough to 'let go' and allow people to experiment with their own ideas with a high degree of autonomy. It is attractive in that it opens up the possibility of radical innovation—doing something different—but it also carries risks since experimentation of this kind will inevitably involve making mistakes. In many ways it is the kind of culture that one might expect to find in an R&D laboratory, but not as a part of the general 'way we do things round here' in the organization as a whole.

Creating the conditions under which people can act autonomously is not easy and in many cases firms have solved this by creating separate units or 'skunk works', where people are encouraged to be 'intrapreneurs' and to challenge the status quo without the need to leave the organization in order to follow up their ideas.

The phrase 'learning organizations' was fashionable in the late 20th century but it has been superseded by other apparently more compelling prescriptions. However, the underlying theme—of mobilizing the full capability of the organization in creating, assimilating, capturing, sharing and using knowledge—remains of critical importance. Chapter 9 looks at the mature high-involvement innovation organization in which innovation is a way of life and where there are multiple mechanisms in place that ensure the high levels of involvement in learning and knowledge management that are needed to become and remain competitive.

Chapter 10 addresses the question of making the journey towards high-involvement innovation. It reports on the experiences of a number of organizations that have been wrestling with this challenge over many years and draws together an approach to such organizational development, which firms can use to maintain momentum in their quest for higher and sustainable levels of participation in innovation.

In the final chapter (Chapter 11) we look at new and emerging challenges in the field of high-involvement innovation. In particular the chapter looks at the changing innovation agenda, where new strategic challenges such as concern for environmental sustainability are coming to the forefront. It also looks at the challenge of building and sustaining high-involvement innovation at the inter-firm level. With an increasing emphasis on networks comes the need to think about and learn to manage beyond the individual organization—and this poses significant questions about how to develop and sustain an innovation culture at network level.

References

Berners-Lee, T. (2000) *Weaving the Web: The Original Design and Ultimate Destiny of the World Wide Web by Its Inventor*. Harper Business, New York.

Bessant, J., S. Caffyn and M. Gallagher (1994) 'Rediscovering continuous improvement,' *Technovation*, **14** (1), 17–29.

Best, M. (1990) *The New Competition*. Polity Press, Oxford.

Best, M. (2001) *The New Competitive Advantage*. Oxford University Press, Oxford.

Boer, H., A. Berger, R. Chapman and F. Gertsen (1999) *CI Changes: From Suggestion Box to the Learning Organization*. Ashgate, Aldershot.

Bright, A. (1949) *The Electric Lamp Industry: Technological Change and Economic Development from 1800 to 1947*. Macmillan, New York.

Christensen, C. (1997) *The Innovator's Dilemma*. Harvard Business School Press, Cambridge, MA.

Cook, P. (1999) *Best Practice Creativity*. Gower, Aldershot.

Coombs, R. and J. Metcalfe (2002) 'Innovation in pharmaceuticals: perspectives on the co-ordination, combination and creation of capabilities,' *Technology Analysis and Strategic Management*, **14** (3), 261–272.

Cooper, R. (1994) 'Third-generation new product processes,' *Journal of Product Innovation Management*, **11** (1), 3–14.

Davenport, T. (1992) *Process Innovation: Re-engineering Work through Information Technology*. Harvard University Press, Boston, MA.

Dodgson, M. (1993) *Technological Collaboration in Industry*. Routledge, London.

Evans, P. and T. Wurster (2000) *Blown to Bits: How the New Economics of Information Transforms Strategy*. Harvard Business School Press, Cambridge, MA.

Feigenbaum, A. (1956) 'Total quality control,' *Harvard Business Review* (November), p. 56.

Francis, D. (2001) *Developing Innovative Capability*. University of Brighton, Brighton.

Freeman, C. and C. Perez (1989) 'Structural crises of adjustment: business cycles and investment behaviour,' in Dosi, G. (ed.), *Technical Change and Economic Theory*. Frances Pinter, London.

Graham, M. and A. Shuldiner (2001) *Corning and the Craft of Innovation*. Oxford University Press, Oxford.

Gundling, E. (2000) *The 3M Way to Innovation: Balancing People and Profit*. Kodansha International, New York.

Hedberg, B. (1981) 'How organizations learn and unlearn,' in Nystrom, H. and Starbuck, W. (eds), *Handbook of Organization Design*. Oxford University Press, Oxford.

Huselid, M. (1995) 'The impact of human resource management practices on turnover, productivity and corporate financial performance,' *Academy of Management Journal*, **38**, 647–656.

Jaikumar, R. (1988) 'From filing and fitting to flexible manufacturing,' WP88-045, Harvard Business School, Cambridge, MA.

Jassawalla, A. and H. Sashittal (1999) 'Building collaborative cross-functional new product teams,' *Academy of Management Executive*, **13** (3), 50–53.

Kanji, G. (1996) 'Implementation and pitfalls of total quality management,' *Total Quality Management*, **7**, 331–343.

Kaplinsky, R. (1984) *Automation—The Technology and Society*. Longman, Harlow.

Kaplinsky, R. and M. Morris (2001). 'A handbook for value chain research.' Institute of Development Studies, Sussex. Available at http://www.ids.ac.uk/ids/global/valchn.html#manuals.

Kay, J. (1993) *Foundations of Corporate Success: How Business Strategies Add Value*. Oxford University Press, Oxford.

Kirkpatrick, D. (1998) 'The second coming of Apple,' *Fortune*, **138**, 90.

Kirton, M. (1989) *Adaptors and Innovators*. Routledge, London.

Moore, G. (1999) *Crossing the Chasm: Marketing and Selling High-Tech Products to Mainstream Customers*. Harper Business, New York.

Oliver, N. and M. Blakeborough (1998) 'Innovation networks: the view from the inside,' in Grieve Smith, J. and Michie, J. (eds), *Innovation, Co-operation and Growth*. Oxford University Press, Oxford.

Piore, M. and C. Sabel (1982) *The Second Industrial Divide*. Basic Books, New York.

Prahalad, C. and G. Hamel (1994) *Competing for the Future*. Harvard University Press, Boston, MA.

Rickards, T. (1997) *Creativity and Problem Solving at Work*. Gower, Aldershot.

Robinson, A. (1991) *Continuous Improvement in Operations*. Productivity Press, Cambridge, MA.

Sapsed, J., J. Bessant, D. Partington, D. Tranfield and M. Young (2002) 'Teamworking and knowledge management: a review of converging themes,' *International Journal of Management Reviews*, **4** (1).

Schroeder, D. and A. Robinson (1991) 'America's most successful export to Japan—continuous improvement programs,' *Sloan Management Review*, **32** (3), 67–81.

Swan, J. (2003) 'Knowledge, networking and innovation: developing an understanding of process,' in Shavinina, L. (ed.), *International Handbook of Innovation*. Elsevier, New York.

Taylor, F. (1947) *The Principles of Scientific Management*, Harper and Row, New York (original published in 1911).

Teece, D. (1998) 'Capturing value from knowledge assets: the new economy, markets for know-how, and intangible assets,' *California Management Review*, **40** (3), 55–79.

Utterback, J. (1994) *Mastering the Dynamics of Innovation*. Harvard Business School Press, Boston, MA.

Van de Ven, A., H. Angle and M. Poole (1989) *Research on the Management of Innovation*. Harper and Row, New York.

Welch, J. (2001) *Jack! What I've Learned from Leading a Great Company and Great People*. Headline, New York.

Wenger, E. (1999) *Communities of Practice: Learning, Meaning, and Identity*. Cambridge University Press, Cambridge.

Womack, J. and D. Jones (1997) *Lean Thinking*. Simon and Schuster, New York.

Womack, J., D. Jones and D. Roos (1991) *The Machine that Changed the World*. Rawson Associates, New York.

Chapter 2

IS IT WORTH IT?

Building and sustaining high-involvement innovation is hard work. Why should organizations bother with this approach? This chapter reports on evidence from a wide variety of countries, sectors and firm sizes to show the significant strategic benefits that come from paying attention to this theme. It focuses particularly on continuous improvement ('doing what we do better'), where examples abound of success with kaizen, lean production, total quality management and other ways of mobilizing involvement and commitment to innovation. But it also covers the challenge of radical innovation—'doing something different'—which can also benefit from a high-involvement approach, not only to creating such change, but also to its successful implementation.

2.1 Do People Really Matter?

What evidence do we actually have that taking care of people and, more importantly, making sure they have the opportunity to get involved in the innovation process actually makes a difference to the organization? It is all very well saying that everyone comes with a free brain and that this potentially could make a difference to the way the organization operates. In practice, the question is quickly raised as to whether the efforts made to bring people into the innovation process actually lead to any significant improvement; or is the investment largely wasted?

There are various kinds of information that we can marshal to help make a case for high-involvement innovation. At a very basic level we could make use of the moral argument, which suggests that it is not particularly pleasant to employ people with high levels of capability to carry out simple, repetitive and mundane tasks. The reaction most people show to the film *Modern Times*, in which at one point Charlie Chaplin literally plays a cog in a machine, gives a strong sense of this. And asking any working group in any organization what they do in their spare time soon reveals the enormous range of talents and capabilities that people have and that could be deployed in the workplace. Whether these capabilities and skills are allowed to make a contribution is of course a very different decision.

In this chapter we will look at evidence from a number of different sources in support of high-involvement innovation, and will draw particularly on:

- Studies of learning and capability development within organizations
- Surveys and multi-organization studies
- Detailed studies of specific high-involvement innovation programmes
- Case studies of experiences from around the world

2.2 Learning about the Learning Curve

One fruitful line of argument lies in looking at the key contributions that people actually make to measurable performance improvement. From the earliest days of organizational behaviour studies it has been clear that the extent to which people feel committed and involved in their working processes has a bearing on the efficiency with which those processes are carried out. For example, the famous Hawthorne studies at the Western Electric plant demonstrated the ability of people to affect productivity and the fact that this could be influenced by a variety of factors including the rather obvious point that, when somebody takes an interest, then people tend to contribute more (Roethlisberger and Dickson 1939).

Of particular relevance to our discussions are the early studies of what has come to be called the learning-curve effect in which the performance of key activities becomes more efficient with practice. This widely known effect was one of the three factors that Adam Smith argued would promote productivity growth with the division of labour. It was studied systematically in the production of airframes in the early part of the twentieth century and the results of these studies translate to some important predictive laws, which suggest that, the more often and more regularly we do something, the easier and more efficient we get. It has been used to great effect in making major strategic decisions about when and how big plants should be built (Arrow 1962).

This is a powerfully established principle, but it depends very much on a series of socio-technical processes operating within the firm. It does not happen by accident, but needs focus and sustained effort to create the conditions under which it can happen and to set the targets towards which it should be directed. As Pavitt and Bell put it, 'technological capability relates to the resources needed to generate and manage improvements in processes and production organization, products, equipment and engineering projects. These are accumulated and embodied in individuals (skills, knowledge, experience) and in organizational systems' (Bell and Pavitt 1993).

For example, when a new product is launched or a new process introduced, the early stages involve a rapid cycle of high-frequency problem-solving activities. The bugs are taken out of the system, the particular limitations on bottlenecks identified and dealt with, minor improvements in usability and reliability identified, and so on. This phase is essentially one of sustained incremental innovation, but one focused on a clear strategic target—that of getting a new product or process to work effectively. Some of this requires the engagement of high-level skills and technical capability, but most of it is the product of a large number of people reflecting on their experience with the new thing and making suggestions as to how that could be improved.

Many documented examples of the learning-curve effect across different industries, in different firm sizes and over a sustained period of time point to the key factor of employee involvement in the process. Indeed, it is possible to find examples where the predicted learning-curve effect did not materialize and in many cases to track this back to a failure to create the structure and conditions within which such involved, focused and committed problem solving can happen (Bell and Scott-Kemmis 1990). So we need to be clear that learning by doing does not simply emerge from repetition, but rather from a much more consciously organized and managed process.

Table 2.1 gives a few examples of more detailed studies that have been carried out to try and identify the significant contribution of sustained incremental change as a result of learning of this type. They concur on the importance of employee involvement and offer a number of examples of the ways in which this involvement can be achieved.

TABLE 2.1   Example studies of learning and performance improvement.

Study	Main focus and findings
Tremblay (1994)	Paper production in several developed and developing country contexts. High importance of incremental innovation, which effect emerges through active employee involvement
Figuereido (2001; 2002)	Detailed comparison of two Brazilian steel companies over a sustained period. Learning and technological capability accumulation in one was much more marked than in the second, attributed to active management of high-involvement innovation
Dutrenit (1998)	Detailed studies of technological development in a Mexican glass producer, highlighting the role of employee involvement in incremental problem finding and solving
McDuffie (Womack *et al.* 1991)	Performance improvement in the automobile industry where one component explaining the difference in performance levels between plants around the world was the level of participation in problem finding and solving around standard operations—kaizen activity

2.3 Performance Improvement through People

'There is no other source of competitive advantage! Others can copy our investment, technology and scale—but NOT the quality of our people . . .'
(Managing Director, British Chrome and Steel, 1998)

Another body of evidence on which we can draw looks at surveys of business performance over a sustained period of time. In a variety of settings—different countries, sectors, firm sizes, etc.—companies that have a track record of investing in employees and in developing the kind of organization in which people can deploy their creativity have done demonstrably better than the average. For example, in the USA Pfeffer (1994) comments on the experiences of a number of firms whose shares performed significantly better then average over a 20 year period (1972–1992). They included a small regional airline (Southwestern), a small publisher (Plenum), an unknown retailer (Wal-Mart), a poultry farmer (Tyson Foods) and a video rental business (Circuit City). Growth was both consistent and high, with the result that some became—like Wal-Mart—major international players.

This is a significant achievement, but it takes on even more importance when set against the performance of the rest of the sectors in which these firms operate. They are not niche businesses but highly competitive and overcrowded—with the result that many firms in such businesses have gone bankrupt and all face serious challenges. To perform well under these conditions takes a particular kind of competitive advantage—one which is highly firm-specific and difficult to imitate. In resource-based strategy theory, such firms have a 'distinctive' capability or competence (Kay 1993).

In these firms it was not the possession of specific assets or market share or scale economy or advanced technology that accounted for success. They achieved (and attribute) their growth through the ways in which they managed to organize and work with their people to produce competitive advantage. This is the conclusion drawn by Mark Huselid, whose large-scale survey work in the USA provides a more up-to-date picture—his conclusion is that advanced human resource practices that emphasize high involvement can '. . . be correlated with superior company performance in terms of sales revenue, shareholder value and profitability' (Huselid 1995). Similar comment on the US experience comes from Ulrich (1998), drawing on a variety of studies. The direction of causality is difficult to establish, but the implication is that success is linked with such human resource practices.

BOX 2.1 Flying high — the benefits of high-involvement innovation.

One of the most competitive business environments is the airline industry where the challenge of finding a sustainable growth model is made even more difficult by problems of overcapacity, differential regulatory pressures, air traffic limitations — never mind the awful legacy of September 11th. In this hostile environment size is by no means the ticket to success, nor is having national flag carrier status; if anything what growth there is is coming through market segmentation and especially in the 'no-frills' low cost area. But there is a risk in this model that other components such as service quality suffer and a further danger that the model has few entry barriers — anyone can join in.

One airline which has consistently managed to make a success from being a low cost niche player is Southwest Airlines which has managed to compete effectively for the past thirty years — despite facing a series of apparent problems and barriers to entry. For example, it did not have access to major international reservation systems, and for many years it was unable to fly in and out of its primary regional airport — Dallas-Fort Worth — and for a long time had to make do with smaller local airports. Its chosen market segment involves trying to sell a commodity product at a low price — yet Southwest has achieved significantly better productivity than the industry average in terms of employees/aircraft, passengers/employee and seat miles/employee. One of its most significant achievements was to slash the turnaround time at airports, getting its planes back in the air faster than others. In 1992 80% of its flights were turned around in only 15 minutes against the industry average of 45 minutes; even now the best the industry can manage is around 30 minutes. All of this is not at a cost to service quality; SWA is one of the only airlines to have achieved the industry's 'triple' crown (fewest lost bags, fewest passenger complaints, best on-time performance in the same month). No other airline has managed the 'triple' yet SWA has done it nine times! Perhaps most significant was that in 2002 in the aftermath of September 11th it was still able to post a profit for the first quarter.

Significantly much of its success comes not through specialized equipment or automation but through high-involvement innovation practices. The company makes a strong commitment to employees — for example, it has never laid anyone off despite difficult times — and it invests heavily in training and teambuilding. An interesting statistic which bears out the attractiveness of SWA as an employer is that it expects to receive around 200 000 job applications per year for a total of about 4000 posts — a 1:50 ratio.

Source: Based on Herskovitz (2002).

This is not an isolated set of examples; many other studies point to the same important message. For example, research on the global automobile industry in the 1980s showed that there were very significant performance differences between the best plants in the world (almost entirely Japanese operated at that time) and the rest. The gaps were not trivial; on average the best plants were twice as productive (based on labour hours/car), used half the materials and space and the cars produced contained half the number of defects. Not surprisingly, this triggered a search for explanations of this huge difference, and people began looking to see if scale of operations, or specialized automation equipment or government subsidy might be behind it. What they found was that there were few differences in areas like automation—indeed, in many cases non-Japanese plants had higher levels of automation and use of robots. However, there were major differences in three areas—design of the product for manufacturability, the way work was organized and the approach taken to human resources.

'... our findings were eye-opening. The Japanese plants require one-half the effort of the American luxury-car plants, half the effort of the best European plant, a quarter of the effort of the average European plant, and one-sixth the effort of the worst European luxury car producer. At the same time, the Japanese plant greatly exceeds the quality level of all plants except one in Europe—and this European plant required four times the effort of the Japanese plant to assemble a comparable product ...'
(Womack *et al.* 1991)

In the UK a major study of high-performance (scoring in the upper quartile on various financial and business measures) organizations drew similar conclusions (DTI 1997). Size, technology and other variables were not particularly significant but 'partnerships with people' were. Of the sample of around 70 firms:

- 90% said that management of people had become a higher priority in the past three years
- 90% had a formal training policy linked to the business plan
- 97% thought training was critical to the success of the business
- 100% had a team structure
- 60% formally trained team leaders so the team system becomes effective more quickly
- 65% trained their employees to work in teams—it does not just happen

As one manager in the study expressed it:

> 'Our operating costs are reducing year on year due to improved efficiencies. We have seen a 35% reduction in costs within two and a half years by improving quality. There are an average of 21 ideas per employee today compared to nil in 1990. Our people have accomplished this.'
>
> (Chief Executive, Leyland Trucks—738 employees—1998)

According to research on firms in the UK that have acquired the 'Investors in People' award, there is evidence of a correlation with higher business performance (Table 2.2). Such businesses have a higher rate of return on capital (RRC), higher turnover/sales per employee and higher profits per employee.

TABLE 2.2   Performance of IiP companies against others.

	Average company	Investors company	Gain
RRC	9.21%	16.27%	77%
Turnover/sales per employee	£64 912	£86 625	33%
Profit per employee	£1815	£3198	76%

Source: Hambledon Group, 2001, cited on DTI website http://www.dti.gov.uk.

A comprehensive study of UK experience (Richardson and Thompson 1999), carried out for the Chartered Institute of Personnel and Development, collected evidence to support the contention that in the 21st century 'Tayloristic task management gives way to knowledge management; the latter seeking to be cost-efficient by developing an organization's people assets, unlike the former which views labour as a cost to be minimized' (CIPD 2001). Caulkin (2001) observes that, although the task of convincing sceptical managers and shareholders remains difficult, '. . . more than 30 studies carried out in the UK and US since the early 1990s leave no room to doubt that there is a correlation between people management and business performance, that the relationship is positive, and that it is cumulative: the more and the more effective the practices, the better the result . . .'.

Other relevant work includes a study carried out by the Institute of Work Psychology at Sheffield University, which found that in a sample of manufacturing businesses, 18% of variations in productivity and 19% in profitability could be attributed to people management practices (Patterson et al. 1997). The study concluded that people management was a better predictor of company performance than strategy, technology or research and development.

Analysis of the national UK Workplace Employee Relations Survey by Guest et al. (2000) found a link between the use of more HR practices and a range of positive outcomes, including greater employee involvement, satisfaction and commitment, productivity and better financial performance. Another UK study concludes that 'Practices that encourage workers to think and interact to improve the production process are strongly linked to increased productivity' (Stern and Sommerblad 1999). Similar findings are also reported by Blimes et al. (1997) and by Wood and de Menezes (1998).

Although encouraging, the CIPD work suggests that there is still a long way to go. They point out that:

'while two-thirds of UK organizations rely strongly on people for competitive advantage, only one in ten prioritizes people over marketing or finance issues. This gap is reflected in a low take-up of even routine HR practices. WERS reported that less than half of companies use a range of standard practices ... According to the 'Future of Work' survey, of 18 progressive practices ranging across areas such as recruitment, training, appraisal, job design, quality and communication, only 1 per cent of companies use three-quarters or more extensively. At the other end of the scale, 20 per cent use fewer than one quarter' (CIPD 2001).

'Despite the popular rhetoric,' concludes the report, 'in the majority of organizations people are not viewed by top managers as their most important assets' (CIPD 2001).

2.4 Mobilizing High-Involvement Innovation

A third source of support for the high-involvement approach can be drawn from the increasing number of studies of employee involvement programs themselves. Studies of this kind concentrate on reports describing structures that are put in place to enable employee involvement and the number of suggestions or ideas that are offered by members of the workforce.

Attempts to utilize this approach in a formal way, trying to engender performance improvement through active participation of the workforce, can be traced back to the 18th century, when the eighth shogun Yoshimune Tokugawa introduced the suggestion box in Japan (Schroeder and Robinson 1991). In 1871 Denny's shipyard in Dumbarton, Scotland employed a programme of incentives to encourage suggestions about productivity-improving techniques; they sought to draw out 'any change by which work is rendered either superior in quality or more economical in cost'. In 1894 the National Cash Register company made considerable efforts to mobilize the 'hundred-headed brain' that their staff represented, whilst the Lincoln Electric Company started implementing an 'incentive management system' in 1915. NCR's ideas, especially around suggestion schemes, found their way back to Japan, where the textile firm of Kanebuchi Boseki introduced them in 1905.

Criticism is often levelled at the Scientific Management school (represented by figures like Frederick Taylor and Frank and Lilian Gilbreth) for helping to institutionalize standardized working practices modelled around a single 'best' way to carry out a task, but this is to mask the significant role that their systematic approach took in encouraging and implementing worker suggestions. It was Frank Gilbreth, for example, who is credited with having first used the slogan 'work smarter, not harder'—a phrase that has since come to underpin the philosophy of continuous-improvement innovation. As Taylor wrote:

'You must have standards. We get some of our greatest improvements from the workmen in that way. The workmen, instead of holding back, are eager to make suggestions. When one is adopted it is named after the man who suggested it, and he is given a premium for having developed a new standard. So, in that way, we get the finest kind of team work, we have true co-operation, and our method ... leads on always to something better than has been known before.'

(Taylor 1912, cited in Boer *et al.* 1999).

Japanese firms have documented their programmes extensively and a number of detailed descriptions exist of how firms like Canon, Bridgestone, Toyota and Nissan organize for high-involvement innovation (Monden 1983; Cusumano 1985; Japanese Management Association 1987; Wickens 1987). Schroeder and Robinson (1993) present a table documenting the top 10 continuous innovation programmes in Japan, with firms like Kawasaki Heavy Engineering (reporting an average of nearly 7 million suggestions per year, equivalent to nearly 10 per worker per week), Nissan (6 million, 3 per worker per week), Toshiba (4 million) and Matsushita (also with 4 million). An interesting element in this study is that these firms gave little financial reward as compared to US firms—indicating the CI had become part of their basic work culture.

Data is also available from industry associations such as the Japan Human Relations Association (JHRA), which tries to track the extent of involvement, the number of suggestions, implementation rates and so on. Figure 2.1 (based on private communication with JHRA) indicates the sustained pattern over a 15 year period from 1981 until 1995.

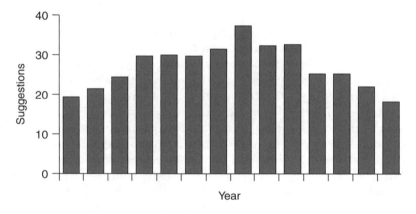

FIGURE 2.1   Suggestions per employee in Japanese industry, 1981–1995.

JHRA observes that high-involvement innovation has developed extensively across Japanese industry, with most growth now coming from the service sector, at least in terms of number of suggestions. This is partly due to the relative lack of emphasis in earlier years in this area: the experience in manufacturing has been that volume precedes quality of ideas and that in more mature companies the numbers of suggestions are lower but their impact higher. For example, Hitachi were receiving suggestions at the level of 100/employee during 1986 but now only have 25; however, these are of significantly higher impact. JHRA also stresses that it is important to put this data in context; these are larger and more experienced firms and represent a fraction of the total 1.6 million firms in Japan. (This information is based on discussions with Professor Yamada of JHRA in 1996.)

Similar data is now available from a wide range of non-Japanese cases; for example, the textile firm Milliken reports receiving an average of one suggestion from each of its employees every week, and they attribute much of their success in winning awards for high and consistent performance to this source. Other examples are reported by several writers, confirming this general trend (Johnson 1998; Schuring and Luijten 1998; Prabhu 2000; Brunet 2002).

BOX 2.2 Suggesting success?

Ideas UK is an independent body which offers advice and guidance to firms wishing to establish and sustain employee involvement programmes. It grew out of the UK Suggestion Schemes Association and offers an opportunity for firms to learn about and share experiences with high-involvement approaches. A recent survey (based on 79 responses from its membership of around 200 firms) indicated a total of 93 285 ideas received during 2000–2001. Not every idea is implemented but from the survey and from previous data it appears that around 25% are — and the savings which emerged as a direct consequence were reported as being £88 million for the period. This pattern has been stable over many years and indicates the type of direct benefit obtained; in addition firms in the survey reported other valuable outcomes form the process of employee involvement including (in order of importance):

- Stimulating Creativity and Innovation
- Assisting Aims of the Organization
- Recognizing Individuals and Teams
- Improving Morale
- Saving Money
- Increased Customer Satisfaction

Source: Personal communication with ideas UK. For more information see the website at http://www.ideasuk.com/.

Whilst much of the reported data on the use of high-involvement approaches relates to Japanese or US experience, a major study was carried out by a group of European and Australian researchers in the late 1990s. This large-scale comparative survey is described in Box 2.3 and Table 2.3 in more detail; its main findings were that continuous innovation (CI) experience has diffused widely and that firms are obtaining significant strategic benefits from it. Importantly the pattern of high involvement has spread but the specific ways in which it is implemented and configured varied widely, reflecting different cultural and historical conditions in different countries.

This theme of transferability of such ideas between locations and into different application areas has been extensively researched by others. It is clear from these studies that the principles of 'lean' manufacturing can be extended into supply and distribution chains, into product development and R&D and into service activities and operations (Lamming 1993; Leonard-Barton, 1992; Leonard-Barton and Smith, 1994; Wheelwright and Clark, 1992). Nor is there any particular barrier in terms of national culture; high-involvement approaches to innovation have been successfully transplanted to a number of different locations (Ishikure, 1988; Kaplinsky *et al.*, 1995; Schonberger, 1985; Schroeder and Robinson, 1991).

BOX 2.3 The CINet survey.

Whilst there are a number of detailed company-level studies of high-involvement innovation, there is relatively little information about the 'bigger picture' (except in the well-reported case of Japan (Imai 1987; Lillrank and Kano 1990; Schroeder and Robinson 1993; Imai 1997)). How far has this approach diffused? Why do organizations choose to develop it? What benefits do they receive? And what barriers prevent them moving further along the road towards high involvement?

Questions like these provided the motivation for a large survey carried out in a number of European countries and replicated in Australia during the late 1990s. It was one of the fruits of a co-operative research network which was established to share experiences and diffuse good practice in the area of high involvement innovation (more information on this network can be found at http://www.continuous-innovation.net/). The survey (the results of which are described in full in Boer et al. (1999)) involved over 1000 organizations in a total of seven countries and provides a useful map of the take-up and experience with high-involvement innovation. (The survey only covered manufacturing, although follow-up work is looking at services as well.) Some of the key findings were as follows.

Overall around 80% of organizations were aware of the concept and its relevance, but its actual implementation, particularly in more developed forms (see Chapter 4), involved around half of the firms.

The average number of years which firms had been working with high-involvement innovation on a systematic basis was 3.8, supporting the view that this is not a 'quick fix' but something to be undertaken as a major strategic commitment. Indeed, those firms that were classified as 'CI innovators' — operating well-developed high-involvement systems — had been working on this development for an average of nearly seven years.

High involvement is still something of a misnomer for many firms, with the bulk of efforts concentrated on shop-floor activities as opposed to other parts of the organization. There is a clear link between the level of maturity and development of high involvement here — the 'CI innovators' group was much more likely to have spread the practices across the organization as a whole. (Again this maps well on to the maturity model introduced in Chapter 4 and described in detail in the second part of the book.)

Motives for making the journey down this road vary widely but cluster particularly around the themes of quality improvement, cost reduction and productivity improvement. This supports the view that high-involvement innovation is an 'engine for innovation' that can be hooked up to different strategic targets (see Chapter 7), but it also underlines its main role as a source of 'doing what we do better' innovation rather than the more radical 'do different' type.

In terms of the outcome of high-involvement innovation, there is clear evidence of significant activity, with an average per capita rate of suggestions of 43/year, of which around half were actually implemented. This is a difficult figure since it reflects differences in measurement and definition, but it does support the view that there is significant potential in workforces across a wide geographical range — it is not simply a Japanese phenomenon. Firms in the sample also reported indirect benefits arising from this including improved morale and motivation, and a more positive attitude towards change.

What these suggestions can do to improve performance is, of course, the critical question and the evidence from the survey suggests that key strategic targets were being impacted upon. On average, improvements of around 15% were reported in process areas like quality, delivery, manufacturing lead time and overall productivity, and there was also an average of 8% improvement in the area of product cost. Of significance is the correlation between performance improvements reported and the maturity of the firm in terms of high-involvement behaviour. The 'CI innovators' — those which had made most progress towards establishing high involvement as 'the way we do things around here' — were also the group with the largest reported gains, averaging between 19% and 21% in the above process areas.

Almost all high-involvement innovation activities take place on an 'in-line' basis — that is, as part of the normal working pattern rather than as a voluntary 'off-line' activity. Most of this activity takes place in some form of group work although around a third of the activity is on an individual basis.

TABLE 2.3   Improvements reported in the CINet survey.

Performance areas (% change)	UK	SE	N	NL	FI	DK	Australia	Average across sample (n = 754 responses)
Productivity improvement	19	15	20	14	15	12	16	15
Quality improvement	17	14	17	9	15	15	19	16
Delivery performance improvement	22	12	18	16	18	13	15	16
Lead time reduction	25	16	24	19	14	5	12	15
Product cost reduction	9	9	15	10	8	5	7	8

2.5 Case Studies

Perhaps it is particularly at the level of the case study that we can see some of the strong arguments in favour of high-involvement innovation. The direct benefits that come from people making suggestions are of course significant, particularly when taken in aggregate, but we need to add to this the longer-term improvements in morale and motivation that can emerge from increasing participation in innovation.

Throughout the book reference will be made to different case studies from a wide range of countries, sectors and firm types, but it will be useful to give a flavour of the case-level experience here in the following examples.

The FMCG Sector

In a detailed study of seven leading firms in the fast moving consumer goods (FMCG) sector, Westbrook and Barwise (1994) reported a wide range of benefits including:

- Waste reduction of £500k in year 1, for a one-off expense of £100k
- A recurrent problem costing over 25k/year of lost time, rework and scrapped materials eliminated by establishing and correcting root cause
- 70% reduction in scrap year on year
- 50% reduction in set-up times; in another case 60–90%

- Uptime increased on previous year by 50% through CI project recommendations
- £56k/year overfilling problems eliminated
- Reduction in raw material and component stocks over 20% in 18 months
- Reduced labour cost per unit of output from 53 pence to 43 pence
- Raised service levels (order fill) from 73% to 91%
- Raised factory quality rating from 87.6% to 89.6%

Capital One

The US financial services group Capital One has seen major growth over the past three years (1999–2002, equivalent to 430%) and has built a large customer base of around 44 million people. Its growth rate (30% in turnover 2000–2001) makes it one of the most admired and innovative companies in its sector. But, as Wall (2002) points out:

> 'Innovation at Capital One cannot be traced to a single department or set of activities. It's not a unique R&D function, there is no internal think-tank. Innovation is not localized but systemic. It's the lifeblood of this organization and drives its remarkable growth ... It comes through people who are passionate enough to pursue an idea they believe in, even if doing so means extending well beyond their primary responsibilities.'

Chevron Texaco

Chevron Texaco is another example of a high growth company which incorporates—in this case in its formal mission—a commitment to high-involvement innovation. It views its 53 000 employees worldwide as 'fertile and largely untapped resources for new business ideas ... Texaco believed that nearly everyone in the company had ideas about different products the company could offer or ways it could run its business. It felt it had thousands of oil and gas experts inside its walls and wanted them to focus on creating and sharing innovative ideas ...' (Abraham and Pickett 2002).

Kumba Resources

In implementing high-involvement innovation in a large South African mining company (De Jager *et al.* 2002), benefits reported included:

- Improvements in operating income at one dolomite mine of 23% despite deteriorating market conditions
- Increase in truck fleet availability at a large coal mine of 7% (since these are 180 ton trucks, the improvement in coal hauled is considerable)
- Increase in truck utilization of 6% on another iron ore mine

'Japanese' Manufacturing Techniques

Kaplinsky (1994) reports on a series of applications of 'Japanese' manufacturing techniques (including the extensive use of kaizen in a variety of developing-country factories in Brazil, India, Zimbabwe, the Dominican Republic and Mexico). In each case there is clear evidence of the potential benefits that emerge where high-involvement approaches are adopted—although the book stresses the difficulties of creating the conditions under which this can take place.

Manufacturing and Service Organizations

Gallagher and colleagues report on a series of detailed case studies of manufacturing and service sector organizations that have made progress towards implementing some form of high-involvement innovation (Gallagher and Austin 1997). The cases highlight the point that, although the sectors involved differ widely—insurance, aerospace, electronics, pharmaceuticals, etc.—the basic challenge of securing high involvement remains broadly similar.

2.6 Summary

> 'For the smallest companies (those with fewer than 50 employees) formal suggestion schemes might seem unnecessary as individual input can usually be captured in other ways. For the rest there is little excuse.'
>
> (CBI 2002)

This chapter has tried to marshal some of the growing evidence that high-involvement innovation offers significant business benefits across a range of dimensions. It represents a small slice of the much wider experience of organizations of all shapes and sizes with this concept and suggests strongly that the challenge is no longer whether or not to aim for high-involvement innovation—but how to go about it. How do we build an innovation culture, one where 'the way we do things around here' is about actively seeking to find and solve problems and look for new opportunities? That question—and a review of some of the forces which make that a difficult task—is the focus of the next chapter.

References

Abraham, D. and S. Pickett (2002) 'Refining the innovation process at Texaco,' *Perspectives on Business Innovation (online)*. Available at http://www.cbi.cgey.com.

Arrow, K. (1962) 'The economic implications of learning by doing,' *Review of Economic Studies*, **29** (2), 155–173.

Bell, M. and K. Pavitt (1993) 'Technological accumulation and industrial growth,' *Industrial and Corporate Change*, **2** (2), 157–211.

Bell, R.M. and D. Scott-Kemmis (1990) *The Mythology of Learning-by-Doing in World War 2 Airframe and Ship Production*. Science Policy Research Unit, University of Sussex, Brighton.

Blimes, L., K. Wetzker and P. Xhonneux (1997) *Value in Human Resources*. Financial Times, London.

Boer, H., A. Berger, R. Chapman and F. Gertsen (1999) *CI Changes: From Suggestion Box to the Learning Organization*. Ashgate, Aldershot.

Brunet, P. (2002) Kaizen in Japan—a target-oriented system, in Smeds, R. (ed.), *Continuous Innovation in Business Processes and Networks*, HUT Press, Heslinki University of Technology, Helsinki.

Caulkin, S. (2001) *Performance through People*. Chartered Institute of Personnel and Development, London.

CBI (2002) *Innovation Potential*. Confederation of British Industry, London, May 2002.

CIPD (2001) *Raising UK Productivity: Why People Management Matters*. Chartered Institute of Personnel and Development, London.

Cusumano, M. (1985) *The Japanese Automobile Industry: Technology and Management at Nissan and Toyota*. Harvard University Press, Cambridge, MA.

De Jager, B., M. Welgemoed, C. De Jager, C. Minnie, J. Bessant and D. Francis (2002) 'Enabling continuous improvement—an implementation case study,' in Smeds, R. (ed.), *Continuous Innovation in Business Processes and Networks*, HUT Press, Helsinki University of Technology, Helsinki.

DTI (1997) *Competitiveness through Partnerships with People*. Department of Trade and Industry, London.

Dutrenit, G. (1998) *From Knowledge Accumulation to Strategic Capabilities*. Science Policy Research Unit, Brighton.

Figuereido, P. (2001) *Technological Learning and Competitive Performance*. Edward Elgar, Cheltenham.

Figuereido, P. (2002) 'Does technological learning pay off? Inter-firm differences in technological capability-accumulation paths and operational performance improvement,' *Research Policy*, **31**, 73–94.

Gallagher, M. and S. Austin (1997) *Continuous Improvement Casebook*. Kogan Page, London.

Guest, D., J. Michie, M. Sheehan and N. Conway (2000) *Employment Relations, HRM and Business Performance: An Analysis of the 1998 Workplace Employee Relations Survey*. Chartered Institute of Personnel and Development, London.

Herskovitz, J. (2002) 'US carrier which invests in people turning a healthy profit,' *Irish Examiner*, Dublin: 14 June, p. 8.

Huselid, M. (1995) 'The impact of human resource management practices on turnover, productivity and corporate financial performance,' *Academy of Management Journal*, **38**, 647–656.

Imai, K. (1987) *Kaizen*. Random House, New York.

Imai, M. (1997) *Gemba Kaizen*. McGraw-Hill, New York.

Ishikure, K. (1988) 'Achieving Japanese productivity and quality levels at a US plant,' *Long Range Planning*, **21** (5), 10–17.

Japanese Management Association (1987) *Canon Production System: Creative Involvement of the Total Workforce*. Productivity Press, Cambridge, MA.

Johnson, M. (1998) 'A case study in continuous improvement,' in Boer, K. and Gieskes, J. (eds), *Continuous Improvement: From Idea to Reality*. Twente University Press, Enschede, The Netherlands.

Kaplinsky, R. (1994) *Easternization: The Spread of Japanese Management Techniques to Developing Countries*. Frank Cass, London.

Kaplinsky, R., F. den Hertog and B. Coriat (1995) *Europe's Next Step*. Frank Cass, London.

Kay, J. (1993) *Foundations of Corporate Success: How Business Strategies Add Value*. Oxford University Press, Oxford.

Lamming, R. (1993) *Beyond Partnership*. Prentice-Hall, London.

Leonard-Barton, D. (1992) 'The organization as learning laboratory,' *Sloan Management Review*, **34** (1), 23–28.

Leonard-Barton, D. and Smith (1994) 'Transforming R&D and manufacturing capabilities,' in Souder, W. and Sherman, J. (eds), *Managing New Technology Development*, McGraw-Hill, New York.

Lillrank, P. and N. Kano (1990) *Continuous Improvement: Quality Control Circles in Japanese Industry*. University of Michigan Press, Ann Arbor, MI.

Monden, Y. (1983) *The Toyota Production System*. Productivity Press, Cambridge, MA.

Patterson, M., M. West, R. Lawthorn and S. Nickell (1997) *The Impact of People Management Practices on Business Performance*. Chartered Institute of Personnel and Development, London.

Pfeffer, J. (1994) *Competitive Advantage Through People*. Harvard Business School Press, Boston, MA.

Prabhu, V. (2000) 'Continuous improvement culture and best practice: implications from a large-scale study of manufacturing companies in N.E. England,' in *From Improvement to Innovation*, Aalborg University Press, Aalborg, Denmark.

Richardson, R. and M. Thompson (1999) *The Impact of People Management Practices on Business Performance: A Literature Review*, Chartered Institute of Personnel and Development, London.

Roethlisberger, F. and W. Dickson (1939) *Management and the Worker*. Harvard University Press, Cambridge, MA.

Schonberger, R. (1985) *World Class Manufacturing*, Free Press, New York.

Schroeder, D. and A. Robinson (1991) 'America's most successful export to Japan—continuous improvement programs,' *Sloan Management Review*, **32** (3), 67–81.

Schroeder, M. and A. Robinson (1993) 'Training, continuous improvement and human relations: the US TWI programs and Japanese management style,' *California Management Review*, **35** (2).

Schuring, R. and H. Luijten (1998) *Re-Inventing Suggestion Schemes for Continuous Improvement. Continuous Improvement—from Idea to Reality*. Twente University Press, Twente, The Netherlands.

Stern, E. and E. Sommerblad (1999) *Workplace Learning, Culture and Performance*. Chartered Institute of Personnel and Development, London.

Taylor, F. (1912) *Scientific Management*. Dartmouth College, Hanover, NH.

Tremblay, P. (1994) *Comparative Analysis of Technological Capability and Productivity Growth in the Pulp and Paper Industry in Industrialised and Industrialising Countries*. University of Sussex, Brighton.

Ulrich, D. (1998) 'A new mandate for human resources,' *Harvard Business Review*, **76** (1), 124–134.

Wall, J. (2002) 'Innovation based sustainability at Capital One Financial,' *Perspectives on Business Innovation*. Available at http://www.cbi.cgey.com.

Westbrook, R. and P. Barwise (1994) *Continuous Improvement in Leading FMCG Companies*. London Business School, London.

Wheelwright, S. and K. Clark (1992) *Revolutionizing Product Development*, Free Press, New York.

Wickens, P. (1987) *The Road to Nissan: Flexibility, Quality, Teamwork*. Macmillan, London.

Womack, J., D. Jones and D. Roos (1991) *The Machine that Changed the World*. Rawson Associates, New York.

Wood, S. and L. de Menezes (1998) 'High commitment management in the UK: evidence from the Workplace Industrial Relations Survey and Employers' Manpower and Skills Practices Survey,' *Human Relations*, **51**, 485–517.

Chapter 3

WHAT'S THE PROBLEM?

At first sight high-involvement innovation is not a problem. Faced with the idea that 'with every pair of hands you get a free brain', any organization would make a high priority of trying to motivate and mobilize that brain to help it achieve its goals. Not for nothing do many organizations make the explicit point in their mission statements, annual reports and other communications that 'people are our most valuable asset!'.

But behind this apparently axiomatic point lies the real difficulty. In practice few organizations can claim to mobilize the full range of creativity and innovative capability that their employees have to offer. This arises not out of a conscious desire to marginalize them, but as a result of the ways in which organizations have evolved—roots that go back hundreds of years and that shape the dominant beliefs about how organizations work. This chapter looks at the blocks and barriers to high-involvement innovation and the need to change 'the way we do things around here'—to develop and sustain a fundamentally different organizational culture.

3.1 Cogs in the Machine?

Whereas a manager looking for the 'free brain' effect is correct in his/her view that everyone has the *potential* to contribute to the innovation process, two trends—industrialization and the increasing specialization of innovation into a science-based activity—have had a major impact on our ideas about participation in the innovation process (Freeman 1982). Although there are documented reports of successful participation, it would be true to say that much of the 20th century was characterized by a lack of involvement of most employees in either product or process innovation. Whilst much of this represented an emergent characteristic of increasingly organized and formalized industrial systems, there are explicit indications of the underlying philosophy. For example, in Frederick Taylor's work on scientific management stress was laid on excluding employees from intervening in the processes within which they worked (Taylor 1947). Henry Ford is reputed to have once complained, 'how come when I want a pair of hands I get a human being as well?' (Melville-Ross 2000). The justification for this separation of hand and brain was that a well-designed system should not be interfered with through the introduction of unnecessary variation. A consequence—easy to see with hindsight but less so in the context of what were significant improvements in productivity and quality—was that many early mass-production factories came to resemble giant machines staffed by an army of human robots. The images in Charlie Chaplin's famous film *Modern Times* provide a picture of this kind of work which is not heavily exaggerated!

3.2 What Makes an Innovative Culture?

'Management that is destructively critical when mistakes are made kills initiative. It's essential that we have many people with initiative if we are to continue to grow.'
(William McKnight, former CEO of 3M)

Concern about how to organize and manage innovation goes back a long way. Ever since the first cavemen began to think about better ways to feed and clothe themselves (and shortly after that to fight others more effectively!) there has been a recognition that new ideas matter. Whilst the lone-inventor model has always been of value—the oddball or crank who lives on the edge of what the rest are doing, but who comes up with a surprising and different way of doing something—it did not take society long to realize the value of trying to organize innovation in more systematic fashion. As Freeman *et al.* (1982) point out, as technologies became more complex in the late 19th century so the idea of the 'lone inventor' became increasingly rare. Whether for purposes of creation or control over 'unlicensed' innovation (as, for example, exerted by various religious groups), attention has been paid to trying to understand how innovation as a shared process operates and how it can be supported (or constrained).

Added to this is the simple psychological effect that comes out of shared problem solving. Take any group of people and ask them to think of different uses for an everyday item—a cup, a brick, a ball, etc. Working alone they will usually develop an extensive list—but then ask them to share the ideas they have generated. The resulting list will not only be much longer, but will also contain much greater diversity of possible classes of solution to the problem. For example, uses for a cup might include using it as a container (vase, pencil holder, drinking vessel, etc.), a mould (for sandcastles, cakes, etc.), a musical instrument, a measure, a template around which one can draw, a device for eavesdropping (when pressed against a wall) and even, when thrown, a weapon!

The psychologist J.P. Guilford classed these two traits as 'fluency'—the ability to produce ideas—and 'flexibility'—the ability to come up with different types of idea (Guilford 1967). The above experiment will quickly show that, working as a group, people are usually much more fluent and flexible than any single individual. When working together people spark each other off, jump on and develop each other's ideas, encourage and support each other through positive emotional mechanisms like laughter and agreement and in a variety of ways stimulate a high level of shared creativity.

This is a common effect demonstrating both the natural human capability for problem solving and also the advantages of doing this in a shared context. It does not always work—when, for example, there are status differences in the group then junior members will tend to keep their mouths shut. Similarly, if the atmosphere is formal and heavily structured, the free flow of ideas will be restricted or, if people feel inhibited or shy, their contribution may not emerge. In other words, achieving this effect is not automatic but requires organization and management. (This is the basis of 'brainstorming' and a wide range of creativity enhancement techniques that have been developed over many years—for more detailed discussion of these and the underlying principles, see Rickards (1997), Cook (1999) and Leonard and Swap (1999).

3.3 Organizing for Innovation

This concern for organizing innovation as a shared activity has been around for a long time—and as a result we can benefit from the many attempts to do it well. As we might expect, there is not a single 'best' way of doing it, not least because all groups are to some extent unique and differ from each other in terms of the personalities involved, the context in which they find themselves, the tasks which they are trying to undertake, etc. However, there are a number of consistent themes, which provide us with a 'blueprint' from which to try and configure innovative organizations.

Table 3.1 summarizes these and gives some indication of the research which describes in more detail the ways in which they operate.

TABLE 3.1 Creating an innovative culture.

Factor	Influence on innovative behaviour	Underpinning research
Motivation	People are driven to make their mark on the world and also motivated by the degree to which they feel able to do so They are also highly motivated by recognition of their contribution from both peers and superiors Need for achievement, need for recognition, etc.	(Maslow 1963; McClelland 1965; Csikszentmihalyi 1988; Amabile 1998; Sternberg 1999)
Availability of 'slack' resources	People need time and space to explore and create They need resources to experiment with and to fail	(Claxton 2001; Gundling 2000)
Leadership	People need role models who exemplify key values—innovators and rule breakers as heroes Leaders who provide resources and motivation and who are consistent—'do as I do not just as I say'. Expression of commitment at strategic level—this is important	(Senge 1990a,b; Bess 1995; Goleman 1998; Cooper 2000)

(continued overleaf)

TABLE 3.1   (*continued*)

Factor	Influence on innovative behaviour	Underpinning research
Direction	Innovation as strategically targeted not just 'moving the deckchairs'. Measurement and improvement motivated from within. Buy in and ownership of challenge	(Dodgson 1989; Johnson and Scholes 1993; Francis 1994; Robert 1995; Mintzberg *et al.* 1998; Hamel 2000)
Self-development	Learning to learn and acquiring and using key skills in context and process	(Wickens 1987; McGill and Warner Weil 1989; Pedler *et al.* 1991)
Enabling tools and resources	Systematic approaches to problem finding and solving Creativity training	(de Bono 1993; Rickards 1997; Cook 1999)
Communication and information exchange	Networking across boundaries Invisible college Knowledge-based organization	(Allen 1977; Wenger 1999)
Knowledge management	Capture and codification Tacit to explicit Display and dissemination	(Nonaka 1991; Tidd 1997; Teece 1998; Krogh *et al.* 2000; Swan 2003)
Cross-boundary working	Linking different knowledge sets Unexpected knowledge, inputs and stimuli Different perspectives and complementary resources Cross-functional working and EI	(Clark and Fujimoto 1992; Blackler 1995; Dyer and Nobeoka 2000; Sapsed *et al.* 2002; Swan 2003)
Appropriate structures	Structures to facilitate interchange and flexibility Project, matrix, line and other choices—need to develop skills in matching tasks to configuration	(Mintzberg 1979; Clark and Fujimoto 1992; Nohria and Eccles 1992; Clark 1993)
Team working	Teambuilding and theory	(Belbin 1984; Bixby 1987; Thamhain and Wilemon 1987; Francis and Young 1988; Hackman 1990; Kharbanda and Stallworthy 1990; Katzenbach and Smith 1992; Holti *et al.* 1995; Tranfield *et al.* 1998; Conway and Forrester 1999; Tranfield *et al.* 2000)
Learning	Embedding a cycle of systematic problem finding and solving Ensuring challenging reflection on experience Building and extending a theory base—understanding and having mental models to guide action Encouraging experiment. Sharing and communication of learning with others	(Kolb 1984; Senge 1990a, b; Garvin 1993; Leonard-Barton 1995)

3.4 The Question of 'Culture'

In the next section we will look at some of the most important themes in a little more detail, but first we need to look a little more closely at what we are trying to build in such organizations—something that is frequently referred to as 'an innovation culture'. The word 'culture' is often very confusing since it is used in widely different ways—much as, in *Alice in Wonderland*, the character of Humpty Dumpty used words to mean whatever he wanted them to mean! For our purposes we are going to think of culture as a shared pattern of behaviour—essentially 'the way we do things around here'.

Such a shared view does not come from nowhere—it results from individuals coming together and working out things that they have in common (shared beliefs and values) and ways in which they agree to behave (group norms). They may disagree at first and the resulting shared view is one which emerges out of such conflict—but the important point is that in an effective group there is a common view of 'the way we do things around here', which shapes how people behave—and when new people join the group, the behaviours that are expected of them. Peer pressure of various forms will act to 'socialize' newcomers into this way of thinking and behaving—and, if people do not conform, the group will tend to exclude or even eject them (Schein 1984; 1992). There is an extensive literature on the theme of organizational culture and how it comes to develop. For more detail on this topic, see Hofstede (1984), Schein (1984), Ekvall (1990), Schein (1992) and Stern and Sommerblad (1999).

This is not 'brainwashing'—people still have their individuality and think and behave in personal and different ways, but where they are working together with others they 'buy in' to a shared way of doing things. Such a shared culture doesn't happen all at once—it depends on a cycle of reinforcement and rehearsal where particular behaviours are repeated over time until they become the norm. Importantly, when a group begins to develop such a shared pattern of behaviour, it creates *artefacts*—things which express their underlying views about how to behave.

This idea borrows from archaeology. We know, for example, a great deal about how ancient Egyptians thought and behaved, in other words their culture. However, all of this emerges not from talking to living people, but from inferring the nature of the culture from the various artefacts found in tombs and other relics. In the same way, the things we see around an organization—the cartoons on the walls, the physical layout of rooms and workplaces, the uniforms or their absence, the presence (or absence) of special parking places for directors, etc.—these all tell us a great deal about the way the organization operates and what it values.

Artefacts emerge as a consequence of how people think and behave in a shared fashion, but we can also use the principle of such reinforcement to help shape the emergence of a culture in a particular direction. The ways in which organizations are structured and in which work processes are defined provide powerful formal ways of doing this—for example, the payment system in a business can be used to send and reinforce the message that 'the only thing that matters is individual output—the faster an individual works, the more he/she will get paid'. This will tend to reinforce a culture of 'every man/woman for him/herself' and one of high output since these are the things that will get rewarded. Alternatively the system may emphasize achievement of high quality, in which everyone shares the responsibility for producing a high-quality item and which requires their working together. These two systems would look very different—piece work as against some form of group bonus scheme for example—but the way they function is by sending messages about patterns of behaviour that the organization is looking to develop till they become routine.

Similarly, the way in which an organization is structured will exert a strong influence on the way people behave. If there is a highly bureaucratic structure with control coming from the top via a series of clearly defined levels of autonomy—people do what they are told and have only limited scope for exercising their own judgement—then the emerging culture will be one of limited initiative and creativity. Equally, if the structure is one that separates out different groups according to the functions they perform, allowing limited contact between them (choosing to co-ordinate their activities at a higher level), then the culture that emerges is likely to be one in which cross-boundary problem solving and innovation do not happen well or often.

The other important point about culture viewed in this way is that it not only takes a long time to develop but also that, once established as 'the way we do things around here', it is extremely difficult to change. Simply talking about doing things differently is unlikely to change the way people think or behave at an individual level, never mind at the shared group level we have been talking about. Without a clear statement of the new values and beliefs backed up with strong and consistent reinforcement through structures and procedures, new ways of behaving are unlikely to emerge or take root.

3.5 The Concept of Behavioural Routines

If culture is about a shared pattern of behaviour, which eventually becomes 'the way we do things around here' driven by what are 'taken for granted' assumptions based on shared beliefs, then we can begin to see the difficulty in moving to a different view and pattern of behaviour. If the dominant pattern has been one characterized by beliefs about the separation of hand and brain, that innovation is the province of specialists, that there is one best way of doing things, etc., then these beliefs will create and reinforce a particular culture. Simply announcing that there might be a different way of looking at things will not change beliefs or behaviour—that will depend on a long-term process of making the new beliefs and values explicit and reinforcing behaviours that support them.

A helpful concept here is the idea of 'behavioural routines'—essentially repeated patterns of behaviour, which eventually become 'the way we do things' and which operate at an almost automatic level. There is growing interest in routines and learning as a way of understanding organizational behaviour (Cohen *et al.* 1996). Winter (1986), for example, defines routines as '. . . a relatively complex pattern of behaviour . . . triggered by a relatively small number of initiating signals or choices and functioning as a recognizable unit in a relatively automatic fashion. . .'. This is not to say that routines are mindless patterns; as Giddens (1984) points out, '. . . the routinized character of most social activity is something that has to be 'worked at' continually by those who sustain it in their day-to-day conduct. . .'. It is rather the case that they have become internalized to the point of being unconscious or autonomous.

As noted by several authors, the development of firm-specific routines is an important determinant of successful innovative performance (Nelson and Winter 1982; Nonaka 1991; Pentland and Rueter 1994). Such clusters of behaviour represent particular abilities in the organization—to generate sustained continuous improvement, to link it to the strategic objectives of the business, etc. But putting routines together to create a different culture is likely to involve an extended learning process.

This is a little like learning to drive. To a child the process looks deceptively simple—just hold the round thing, press the pedals and off you go. But acquiring the ability to drive involves extensive learning over a sustained period. First, you have to master the individual and unfamiliar controls—not as easy as they look. Then you have to link these individual actions together into sequences like changing gear—remember how much fun learning the hill start was? And finally, after much practice and a lot of ground gears, burnt rubber and irate drivers in front of whom you've stalled for the thirteenth time, you get as far as the driving test and acquire a licence. But this is only the beginning; having demonstrated a basic level of competence, you then have to go on learning—about driving on different roads, under different conditions, in different cars, on foreign motorways and dirt tracks—until after a long period of learning you might consider yourself reasonably good.

The process continues, rehearsing and reinforcing, integrating new behaviours into old routines, extending the repertoire, until one day you are driving along a road, listening to the radio or chatting to a friend and you realize that you have not been consciously thinking about driving at all—it is something that has become nearly automatic. (Fortunately as psychologists will confirm, this is not inattention, but rather the effect of driving having become a routine activity!)

This raises an apparent paradox—how can innovation (with its emphasis on creativity and spontaneity) be compatible with routine patterns of behaviour? What we mean is that the behavioural patterns through which innovation can emerge become accepted as 'the way we do things around here'—for example, spending time playing with novel ideas, or meeting with people with different perspectives, or carrying out experiments or 'just' daydreaming. Making these the norm requires careful attention to constructing and reinforcing such behaviours and putting in place structures and procedures to enable them to happen.

3.6 Building an Innovation Culture

With the above picture in mind we can see that the effort to build an innovation culture is essentially an exercise in finding what can enable and support the development of innovative behaviours across the organization to the point where they become routines. It is also clear that doing so will involve much more than simply wishing for it, or assuming that it will happen naturally. Whilst everyone is potentially capable of innovative behaviour and groups can offer more fluency and flexibility in idea generation, etc., the fact remains that there are plenty of elements in the fabric of organizational life that act to suppress this kind of behaviour. For example:

- At the individual level people may not feel able to innovate (and if they do not believe they can, then they will not behave in that way) for reasons that include:

- They do not know how
- They are not permitted to express opinions or offer ideas—do as you're told
- They feel shy or anxious about offering an idea
- They feel it is not their place—someone else's job
- They fear what others in the group might say or do—peer pressure
- They feel it is not worth their while—why bother?

If we are to deal with these, then we need to try and construct routines that allow development of skills (through training, for example), safe and low-risk expression of ideas (for example, through brainstorming or similar sessions), acceptance of responsibility for implementing ideas (for example, through job enlargement and team-based activities) and motivation (for example, through changing the reward/recognition system)

- At the workgroup level people may not feel able to innovate for reasons that include:
  - It is not the done thing (group norms do not support it)
  - No time or space to make it happen—too busy doing the 'real' job
  - No reward—why should we bother?
  - Lack of skills—do not know how to do it except on an occasional basis
  - The structures and procedures here do not support it

If we are to deal with these then we need to try and construct routines that allow space and time (for example, through allocating time and other resources to innovative activities within the working day), provide motivation (for example, through changing the reward/recognition system), offer supporting structures (for example, by introducing a formal innovation involvement process or group-based suggestion scheme) and equipping people with skills (for example, through training and development work)

- And at the organizational level reasons include:
  - There is no sharing of learning, so the same problems are confronted and solved again and again in different places—'re-inventing the wheel'
  - There is no tradition of reflecting and reviewing in order to learn, so the same mistakes keep getting made
  - Only certain people feel empowered or authorized to innovate—the rest feel that it is not their job, or that they are not allowed to
  - Lack of communication
  - Lack of understanding of the overall strategic direction—people feel there is no point in making changes
  - Etc.

Dealing with these might involve implementing routines such as cross-functional teamworking, post-project review meetings to capture learning, establishing new communication paths, staff rotation, etc.

Kanter (1997) provides a list of environmental factors which contribute to stifling innovation; these include:

- Dominance of restrictive vertical relationships
- Poor lateral communications
- Limited tools and resources
- Top-down dictates
- Formal, restricted vehicles for change

- Reinforcing a culture of inferiority (i.e. innovation always has to come from outside to be any good)
- Unfocused innovative activity
- Unsupporting accounting practices

and these are similar to the list offered by Amabile (1998). They offer powerful challenges to the current ways in which organizations are structured and operate and suggest directions for trying to establish routines that would be more supportive of innovation.

BOX 3.1 'Killer phrases'.

A good way of capturing the ways in which organizations have cultures that inhibit innovation is to ask people to tell you their favourite 'killer phrases'. These are the many different ways in which an organization says 'no' to an idea—and in doing so sends out a signal that negatively reinforces the kind of behaviour we are trying to develop. If people keep getting told 'no', then they will quickly stop coming up with ideas and offering them.

Killer phrases always have the same structure—'that's a great idea ... **BUT**...' and this 'yes, but' approach is powerful since it works at all levels.

Individuals have killer phrases running inside their heads—for example:

- I've got a good idea—but:
  - No-one will listen to me
  - It's not my job to offer ideas
  - Someone else must have already thought of it
  - I'll look stupid if I say anything

At the level of the group and the organization we have many more, for example:

- That's a great idea BUT:
  - We've already tried it
  - We've never tried it
  - We don't have the time/money/people/other resources
  - X wouldn't like it
  - X would like it (!)
  - It's not the way we do things around here
  - We did that last year and look what happened

I am grateful to Dr George Lester and Professor Tudor Rickards of Manchester Business School for introducing me to this fascinating topic.

3.7 Learning to Manage Innovation

At the heart of developing an innovation culture is the attempt to establish and reinforce behaviour patterns to the point where they become routines—they become, simply, 'the way we do things around here'. What we have learned over many years and through the experience (both successful and less so) of many different organizations is a set of enabling elements—structures, procedures, etc.—which help enable and facilitate the development of an innovation culture. These were outlined in Table 3.1. a little earlier in the chapter.

It is important to recognize that this is not an exact science—knowing the basic blueprint for these enablers does not mean that every firm which adopts them will succeed in creating an innovation culture. Organizations differ widely in terms of what they do, the environment in which they operate, their patterns of leadership and strategic direction and their assets—particular knowledge, physical resources and, above all, people. Each organization needs to develop its own version of them, shaping and configuring them to suit its own particular circumstances and reviewing and developing them through its own learning process.

For example, in the car industry during the late 1980s it became clear that there was a significant advantage associated with Japanese and Japanese owned plants—an advantage of around 2:1 in terms of better quality, productivity, etc. Extensive research on the gap suggested that firms like Toyota were achieving this through a high level of employee involvement in innovation—on average Toyota was receiving around 2 million improvement suggestions every year from its workforce. This kaizen—continuous improvement—was clearly something other firms wished to acquire and they looked closely at the ways Toyota and others had achieved it—through the widespread use of quality circles, policy deployment and other approaches. But simply adopting them did not bring the expected benefits. Indeed, the early experience was often of an initial 'honeymoon effect', where a flow of suggestions began to emerge, followed by a rapid decline to the earlier status—or even worse. What was going on was an attempt to simply copy rather than to adapt and develop—to learn.

In similar fashion the 3M company's ability to maintain a steady rate of innovation over a century of business life is a remarkable achievement and, not surprisingly, many companies try to emulate its success by looking closely at what it does. Most fail—and in large measure this is because they try to copy blindly rather than adapting and configuring the 3M blueprint to their own (often very different) circumstances. Just because 3M is able to benefit from a policy that gives its staff 15% of their time as 'free' space in which to pursue curiosity-driven projects and ideas, this does not mean that allocating this level of resource in another firm will have the same effect. (As Box 3.2 shows, the 3M success is derived from many years of reinforcement and development of an innovation culture, which is enabled by a wide range of supporting mechanisms.)

This raises the other key point in building an innovation culture—it is not the product of doing one thing well but of changing and reinforcing a wide set of different behaviours. (It is also important to note that the 'recipes' for success at one point in time may not be appropriate for another—organizations also need to review whether their culture is still appropriate for new circumstances and need to be prepared to adapt or even abandon it.)

BOX 3.2 3M as an example of an innovative culture.

'As our business grows, it becomes increasingly necessary to delegate responsibility and to encourage men and women to exercise their initiative. This requires considerable tolerance.

Those men and women, to whom we delegate authority and responsibility, if they are good people, are going to want to do their jobs in their own way.

Mistakes will be made. But if a person is essentially right, the mistakes he or she makes are not as serious in the long run as the mistakes management will make if it undertakes to tell those in authority exactly how they must do their jobs.'

These comments are from William McKnight, who was CEO of 3M from 1949 but who joined the company as a book-keeper in 1907. He is widely credited with having articulated some of the key principles on which the company culture is based and which have led to such an effective track record in innovation. It is often cited as an example of successful and consistent innovation drawing on what is clearly a highly innovative culture. 3M has around 50 000 products in its range and yet is so confident of its ability to innovate that it sets the stretching target of deriving half of its sales from products it develops and introduces during the last three years. Not only is 3M able to keep this ambitious flywheel of innovation turning, but it does so with a mixture of product improvements and breakthrough radical new product concepts.

Significantly 3M does not attribute its success to a single organizational 'lever'. Although it is famous for its '15%' rule in which people are encouraged to explore and play with ideas that may not be directly relevant to their main job, this space for innovation is only one element of a complex culture. Other components include policies to allow people to progress their ideas if they feel a personal commitment and are prepared to champion them — this is enabled through a rising series of funding options from simple 'seed' money through to more extensive resources made available if the Board can be convinced by the ideas and the enthusiasm of the proposal. There is a deliberate attempt to create a sense of company history based on valuing as heroes and heroines those people who challenged the system — and a deliberate policy of encouraging 'bootlegging' behaviour, progressing projects that do not necessarily have official sanction but that people pursue often in highly innovative and improvisational mode.

The complex set of behaviours which the firm has discovered works and their subsequent embodiment in a set of reinforcing processes, structures and mechanisms make it difficult for others to imitate the 3M approach — it is not simply a matter of copying but rather of learning and configuring to suit particular circumstances.

For a detailed discussion of how 3M has built an innovative culture, see Mitchell (1991), Kanter (1997) and Gundling (2000).

3.8 High Involvement vs. Focused Development of Innovation Culture

So far we have seen that there is considerable scope for innovative behaviour amongst any group of people, and that the fluency and flexibility of idea generation increases with the numbers involved, but capturing this potential depends on creating an innovation culture, which is not an easy task. The killer phrases described in Box 3.2 are just one humorous expression of the strong forces that act against developing and sustaining a belief in innovation and the practices which would follow from that. Most organizations are established to try and achieve a measure of stability and reinforce doing more of the same, not doing things differently or doing different things. So there is inevitably a tension that has to be managed and this represents a significant challenge when applied across the entire workforce of an organization.

The nature of this tension—and the implications which it has for organization design and management—has occupied researchers for many years. One of the pioneering studies was that carried out by Burns and Stalker in the 1960s, looking at innovation organization in both a mature industry (textiles) and a new and rapidly growing one (electronics) (Burns and Stalker 1961). Their conclusions were that all organizations need to have innovative capability, although for some sectors (like electronics in their study) there is a greater sense of urgency. But organizing for it uncovers a tension between two differing organizational 'archetypes'—what they termed 'organic' and 'mechanistic'. The one (mechanistic) is concerned with maintaining the status quo and managing the operations that keep the business going, whilst the other (organic) is concerned with creating the future products and processes. It is important to stress that these are 'ideal types'—they do not exist in such a form in real organizations but they serve to clarify the two points on a spectrum around which real organizations have to organize themselves.

The relevance of Burns and Stalker's model can be seen in an increasing number of cases where organizations have restructured to become less mechanistic. For example, General Electric in the USA underwent a painful but ultimately successful transformation, moving away from a rigid and mechanistic structure to a looser and decentralized form (Moody 1995). ABB, the Swiss–Swedish engineering group, developed a particular approach to their global business based on operating as a federation of small businesses, each of which retained much of the organic character of small firms (Champy and Nohria 1996). Other examples of radical changes in structure include the Brazilian metalworking firm Semco and the Danish hearing aid company Oticon (Semler 1993; Kaplinsky et al. 1995). Importantly, these changes helped the firms adapt to their particular environmental circumstances, but later developments required other changes and not all of the firms—particularly ABB—were successful in making them.

Related to this work has been another strand, which looks at the relationship between different environments and organizational form. Once again the evidence suggests that the higher the uncertainty and complexity in the environment, the greater the need for flexible structures and processes to deal with it (Miles and Snow 1978; Lawrence and Dyer 1983). This partly explains why some fast-growing sectors, for example, electronics or biotechnology, are often associated with more organic organizational forms, whereas mature industries often involve more mechanistic arrangements.

The nature of much advanced technology is also an important factor here, with its emphasis on integration and networking and the increasing availability of information in distributed and widely available form (Woodward 1965; Thompson 1967; Mintzberg 1979; Kaplinsky 1984; Ettlie 1988; Bessant et al. 1991). This underlines a tendency towards more open and participative forms of co-ordination and management and creates better foundations for high-involvement approaches (Woodward 1965; Thompson 1967; Mintzberg 1979; Best 2001). A number of case studies bear this out—for examples, see Clark (1995), Preece (1995) and McCloughlin (1998).

Table 3.2 lists some of the key differences between the two archetypes of mechanistic and organic systems. The tensions between them and the difficulties

TABLE 3.2 Organic and mechanistic systems (based on Burns and Stalker 1961).

Mechanistic	Organic
Specialized differentiation of functional tasks into which the problems and tasks facing the concern as a whole are broken down	Specialist knowledge is shared across team members and made available to deal with the common task of the concern
The abstract nature of each individual task is pursued with techniques and purposes more or less distinct from those of the concern as a whole	The 'realistic' nature of the individual task is seen as set by the total situation of the concern
The reconciliation for each level in the hierarchy of the distinct performance of each task by immediate superiors, who are also in turn responsible for seeing that each is relevant in their own special part of the main task	Adjustment and continual re-definition of individual tasks through interaction with others
The precise definition of rights and obligations and the technical methods attached to each functional role	The shedding of 'responsibility' as a limited field of rights, obligations and methods—problems may not be posted somewhere else as someone else's responsibility
Hierarchical structure of control, authority and communication	A network structure of control, authority and communication
Reinforcement of the hierarchical structure by location of knowledge of actualities exclusively at the top of the hierarchy, where the final reconciliation of distinct tasks and assessment of relevance is made	Omniscience is no longer imputed to the head of the concern; knowledge about the technical or commercial nature of the here and now task may be located anywhere in the network; this location becoming the *ad hoc* centre of control, authority and communication
Tendency for interaction between members of the concern to be vertical, i.e. superior/subordinate	A lateral rather than vertical direction of communication through the organization, communication between people of different ranks, also resembling consultation rather than command
A tendency for operations and working behaviour to be governed by the instructions and decisions issued by superiors	Content of communication, which consists of information and advice rather than instructions and decisions
Insistence on loyalty to the concern and obedience to superiors as a condition of membership	Commitment to the concern's tasks and to the 'technological ethos' of material progress and expansion is more highly valued than loyalty and obedience
Greater importance and prestige attached to internal (local) than to general (cosmopolitan) knowledge, experience and skill	Importance and prestige attached to affiliations and expertise valid in the industrial and technical and commercial milieux external to the firm

in balancing the two fundamentally different cultures that they represent can be readily seen.

It is very important to stress that this is not an 'either/or' pattern—in practice, organizations need aspects of both organic and mechanistic approaches. The challenge is to identify the particular needs of the context in which the organization (or its sub-element) is working and then to create a system best suited to this. In innovation terms the conditions needed for a 'pure' research laboratory will be different to those for shop-floor innovation work, yet both are essential to overall success in innovation.

One resolution that has been widely applied is to focus attention on creating an innovation culture amongst a relatively small but influential group within the organization. These 'licensed' innovators may be in the R&D area, or in systems engineering, or in marketing, but in each case the principle is one that tries to concentrate efforts to develop innovation culture in areas where such a culture will yield 'big hits' in terms of innovation impacts. There is much to be said for this approach—creating the new blockbuster product or revolutionary process or opening up the new market niche all have significant strategic impacts on the business. For example, a company like GlaxoSmithKline can expect to earn several million dollars daily from the sales of a blockbuster drug, whilst the Pilkington company transformed its fortunes through the development and later licensing of the radical float-glass process.

Much experimentation around developing innovation culture has been done with separate and specialized groups like these, for example in the field of R&D management (Roussel *et al.* 1991). The argument for them is based on establishing a virtuous circle in which highly skilled and qualified people are enabled to deploy their individual and especially their shared creativity through structures and procedures that are often very different to those which operate in the rest of the organization.

Such models have often been very successful—as a variety of case histories testify. Whether it is Lockheed's pioneering of radical new aircraft designs and technologies through its 'skunk works' (Rich and Janos 1994), Data General developing major new product concepts in mini-computers (Kidder 1981) or Hewlett-Packard setting up radical innovation teams (Leifer *et al.* 2000), it is clear that careful attention to creating a focused innovation group can pay big dividends.

But these approaches also have their limitations, particularly in terms of bringing back into the mainstream the benefits of highly focused innovation.

3.9 High-Involvement Innovation

One argument that can be advanced in favour of this 'specialist innovator' approach is that it works, so why tinker with it? If it is difficult to resolve the implicit tensions in the organization, then why not concentrate on a model in which a small percentage of big hitters act as innovators for the rest of the organization? What is the extra benefit in aiming for higher levels of involvement (see Figure 3.1) when achieving that may involve significant extra managerial efforts to create, enable and sustain a high-involvement innovation culture? This is a viable—and fairly common—view, but it may be worth challenging it in three particular ways:

- The nature of the innovation task
- Change receptivity
- Creative combinations

The Nature of the Innovation Task

First, even though some elements of innovation, particular involving radical concepts and high technologies, may require specialist knowledge and skills, much of the innovation task in any organization is about problem finding and solving. It is about ironing out the many bugs that lie on the road between idea and successful technical and/or commercial reality. Whilst novelty may be high at the start of this journey, much of the subsequent work is essentially incremental in nature. In addition, much valuable innovation is of the 'do what we do better' variety—wringing a stream of performance improvements from existing machinery or products through continuous review and modification.

This is, for example, the underlying driver for the well-known learning and experience effects in manufacturing where the costs of production fall with increased volume (Bell and Scott-Kemmis 1990); see Chapter 2 for more on this. What actually takes place is a rapid learning process, involving extensive problem solving to 'streamline' the product or process—but it is a process that depends on high levels of involvement in this activity. Joseph Juran, one of the pioneers of the quality movement in the USA and Japan, pointed out the significance of 'the gold in the mine', suggesting that each worker in a factory could potentially contribute a valuable and continuing stream of improvements—provided they were enabled to do so (Juran 1951).

Although there is evidence that this kind of participation has always taken place on an individual firm basis, it is fair to say that it was brought to the world's attention through the experience of Japanese manufacturing in the post-war period. From a position in which Japanese manufactured goods were seen as cheap and of poor quality the industry transformed itself into a world leader, setting radically new standards in quality, productivity and flexibility. There are many reasons to help explain this but a dominant theme is that of employee involvement in the core operations of the firm. Perhaps because Taylorism had never really established itself in Japan (where industrialization took place much later than in the West) the separation of hand and brain was not so marked; the scarcity of resources in the post-war period also put a premium on finding innovative ways around problems of design and production. Although some of the key ideas behind, for example, quality improvement were introduced on the back of post-war aid programmes, it is important to see that their success lay in finding fertile ground in Japanese factories. As Juran comments,

> '... I am agreeably flattered but I regard the conclusion as ludicrous. I did indeed lecture in Japan as reported, and I did bring something new to them—a structured approach to quality. I also did the same thing for a great many other countries, yet none of these attained the results achieved by the Japanese. So who performed the miracle?'
>
> (Juran 1951)

Underpinning the 'miracle' was, of course, hard work. Success was due not to one or two radical innovations but to a continuing stream of incremental improvements, tightening up and extending process and product performance. Shingo's account of how Toyota managed to solve the classical set-up time problem associated with batch manufacturing is instructive (Shingo 1983). In the early days of car manufacturing the giant body presses took around a day to set up for a different model—with consequent impacts on productivity and flexibility in the factory. The task of reducing this set-up time was critical to Toyota's development and over a 20 year period Shingo and his team were able to cut the time down to minutes—developing the 'Single Minute Exchange of Die' (SMED) approach. There were no radical breakthroughs during this period, but rather a systematic cycle of problem finding and solving driving the time down; the 'engine' for this was the creativity of the shop-floor teams working with the presses themselves.

Although the experience of the car industry has been well documented, similar patterns have been reported across Japanese industry (Schonberger 1982; Japanese Management Association 1987; Ishikure 1988; Suzaki 1988).

Change Receptivity

The second point relates to the theme of change management. Much concern is expressed about how to introduce change in ways that will gain the acceptance and co-operation of those affected, and a whole industry of consultancy has been built up around the techniques of effective change implementation (Smith and Tranfield 1990; Burnes 1992). This is not a simple task; as Mintzberg and colleagues comment, 'change can't be managed. Change can be ignored, resisted, responded to, capitalized upon, and created. But it can't be managed and made to march to some orderly step-by-step process' (Mintzberg *et al.* 1998). One of the arguments in favour of high-involvement innovation is that people become used to change not as an occasional and dramatic challenge to their world—one which quite naturally may trigger defensive behaviour responses—but as a regular and accepted feature. 'The way we do things around here' includes the notion of change as an accepted element. There is considerable evidence to support the view that employee involvement is a key element in organizational development programmes (French and Bell 1995) and the theme of participation in ensuring effective adoption of new technologies is also well documented (Mumford 1979; Kidd 1994; Dawson 1996). A number of writers have drawn attention to the positive benefits which instilling a culture of high-involvement innovation can have in respect of preparing the ground for more radical changes; see, for example Leonard-Barton (1992) and Kofoed and Gertsen (2000).

Creative Combinations

Third, the history of innovation is about unexpected combinations. Seeing new possibilities in existing frames and then enabling a new synthesis is the story of human development. Such radical—'do different'—innovation is not the monopoly of highly trained scientists, engineers and other professionals; it sometimes needs the perspective of distance to see the wood for the trees and pick up the signal from the background noise. Evidence is accumulating to suggest that the scope for participation in innovation is not just confined to incremental 'do better' kinds but—given relevant training and support—also available at higher levels of novelty.

Figure 3.1 provides a graphical representation of the challenge. Until recently the norm was to concentrate on low involvement and high impact and to develop

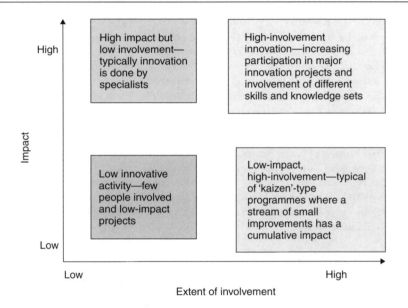

FIGURE 3.1 Options for involvement in the innovation process.

'good practice' in enabling a small number of specialists to innovate on behalf of the organization. The late 20th century saw a growing realization of the additional benefits that might come from enabling higher levels of participation in low-impact innovation of the 'do better' variety—and there has been a development of good practice in this area too. One of the biggest challenges in innovation management in the 21st century is going to be to try and increase the level of involvement of a significant number of people in high-impact innovation—creating and operating a real learning organization.

3.10 Summary

High-involvement innovation is not about occasional radical innovation break-throughs but about creating a culture in which innovation is a way of life. In order for this to happen there is much that needs to be done to create the under-lying conditions in which innovation can happen—in terms of the structure and systems within the organization. But—to borrow a theatrical analogy—it is not simply a matter of good stage management, assembling the props and scenery in a well-endowed theatre. High-involvement innovation also needs a cast—and they need to be rehearsed in their roles as active participants in the innovation process. This focus on behaviour patterns forms the basis of the next chapter.

References

Allen, T. (1977) *Managing the Flow of Technology*. MIT Press, Cambridge, MA.

Amabile, T. (1998) 'How to kill creativity,' *Harvard Business Review*, September/October, 77–87.

Belbin, M. (1984) *Management Teams—Why They Succeed or Fail*. Heinemann, London.

Bell, R. M. and D. Scott-Kemmis (1990) *The Mythology of Learning-by-Doing in World War 2 Airframe and Ship Production*. Science Policy Research Unit, University of Sussex, Brighton.

Bess, J. (1995) *Creative R&D Leadership: Insights from Japan*. Quorum Books, Westport, CT.

Bessant, J., S. Smith, D. Tranfield and P. Levy (1991) 'A new paradigm for the organisation of manufacturing,' *International Journal of Integrated Manufacturing Systems*, **2** (2).

Best, M. (2001) *The New Competitive Advantage*. Oxford University Press, Oxford.

Bixby, K. (1987) *Superteams*. Fontana, London.

Blackler, F. (1995) 'Knowledge, knowledge work and organizations,' *Organization Studies*, **16** (6), 1021–1046.

Burnes, B. (1992) *Managing Change*. Pitman, London.

Burns, T. and G. Stalker (1961) *The Management of Innovation*. Tavistock, London.

Champy, J. and N. Nohria (eds) (1996) *Fast Forward*. Harvard Business School Press, Cambridge, MA.

Clark, J. (ed.) (1993) *Human Resource Management and Technical Change*. Sage, London.

Clark, J. (1995) *Managing Innovation and Change: People, Technology and Strategy*. Sage, London.

Clark, K. and T. Fujimoto (1992) *Product Development Performance*. Harvard Business School Press, Boston, MA.

Claxton, G. (2001) 'The innovative mind,' in Henry, J. (ed.), *Creative Management*. Sage, London.

Cohen, M., R. Burkhart, G. Dosi, L. Marengo, M. Warglien and S. Winter (1996) 'Routines and other recurring patterns of organization,' *Industrial and Corporate Change*, **5** (3).

Conway, S. and R. Forrester (1999) *Innovation and Teamworking: Combining Perspectives through a Focus on Team Boundaries*. University of Aston Business School, Birmingham.

Cook, P. (1999) *Best Practice Creativity*. Gower, Aldershot.

Cooper, R. (2000) *Product Leadership*. Perseus Press, New York.

Csikszentmihalyi, M. (1988) 'Motivation and creativity,' *New Ideas in Psychology*, **6** (2), 159–176.

Dawson, P. (1996) *Technology and Quality: Change in the Workplace*. International Thomson Business Press, London.

de Bono, E. (1993) *Serious Creativity*. Harper Collins, London.

Dodgson, M.E. (1989) *Technology Strategy and the Firm*. Longman, Harlow.

Dyer, J. and K. Nobeoka (2000) 'Creating and managing a high-performance knowledge-sharing network: the Toyota case,' *Strategic Management Journal*, **21** (3), 345–367.

Ekvall, G. (1990) 'The organizational culture of idea management,' in Henry, J. and Walker, D. (eds), *Managing Innovation*. Sage, London, pp. 73–80.

Ettlie, J. (1988) *Taking Charge of Manufacturing*. Jossey-Bass, San Francisco, CA.

Francis, D. (1994) *Step by Step Competitive Strategy*. Routledge, London.

Francis, D. and D. Young (1988) *Top Team Building*. Aldershot, Gower.

Freeman, C. (1982) *The Economics of Industrial Innovation*. Frances Pinter, London.

Freeman, C., L. Soete and J. Clark (1982) *Unemployment and Technical Change*. Frances Pinter, London.

French, W. and C. Bell (1995) *Organizational Development: Behavioural Science Interventions for Organization Improvement*. Prentice Hall, Englewood Cliffs, NJ.

Garvin, D. (1993) 'Building a learning organization,' *Harvard Business Review*, July/August, 78–91.

Giddens, A. (1984) *The Constitution of Society*, University of California Press, Berkeley, CA.

Goleman, D. (1998) 'What makes a leader?,' *Harvard Business Review*, November, 93–102.

Guilford, J. (1967) *The Nature of Human Intelligence*. McGraw-Hill, New York.

Gundling, E. (2000) *The 3M Way to Innovation: Balancing People and Profit*. Kodansha International, New York.

Hackman, J. (ed.) (1990) *Groups That Work (and Those That Don't): Creating Conditions for Effective Teamwork*. Jossey Bass, San Francisco, CA.

Hamel, G. (2000) *Leading the Revolution*. Harvard Business School Press, Boston, MA.

Hofstede, G. (1984) *Culture Consequences*. Sage, London.

Holti, R., J. Neumann and H. Standing (1995) *Change Everything at Once: The Tavistock Institute's Guide to Developing Teamwork in Manufacturing*. Management Books 2000, London.

Ishikure, K. (1988) 'Achieving Japanese productivity and quality levels at a US plant,' *Long Range Planning*, **21** (5), 10–17.

Japanese Management Association (1987) *Canon Production System: Creative Involvement of the Total Workforce*. Productivity Press, Cambridge, MA.

Johnson, G. and K. Scholes (1993) *Exploring Corporate Strategy*. Prentice Hall, Hemel Hempstead.

Juran, J. (1951) *Quality Control Handbook*. McGraw-Hill, New York.

Kanter, R. (ed.) (1997) *Innovation: Breakthrough Thinking at 3M, DuPont, GE, Pfizer and Rubbermaid*. Harper Business, New York.

Kaplinsky, R. (1984) *Automation—The Technology and Society*. Longman, Harlow.

Kaplinsky, R., F. den Hertog and B. Coriat (1995) *Europe's Next Step*. Frank Cass, London.

Katzenbach, J. and D. Smith (1992) *The Wisdom of Teams*. Harvard Business School Press, Boston, MA.

Kharbanda, O. and M. Stallworthy (1990) *Project Teams*. NCC-Blackwell, Manchester.

Kidd, P. (1994) *Agile Manufacturing—Forging New Frontiers*. Addison Wesley, Reading, MA.

Kidder, T. (1981) *The Soul of a New Machine*. Penguin, Harmondsworth.

Kofoed, L. and F. Gertsen (2000) 'The role of CI and learning in a radical change process,' in Gertsen, F. (ed.), *CI 2000: From Improvement to Innovation*. Aalborg University Press, Aalborg, Denmark.

Kolb, D. (1984) *Experiential Learning*. Prentice-Hall, Englewood Cliffs, NJ.

Krogh, G., K. Ichijo and I. Nonaka (2000) *Enabling Knowledge Creation: How to Unlock the Mystery of Tacit Knowledge and Release the Power of Innovation*. Oxford University Press, Oxford.

Lawrence, P. and P. Dyer (1983) *Renewing American Industry*. Free Press, New York.

Leifer, R., C. McDermott, G. O'Conner, L. Peters, M. Rice and R. Veryzer (2000) *Radical Innovation*. Harvard Business School Press, Boston, MA.

Leonard, D. and W. Swap (1999) *When Sparks Fly: Igniting Creativity in Groups*. Harvard Business School Press, Boston, MA.

Leonard-Barton, D. (1992) 'The organization as learning laboratory,' *Sloan Management Review*, **34** (1), 23–38.

Leonard-Barton, D. (1995) *Wellsprings of Knowledge: Building and Sustaining the Sources of Innovation*. Harvard Business School Press, Boston, MA.

Maslow, A. (1963) 'The creative attitude,' *Structuralist*, **3**, 4–10.

McClelland, D. (1965) *The Achieving Society*. Van Nostrand Rheinhold, New York.

McCloughlin, I. (1998) *Creative Technological Change*. Routledge, London.

McGill, I. and S. Warner Weil (1989) *Making Sense of Experiential Learning*. Open University Press, London.

Melville-Ross, T. (2000) 'Forget the cliches, people management works,' *The Independent*, **4**.

Miles, R. and C. Snow (1978) *Organizational Strategy, Structure and Process*. McGraw-Hill, New York.

Mintzberg, H. (1979) *The Structuring of Organizations*. Prentice Hall, Englewood Cliffs, NJ.

Mintzberg, H., J. Lampel and B. Ahlstrand (1998) *Safari Strategy*. Jossey Bass, San Francisco, CA.

Mitchell, R. (1991) 'How 3M keeps the new products coming,' Henry, J. and Walker, D. (eds), *Managing Innovation*. Sage, London.

Moody, F. (1995) *I Sing the Body Electronic*. Hodder and Stoughton, London.

Mumford, E. (1979) *Designing Human Systems*. Manchester Business School Press, Manchester.

Nelson, R. and S. Winter (1982) *An Evolutionary Theory of Economic Growth*, Harvard University Press, Cambridge, MA.

Nohria, N. and R. Eccles (1992) *Networks and Organizations: Structure, Form and Action*. Harvard Business School Press, Boston, MA.

Nonaka, I. (1991) 'The knowledge creating company,' *Harvard Business Review*, November–December, 96–104.

Pedler, M., T. Boydell and J. Burgoyne (1991) *The Learning Company: A Strategy for Sustainable Development*. McGraw-Hill, Maidenhead.

Pentland, B. and H. Rueter (1994) 'Organizational routines as grammars of action,' *Administrative Science Quarterly*, **39**, 484–510.

Preece, D. (1995) *Organizations and Technical Change*. Routledge/International Thompson, London.

Rich, B. and L. Janos (1994) *Skunk Works*. Warner Books, London.

Rickards, T. (1997) *Creativity and Problem Solving at Work*. Gower, Aldershot.

Robert, M. (1995) *Product Innovation Strategy—Pure and Simple*. McGraw-Hill, New York.

Roussel, P., K. Saad and T. Erickson (1991) *Third Generation R&D: Matching R&D Projects with Corporate Strategy*. Harvard Business School Press, Cambridge, MA.

Sapsed, J., J. Bessant, D. Partington, D. Tranfield and M. Young (2002) 'Teamworking and knowledge management; a review of converging themes,' *International Journal of Management Reviews*, **4** (1).

Schein, E. (1984) 'Coming to a new awareness of organizational culture,' *Sloan Management Review*, Winter, 3–16.

Schein, E. (1992) *Organizational Culture and Leadership*. Jossey Bass, San Francisco, CA.

Schonberger, R. (1982) *Japanese Manufacturing Techniques: Nine Hidden Lessons in Simplicity*. Free Press, New York.

Semler, R. (1993) *Maverick*. Century Books, London.

Senge, P. (1990a) *The Fifth Discipline*. Doubleday, New York.

Senge, P. (1990b) 'The leader's new work: building learning organizations,' *Sloan Management Review*, **32** (1), 7–23.

Shingo, S. (1983) *A Revolution in Manufacturing: The SMED System*. Productivity Press, Cambridge, MA.

Smith, S. and D. Tranfield (1990) *Managing Change*. IFS Publications, Kempston.

Stern, E. and E. Sommerblad (1999) *Workplace Learning, Culture and Performance*, Chartered Institute of Personnel and Development, London.

Sternberg, R. (ed.) (1999) *Handbook of Creativity*. Cambridge University Press, Cambridge.

Suzaki, K. (1988) *The New Manufacturing Challenge*. Free Press, New York.

Swan, J. (2003) 'Knowledge, networking and innovation: developing an understanding of process,' in Shavinina, L. (ed.), *International Handbook of Innovation*. Elsevier, New York.

Taylor, F. (1947) *The Principles of Scientific Management*. Harper and Row, London (original published in 1911).

Teece, D. (1998) 'Capturing value from knowledge assets: the new economy, markets for know-how, and intangible assets,' *California Management Review*, **40** (3), 55–79.

Thamhain, H. and D. Wilemon (1987) 'Building high performing engineering project teams,' *IEEE Transactions on Engineering Management*, **EM-34** (3), 130–137.

Thompson, J. (1967) *Organizations in Action*. McGraw-Hill, New York.

Tidd, J. (1997) 'Complexity, networks and learning: integrative themes for research on innovation management,' *International Journal of Innovation Management*, **1** (1), 1–22.

Tranfield, D., I. Parry, S. Wilson, S. Smith and M. Foster (1998) 'Teamworked organizational engineering: getting the most out of teamworking,' *Management Decision*, **36** (6), 378–384.

Tranfield, D., S. Smith, M. Foster, S. Wilson and I. Parry (2000) 'Strategies for managing the teamworking agenda: developing a methodology for team-based organization,' *International Journal of Production Economics*, **65**, 33–42.

Wenger, E. (1999) *Communities of Practice: Learning, Meaning, and Identity*. Cambridge University Press, Cambridge.

Wickens, P. (1987) *The Road to Nissan: Flexibility, Quality, Teamwork*. Macmillan, London.

Winter, S. (1986) 'The research program of the behavioural theory of the firm: orthodox critique and evolutionary perspective,' in Gilad, B. and Kaish, S. (eds), *Handbook of Behavioural Economics, Vol A. Behavioural Microeconomics*. JAI Press, Greenwich, CT.

Woodward, J. (1965) *Industrial Organization: Theory and Practice*. Oxford University Press, Oxford.

Chapter 4

A MODEL FOR HIGH-INVOLVEMENT INNOVATION

Without a framework against which to measure it, high-involvement innovation remains simply a worthy sentiment. This chapter presents a research-based model, which allows organizations to position themselves and to think about how they might carry forward the development of a high-involvement innovation culture. It is described in detail in the Appendix, but this chapter will introduce the basic features.

The model has two dimensions—performance and practice. The former refers to the measurable indicators of innovation, whilst the latter deals with the extent to which an innovation culture has been developed and implemented. Organizations can use this framework to position themselves and 'benchmark' themselves against others and/or a model of good practice and performance.

The value of the model is that it recognizes that firms differ in a number of ways (including how far along the journey to high involvement they have already travelled) and that there is no single solution that will fit all of them. Instead, it uses a series of 'archetypes' of organizations at different stages in their development and examines typical blocks and barriers associated with these stages and how they can be dealt with.

These archetypes, and progress between them as stages on the journey towards a successful and sustainable innovation culture, are described in the next five chapters.

4.1 Measuring Innovation Culture

As we saw in the previous chapter, one of the big challenges facing organizations is to build a shared pattern of beliefs and behaviours that support innovation and become 'the way we do things around here'. To some extent we can help create the conditions for establishing such a culture through clear strategic leadership, the use of enabling mechanisms such as structures or procedures and, most importantly, by consistent reinforcement and encouragement to enable these behaviours to take root. But we need some way of positioning where we are in terms of such development, and which areas to work on to extend capability. Some form of measurement framework through which we can assess the extent of development of innovative capability would not only help with this 'positioning' activity but would also help ensure that we selected suitable development strategies to fit our particular circumstances rather than assuming that 'one size fits all'.

Studies of innovative groups—such as research teams or engineers—and how they can be supported and enabled give us some clues as to how such audits might be constructed. For example, Ekvall's work on fostering creative climate suggests a series of behaviours that can be supported and developed and his audit is complemented by a number of others working in the area of creative climate (Bessant and Rickards 1980; Ekvall 1990; Cook 1999; Leonard and Swap 1999). Kanter and others discuss structural arrangements that can support or undermine innovative behaviour, whilst Chiesa *et al.* take a process-based approach to auditing (Chiesa *et al.* 1996; Kanter 1997). A number of public policy approaches to improving organizational structure and climate around innovation make use of some form of assessment, often with a self-administered component, (DTI 1994; 1997; Design Council 2002), whilst there is increasing use of overarching assessment frameworks such as the European Quality Award (website: http://www.efqm.org). Francis (2001) provides a comprehensive review of such audit-based approaches to innovation.

The challenge is to build such supportive environments across a wider section of the organization—to try and get levels of involvement such that the whole organization starts to behave as if it were a giant R&D laboratory or product development environment. Questions of how far this can, should or could be done are important in configuring a high-involvement innovation culture in particular organizations, because it is clear that one standard model is unlikely to work for all organizations. For example, the idea of empowering every individual to have the same degree of freedom to experiment as a research scientist currently has may help in a service environment, where they may come up with a novel way of delighting a particular customer. But would the same be true if they were an employee in the pharmaceutical industry who decided to experiment with the formulation of a life-saving drug?

In this chapter we will look at a framework for reviewing the extent of development of key innovative behaviours in an organization. It clusters some of the behaviours that have consistently been shown to be positively associated with innovation in eight core groups (abilities) and offers some measurement of the extent to which they are or could be developed. As we saw in Chapter 3, success comes not from doing one or two of these well but from the ability to develop capability across the spectrum.

4.2 Developing a Model

'If you don't know where you're going, then you'll probably end up somewhere else!'
(comment made by frustrated manager reporting on his experience with trying to develop innovation capability)

The metaphor of the journey is often used when people talk about making progress towards high-involvement innovation in its various guises. For example, it is commonplace to hear people say that 'total quality management is a journey, not the destination'. This idea of a journey provides a helpful model because it reminds us first that, however devoutly we may wish it, making the move from one kind of organization (low involvement) to another is not something we can accomplish overnight. Realizing the kinds of benefits we saw in Chapter 2 inevitably requires us to address the problem issues that Chapter 3 raised. More important, such a metaphor focuses our attention on the need for a map. If moving to high-involvement innovation represents a journey, then we need to ask answer questions like:

- Between where and where?
- With what stages on the way?
- How far can we go?
- How fast?
- What will help us and what will slow us down?
- If others have travelled that road, can they help us avoid obstacles we might trip over?

Research (see Box 4.1) which we have carried out at the Centre for Research in Innovation Management, University of Brighton (CENTRIM—for more details on CENTRIM's activities see http://centrim.bus.brighton.ac.uk/) over the past ten years has been trying to produce such a map, working alongside a variety of organizations from different sectors and in different size brackets. Although widely different, what these organizations share is a concern to develop and sustain higher levels of involvement in innovation. Much like early mapmakers, our first attempts were sketchy and inaccurate (to say the least!), but we found that the process of continuous improvement has helped us create a basic map that organizations can use to navigate as they make their way along their own versions of this journey.

BOX 4.1 The CIRCA research programme.

A key theme in the literature surrounding employee involvement in innovation is the difficulty of translating the simple concept into a sustainable set of organizational practices. Case studies and interviews with practitioners regularly highlight the difficulties in implementation and there are a number of reports of failures in programmes aimed at engendering employee involvement in what is often termed 'continuous improvement' (CI). The problem of implementation is not simple and the solutions clearly involve more than simple inputs of training or the application of proven tools and techniques.

Concern with these problems of implementation led to the establishment of a major research activity in the UK in the 1990s. The CIRCA (Continuous Improvement Research for Competitive Advantage) programme at the University of Brighton has been working with a range of industrial organizations over a sustained period in what might be termed 'action research' aimed at understanding the problems in establishing and sustaining CI and in developing a methodology to support this.

In particular the programme has involved in-depth research with a small number of core case-study companies and experience sharing and 'snapshot' case-study work with a wider network of around 100 firms (Bessant *et al.* 2001). A broader perspective was gained through participating in a European Network for research on CI ('EuroCInet') established under the EUREKA programme, which has been running a large sample survey of CI experience and practice. In the UK we surveyed (in conjunction with *Works Management* magazine) a sample of 142 firms; the results were collated with those from other countries and published (Boer *et al.* 1999). One other element in the research was the setting up of what has become a 'learning network' for exchange of experience and ideas about implementing CI; membership grew from a planned group of 20 firms to over 70 organizations participating in some aspect of the Network's activities (Bessant 1995).

The main aim in the research was to capture experience with CI and particularly to collect data around the following basic themes:

- Background data characterizing the organization and its products, markets, etc.
- History of CI, especially reconstructing the process of evolution (including any stops, false starts, and stalling points)
- Performance measures, both in terms of the level of CI activity (how many suggestions, how much involvement, etc.) and in terms of impact on the business (at local and strategic level)
- Practice measures, exploring the extent to which CI behaviours were in place and had become 'routinized'
- Key blocks and barriers to maintaining or developing CI
- Key enabling factors facilitating progress

Two criticisms can be made of the methodology used. In the first place, the extended nature of the research meant that the model frameworks used to shape the interview questions were less developed in the early stages than later in the work. (The evolution of the model development is described in Caffyn (1998).) Second, the work focused on intra-firm behaviours and so far the influence of product/market or of firm size has not been fully explored.

Having a map was important for firms we spoke to who were trying to enable high-involvement innovation. It was not just that they wanted to ensure that their investments in trying to make something happen were leading to real progress but also that this was progress in the right direction. Many were aware of, or had experienced, the problem of running out of steam and were looking to identify where they had got to, and how best to target any relaunch of their activities. Others were aware that, although they had achieved a measure of sustained benefits, there might be more to aim at. In general, firms expressed two concerns, both of which would benefit from having a map:

- How to measure and direct progress
- How to motivate and target for the next level

4.3 Creating the Model

Our early interest in high-involvement innovation (HII) led us to look at a range of organizations that were trying to make it happen. However, it quickly became clear to us that we were not dealing with a binary state, a simple 'on/off' switch.

The *extent* of involvement—and more importantly, the sustained *benefits* arising from it—varied widely. So we began to cluster their experiences and found a pattern emerging; put simply, the more mature and developed the organizational context for high-involvement innovation is, the greater the benefits (both in terms of impact and sustainability).

One way of assessing the impact on performance of the organization is to measure things like the number and frequency of ideas suggested, the direct performance improvement resulting from particular suggestions, the number of people involved, etc. This was possible with many of the cases but some were also able to make more sophisticated measurements of the performance impact. Because they had begun to target the various HII activities towards strategic goals in the organization (like cost, speed, quality, etc.) and to measure their change over time, more direct 'bottom line' links could be drawn. In this way we could construct a simple measurement scale for the performance improvement dimension of HII.

Establishing one dimension was helpful, but it was apparent that we needed something else to explain how and why some firms were able to achieve significant scores on this performance dimension whilst others were not. Clearly something was developing amongst some of the firms to enable them to achieve such benefits and our original thought was that this simply involved time. That is, the longer firms had been trying, the more developed their high-involvement innovation capability became. However, it became clear that time was not on its own an effective predictor—some firms spent ages trying to make high-involvement innovation happen but made little progress, whilst others moved rapidly towards higher levels of performance.

We then suggested that what was evolving in terms of capability was the underlying *behaviour* of the organization. High-involvement innovation is all about what people *do* in the organization and about understanding and institutionalizing that across more than the traditional groups associated with innovation.

Drawing on these observations, we began working with a model that classified experience with developing high-involvement innovation into five ascending levels. We described them as below and linked them with the 'performance' dimension described above (see Figure 4.1):

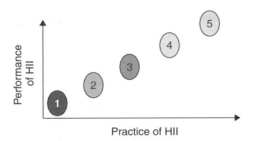

FIGURE 4.1 The five-stage model.

- Level 1 Precursor ('natural' or background improvement, *ad hoc* and short-term)
- Level 2 Structured (formal attempts to create and sustain HII)
- Level 3 Goal oriented (HII directed at company goals and objectives)

- Level 4 Proactive (HII largely self-driven by individuals and groups)
- Level 5 Strong innovation capability (HII is the dominant culture—'the way we do things around here')

Box 4.2 gives brief sketches of each of a series of five 'archetypes'—drawn from a study of these performance and practice patterns—each of which represents a more advanced stage of development.

BOX 4.2 Archetypes of high-involvement innovation capability.

Does your organization look like this?

Level 1

You believe that people have a much bigger contribution to make to finding and solving problems than they are currently able to make. There must be ways of getting them to chip in their ideas for improving things instead of leaving it up to you and your specialists.

Perhaps you have seen examples in other organizations; perhaps you have read about it; perhaps you have been told by one of your customers that they'd like to see more evidence of this. Everyone seems to be doing it, and there is some logic in trying to get people to contribute their ideas for improvements — rather than hanging their brains up on the coat hook as they arrive in the morning!

You're not sure how to put this into practice but you are prepared to give it a try — 'nothing ventured, nothing gained'. It's probably going to take more than just talking to people to get them to chip in their ideas, and you are prepared to invest a bit of time and money in training, perhaps with the help of a consultant.

Your expectations are not too high — this is only an experiment and, if it doesn't work, you can always go back to the tried and tested ways of working in the organization. You don't really have a strategic view on this — if it takes off, then there will be time to put some real resources behind it. As long as it doesn't rock the boat too much, and particularly doesn't get in the way of the real tasks of the business, it's worth a try.

Level 1/2

For whatever reasons, you have decided to try and do something about involving people in problem finding and solving within your organization. You're reasonably convinced by the experience of others and by the idea that 'with every pair of hands you get a free brain!' — your problem is how to put that into practice. You are trying a few things to get the idea across, but you are also aware that this is a big change to the established 'way we do things around here' so it isn't going to be easy.

You've started with a pilot activity rather than trying to change the whole organization in one go. You've picked a group or groups of people as 'guinea pigs' — some of them are more enthusiastic than others — and they are going through a short programme of training and project work on simple problem finding and solving. You may be doing this on a DIY basis, but the chances are that you have hired in some expertise to help with the training and other activities.

People seem to be having fun and they are learning some new tools and techniques; they are also keen to try and make a difference in the project areas they have been tackling. The results are interesting and in some cases you are agreeably surprised by what they have been able to achieve in a relatively short period of time. Many of the solutions they have introduced have a 'why didn't we think of that before?!' quality about them — and you are encouraged to think that it might be worth trying to capture this latent knowledge and capability on a more systematic basis.

But there lies your dilemma. Up till now it has been a (relatively) low cost exercise — an experiment that has not really disrupted things and that has motivated people and produced some interesting results. It confirms your views that it might be worth going down this path further — but the next step is a much bigger one. Somehow you have to spread the activity and enthusiasm across the rest of the workforce, and make the problem finding and solving a part of their day-to-day activity rather than just a one-off project. And if you're going to do that then you need to put some structure into the programme — you need regular training, you need some way of helping and supporting the groups, you need to think about how to manage the flood of ideas which might result so you don't turn people off when their ideas don't get implemented — the list goes on and on! And there is the big question which someone is bound to raise — 'what's in it for me?!!!'. People are bound to ask what they are going to get in return for giving their good ideas — so you need to think carefully about some form of recognition for their participation.

On top of that you have to convince your colleagues that this is a worthwhile invest-ment — because it is clear that moving to the next stage will cost time and money, not to mention the need for continuing top-management support. All in all, what started as an interesting experiment has now led you to a major strategic decision — the potential benefits have been shown by the experiment but now you have to decide whether to move on to a much higher level of commitment.

Level 2

You have been working in a fairly systematic fashion with the idea of employee involvement in 'continuous improvement' for a while now. You originally set up a project team with the responsibility for designing and implementing a high-involvement innovation (HII) system within the organization, and your role is primarily to provide support and backing (not to mention finding the resources to keep it going!). The team is made up of staff from various parts and levels in the organization and they are seconded for a significant part of their time to the HII programme. They originally designed a system which they spent several months planning before launching, first in a pilot project and then rolling it out to the rest of the organization. Their work now is around monitoring and fine-tuning it, which they do through a monthly review meeting that you also attend.

The 'HII system' is made up of:

- A small group of facilitators (drawn from the project team), whose role is to help train and support the various HII teams. Initially their role was very much 'hands on', but as the teams gain in confidence so the facilitators can work on fine-tuning, helping introduce new tools, helping extend participation, etc.
- A problem finding and solving approach, which defines a systematic process for all the teams to use. This is a simple variation on Deming's famous 'plan, do, check, act', which the project team have modified to suit the organization. Everyone receives training in this at the start of their involvement in the HII programme, and they are encouraged to start using it immediately on workplace problems

- Training in a suite of simple problem finding and solving tools, which teams can quickly use to help them in their HII activities. Examples of the tools are fishbone charts, brainstorming and process mapping
- A team-based approach, where groups of five to six people are drawn from a work area and trained together to become a HII team. To help them work as a group they are given some basic training (half day) in tools to help run meetings — agenda setting, action planning, etc. Initially the facilitators help them run their HII sessions but the teams gradually take over and become self-managing; most try and meet once a week for about 45 minutes
- An idea management system, which the project team designed to deal with the high volume of ideas that began to flow once the programme got under way. Essentially the system is geared to try and provide some response as quickly as possible to anyone who has made a suggestion. The response may be simple — an acknowledgement and a go ahead for implementation by the team itself (this accounts for a substantial proportion of all ideas). The next level is those ideas that need additional help or resources — perhaps a skilled craftsman or technician. These are acknowledged and put on a priority list for action when the relevant resource people become available. Finally, there are those major changes that form the basis of a special action team — a cross-functional group aimed at tackling a big problem issue. (The 'idea management system' (IMS) also has mechanisms for helping say no quickly and clearly to those ideas that — for whatever reasons — are not feasible or desirable.)
- A recognition system, which aims to help maintain motivation amongst the staff to contribute their ideas. Although the group looked at a monetary-based reward system (linked to the value of improvements suggested), they decided that this would not be the most effective, not least because it might be divisive and would tend to encourage people only to offer their 'big' ideas. Instead, the system is designed to try and encourage the behaviour of suggesting — which it does by providing simple token rewards for any suggestion made (without attempting to evaluate them). The rewards here vary but include a free cup of coffee, a coffee mug, a T shirt, etc.; one of the most successful has been a scheme where the company contributes £1 to a nominated charity for every idea suggested in the HII teams. For those ideas that have more significant potential there is a bigger reward, the size and nature of which is decided upon by a panel including the HII project team; this award is made to the group as a whole. (Examples here include money but also other things like a meal out for all the team members or a place on a training course for each member of the team.)
- A communication system, where the results of individual projects can be shared with others. This takes several forms — teams make up 'storyboards' about their particular projects, which they display in their areas; there is an in-house newsletter, etc.

Things are going fairly well with the current system — the majority of people are involved, although there is a spread of enthusiasm from a few fanatics right across to a handful of people who are really not interested and in some cases actively hostile. Overall, it seems as though people have got the hang of the basic problem finding and solving approach and the tools that support it; if you look around the organization you can sometimes see the evidence in the form of flip charts or pictures on the walls, or people going into a huddle during a coffee break to try and crack a particular problem issue. There have been one or two big wins — projects where the team has been able to make a significant impact on a particular area — and these big hits in terms of improved quality or reduced costs help you to keep the rest of the management team convinced that the (still significant) investment in HII is worth maintaining.

Although it has gone well and has undoubtedly started to change the way people think and behave around the organization, you have some concerns, which the HII team in different ways share. The programme isn't really going anywhere — and in some cases it appears to be falling back. Whereas, when you started around a year ago, there was a lot of enthusiasm, things now feel a little stale. In the same way, whereas people used to make time and give priority to HII sessions, these are increasingly being pushed aside as urgent work comes along. The team can do some things to help maintain momentum — for example, extra training sessions and the introduction on some new tools — but there is a growing sense that the programme is running out of steam.

This isn't helped by the fact that many of the projects that teams have been proposing are put into the queue for specialist action teams — and there simply isn't enough capacity amongst the specialists to respond quickly. The growing delay between teams suggesting things and something getting down about their ideas is setting up a climate where they start to ask whether it's worth bothering — no-one does anything with our ideas anyway.

You are also concerned that the benefits, although useful in terms of overall morale, are not really producing a big impact on the bottom line. Most of the gains are modest and confined to a local level — and you are finding it increasingly difficult to justify continuing to commit resources to HII when the matter comes up for discussion amongst your senior colleagues.

Level 3

Your organization has been systematically working at involving staff in problem finding and solving for some time, and there is a well-developed framework to support such activity. This includes:

- A HII project team whose task is to monitor and support the continuing development of employee involvement in problem solving
- A common systematic approach to problem finding and solving, which is used by teams and individuals
- Regular training and updating in the use of simple tools and techniques for problem finding and solving
- An idea management system, to manage and progress the various suggestions made from different groups
- A recognition system which provides feedback and some form of acknowledgement/reward to individuals and teams contributing suggestions
- A communication system, which captures and shares some of the ideas and experiences

After operation of such a systematic approach for a while, it became clear that there was a lack of strategic focus to the problem-solving activity and that, as a consequence, the benefits achieved were confined to a local level. In trying to move on from this and to break out of a growing sense that the HII activity was running out of steam, the organization embarked upon a policy deployment programme. This was a major exercise involving linking the 'top-down' strategic planning of the business to the 'bottom-up' capability for finding and solving problems.

In essence, the process involves a top-level set of clear business objectives and targets, which provide the focus for the HII activity. These clear targets are then broken down into project areas and further disaggregated into individual improvement tasks; in other words, the overall strategy is systematically broken down into 'bite-sized' chunks, which different HII teams can work on right across the organization. The process of developing this is interactive with briefing sessions cascading down through the organization so that everyone knows what the objectives are and why they are chosen, and so that everyone can explore how they and their HII activity can make an impact on these targets.

The result is an extended matrix of potential HII projects, each of which links to a strategic objective. The effect is to connect up the 'engine' of problem finding and solving with the current strategic needs of the business — for example, for cost reduction, quality improvement, or time saving.

A key component in making this approach work has been the introduction of a 'measurement culture'. In the early days of HII some teams had used local measures to help guide their improvement activities, but this was not done on a widespread or systematic basis. However, in policy deployment it is essential that measurement is introduced throughout the process — otherwise there is no way of knowing whether or not the objectives have been achieved. The types of measurement vary from very simple counting and checking through to more complex and precise approaches, but the underlying principle is the same — to ensure that progress is being made and to identify how much further improvement is needed. This has important implications for the problem of 'proving' the value of HII to the bottom line; once strategic targets are set and progress against them is monitored and measured, it becomes possible to 'prove' the value of investing in HII.

In general the system works very well; clear targets are now set and reviewed regularly and the HII teams 'buy in' to the overall strategy and translate it into particular objectives for their problem-solving work. Much of the monitoring and measurement work is done by the groups themselves, and the contribution of individuals to HII activity towards these organization objectives now forms part of the annual appraisal process. In this way HII has become much more part of the day-to-day 'way we do things around here' than a special initiative.

There are some areas where it could develop further. It still works best within specific areas and the distribution of enthusiasm and involvement varies across the organization. There are some cross-functional projects and even some that involve working with people outside the firm on joint projects — but these are still in their infancy. Increasingly, it seems as though the 'big hits' are likely to come from dealing with problems like these, which span different areas and organizations.

HII also still needs quite a bit of external support and facilitation — helping define and agree objectives, providing training and development support to teams, steering and guiding the process. It is also very much about achieving performance improvements through a lot of small ideas, often resulting from a systematic attack on and elimination of all sorts of waste and inefficiency. Whilst this is of immense positive value, there may be scope for extending the process to a more proactive search for radical new ideas.

Level 4

Your organization has been working with HII for some time and has established the basic process of finding and solving problems as a key part of 'the way we do things around here'. HII is not a special initiative but part of the way of life in the organization and groups often find and solve problems in systematic fashion without consciously thinking about how they do it. It is normal to go into groups, do some brainstorming, collect some data, follow a systematic approach — that's just how we do it.

Whilst there is a high degree of involvement in problem finding and solving activity, it is linked to the overall strategy of the business. There is a clear process of policy deployment, where the top-level objectives and targets are shared with everyone in the organization (so people know why certain things have to be improved); these high-level targets are broken down systematically into projects with which different HII teams can engage. Monitoring and measuring of progress towards achieving them is handled by the teams themselves and the results are displayed and shared so everyone has a sense of progress towards meeting the strategic objectives.

Teams are experienced and the organization continues to invest in regular training and updating of skills relevant to HII. For this reason they are largely self-facilitating, able to take on loosely defined strategic projects and use a variety of different approaches to carrying them out. They feel empowered to experiment with different solutions (not all of which work) and they share the results of their efforts with other teams so that there is little re-inventing of the wheel and so that groups can avoid falling into the same traps as their colleagues. There is a sense of top-management support, which extends to empowering the groups to choose how their solutions will be implemented and often to spending the money to get something done. There is a high degree of trust — the underlying thinking being that the teams are well trained in HII, they have a clear sense of the strategic objectives and they will try different approaches to find a solution, so they do not need a heavy hand on the tiller from outside.

The 'buy-in' to the strategy is helped through the reward system, which acknowledges that if the organization can achieve its (stretching) strategic objectives it must have done so as a result of the collective efforts of the HII teams. For this reason, there is a simple bonus scheme based on a profit-share of profits over and above the agreed target levels. This provides a powerful incentive to the teams themselves.

This approach has worked well and there is a high degree of motivation amongst the workforce. Labour turnover is low and performance levels are high. There are still areas for further development, however, particularly between different areas within the organization and certainly outside in its relationships with others. Problem finding and solving in the value stream is an important priority. A second area for extending the approach is in the development of new products and services; at present almost all the HII work has concentrated on making processes efficient and lean — high quality, fast and low cost. However, there is also scope for using the ideas and techniques — the HII capability — in other areas and aspects of the business.

Level 5

The organization has been involved in HII for some time and has established systematic finding and solving problems as a key part of 'the way we do things around here'. This approach is strategy-linked — improvements are made regularly and continuously and they make a contribution to the various strategic objectives of the organization. There is a clear link between overall strategy and its deployment down to the various problem-solving teams. HII is also part of individual behaviour — people are often involved in several different activities, from a personal, through a work-group team to cross-functional and even inter-organizational teams. The whole ethos is one of change — constantly searching for ways to improve things and not leaving things as they are unless there is a good reason. The motto could almost be 'if it ain't being fixed, it's broke!' — recognizing that the world outside is constantly moving on and survival and growth of the organization depend on constant learning and change.

People feel a high degree of empowerment — they are skilled and the organization invests regularly in training and equipping them with the skills they need to understand, to find and to solve problems. They are also not afraid to experiment — the organization takes the view that it is important to make mistakes whilst trying things out and that this is to be encouraged, not blamed. The only 'crime' is to make the same mistake twice, so people are encouraged to capture and share whatever they learn through experiment.

Knowledge is at the heart of this organization. It is constantly looking for better ways of doing things, for better ideas in its products and services, and it has people skilled and experienced in the tools and techniques of systematic problem finding and solving to support this. However, it also ensures that the lessons of this constant learning process are captured and shared for others to use — accomplishing this through regular meetings and discussion, documentation, displays, newsletters and other communications media, etc.

Part of the looking process involves getting access to new sources of information and seeing things from new perspectives. So the organization encourages job rotation and secondment, brings in people with deliberately different backgrounds to provide fresh perspectives, sends people out to visit and talk with customers, supplier, competitors, etc. It is very open to new sources of ideas and knowledge and to ways of seeing the existing patterns in different ways.

Not only is systematic and strategically aligned HII a way of life, it pervades every aspect of the organization. Involvement levels are very high and the approach is used within work areas, between different areas and out into the supply and distribution chain. The concept of value streams and the strategic improvement of these rather than local problem solving is central.

4.4 Developing High-Involvement Practice

Having established the idea of firms developing their practice of high involvement to the different levels of capability, we needed to understand *what* was being developed in more detail. Our view was that it was the overall pattern of behaviour in the organization—the collection of 'routines' that made up the culture—'the way we do things around here' (see Chapter 3). From the research companies it became clear that specific behaviours cluster together and reinforce each other to create an ability within the organization to do something important in making high-involvement innovation happen—for example, to link it to the overall strategy of the business or to work creatively across organizational boundaries.

Figure 4.2 shows the model in diagrammatic form—essentially we can consider the behaviours as streams that flow into tributaries and eventually into a major river. It is possible to have water flowing in the river even if some of the streams are blocked or dried up, but it is obviously valuable to try and identify where this is happening and to do something about it.

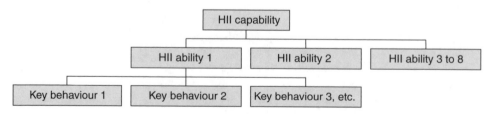

FIGURE 4.2   Behavioural model of HII capability.

TABLE 4.1 Key behaviour abilities for levels in the model.

Key behaviour abilities	Level in the model				
	1	2	3	4	5
Cluster 1	Indicators of typical behaviour patterns and consequences at each of the different levels				
'Understanding high-involvement innovation'					
Clusters 2 to 8 'Getting the habit', 'focusing' etc. (see Appendix)	As above				

The five levels of capability development relate to the extent to which these many behaviours are developed and have become routines within the organization. So the model becomes like that shown in Table 4.1.

4.5 Components of High-Involvement Capability

The last piece of the puzzle was to try and identify which particular behaviours and clusters of behaviours were important in determining these abilities and contributing to overall high-involvement capability. In trying to establish these we drew on a number of sources:

- A literature survey of relevant work in the field of innovation research and practice, which looked at the behaviours associated with innovation and the organizational structures and processes that supported them. The focus here tended to be on 'traditional' types of innovation specialists
- A literature survey of attempts to establish more extensive involvement in the innovation process—for example, through total quality programmes that aimed to involve people at least at the level of continuous improvement—'do what we do better' innovation
- Analysis of case studies within the CIRCA research project, and testing via feedback with companies within the network (see Box 4.1 for details)
- Validation of the emerging model via parallel research work in the EuroCInet programme across several European countries and Australia (described in detail in Chapter 2 but, for further information, see Boer *et al.* 1999)

TABLE 4.2 Key abilities in developing high-involvement innovation capability.

Ability	Constituent behaviours
'Understanding'—the ability to articulate the basic values of continuous high-involvement innovation (HII)	People demonstrate a shared belief in the value of small steps and that everyone can contribute, by themselves being actively involved in making and recognizing improvements
	When something goes wrong the natural reaction of people at all levels is to look for reasons why etc., rather than to blame individual(s)

(continued overleaf)

TABLE 4.2   (*continued*)

Ability	Constituent behaviours
'Getting the HII habit'—the ability to generate sustained involvement in HII	People make use of some formal problem finding and solving cycle People use appropriate tools and techniques to support HII People use measurement to guide the improvement process People (as individuals and/or groups) initiate and carry through HII activities—they participate in the process Closing the loop—ideas are responded to in a clearly defined and timely fashion—either implemented or otherwise dealt with
'Focusing HII'—the ability to link HII activities to the strategic goals of the company	Individuals and groups use the organization's strategic goals and objectives to focus and prioritize improvements Everyone understands (i.e. is able to explain) what the company's or department's strategy, goals and objectives are Individuals and groups (e.g. departments, HII teams) assess their proposed changes (before embarking on initial investigation and before implementing a solution) against departmental or company objectives to ensure that they are consistent with them Individuals and groups monitor/measure the results of their improvement activity and the impact it has on strategic or departmental objectives HII activities are an integral part of the work of individuals or groups, not a parallel activity
'Leading HII'—the ability to lead, direct and support the creation and sustaining of HII behaviours	Managers support the HII process through allocation of time, money, space and other resources Managers recognize in formal (but not necessarily financial) ways the contribution of employees to HII Managers lead by example, becoming actively involved in design and implementation of HII Managers support experiment by not punishing mistakes but by encouraging learning from them
'Aligning HII'—the ability to create consistency between HII values and behaviour and the organizational context (structures, procedures, etc.)	Ongoing assessment ensures that the organization's structure and infrastructure and the HII system consistently support and reinforce each other The individual/group responsible for designing the HII system designs it to fit within the current structure and infrastructure Individuals with responsibility for particular company processes/systems hold ongoing reviews to assess whether these processes/systems and the HII system remain compatible People with responsibility for the HII system ensure that, when a major organizational change is planned, its potential impact on the HII system is assessed and adjustments are made as necessary
'Shared problem-solving'—the ability to move HII activity across organizational boundaries	People co-operate across internal divisions (e.g. cross-functional groups) in HII as well as working in their own areas. This is also extended to inter-organizational relationships People understand and share a holistic view (process understanding and ownership) People are oriented towards internal and external customers in their HII activity Specific HII projects with outside agencies—customers, suppliers, etc.—are taking place Relevant HII activities involve representatives from different organizational levels

TABLE 4.2   *(continued)*

Ability	Constituent behaviours
'Continuous improvement of continuous improvement'—the ability to strategically manage the development of HII	The HII system is continually monitored and developed; a designated individual or group monitors the HII system and measures the incidence (i.e. frequency and location) of HII activity and the results of HII activity
	There is a cyclical planning process whereby the HII system is regularly reviewed and, if necessary, amended (single-loop learning)
	There is periodic review of the HII system in relation to the organization as a whole, which may lead to a major regeneration (double-loop learning)
	Senior management make available sufficient resources (time, money, personnel) to support the ongoing development of the HII system
'The learning organization'—generating the ability to enable learning to take place and be captured at all levels	People learn from their experiences, both positive and negative
	Individuals seek out opportunities for learning/personal development (e.g. actively experiment, set their own learning objectives)
	Individuals and groups at all levels share (make available) their learning from *all* work experiences
	The organization articulates and consolidates (captures and shares) the learning of individuals and groups
	Managers accept and, where necessary, act on all the learning that takes place
	People and teams ensure that their learning is captured by making use of the mechanisms provided for doing so
	Designated individual(s) use organizational mechanisms to deploy the learning that is captured across the organization

Table 4.2 summarizes the findings from these different studies, from which it can be seen that we concentrated on *eight* key abilities or clusters of behaviour as providing the underpinning for high-involvement innovation capability. The Appendix provides a more detailed description of the key behaviours in each case.

4.6 Towards a 'Reference Model' for High-Involvement Innovation

These eight clusters of behaviours—key abilities—are things that we can see high-performing innovation organizations doing extensively. Importantly, they have found ways to spread these behaviours beyond the 'traditional' innovation specialist groups to less familiar areas and to people who are less experienced or who have previously not been involved in innovative activities. Our case-study research indicated that different firms had developed these abilities to a greater or lesser extent, and this development of practice had some bearing on the likely performance improvements that they could expect. From this experience it seems that the development of high-involvement innovation is essentially an evolutionary process involving gradual learning and embedding of an increasing number of behavioural abilities.

Using these, we could turn the descriptive model of Table 4.1 into a staged development model, which identifies particular levels of evolution of these behaviours and tries to connect them with likely performance impacts. These levels match up with the archetypes described earlier and which are illustrated in Figure 4.1. Table 4.3 describes their performance and practice characteristics in outline.

TABLE 4.3   An explanation of the different levels in the reference model.

Level	Performance	Practice
0 = No high-involvement innovation activity	No impact from high-involvement innovation	Problem solving random No formal efforts or structure Occasional bursts punctuated by inactivity and non-participation Dominant mode of problem solving is by specialists Short-term benefits No strategic impact
1 = Trying out the ideas	Minimal and local effects only Some improvements in morale and motivation	High-involvement innovation happens as a result of learning-curve effects associated with a particular new product or process—and then fades out again. Or it results from a short-term input—a training intervention, for example—and leads to a small impact around those immediately concerned with it. These effects are often short-lived and very localized
2 = Structured and systematic high-involvement innovation	Local-level effects Measurable high-involvement innovation activity, e.g. number of participants, ideas produced, etc. Measurable performance effects confined to projects Little or no 'bottom line' impact	Formal attempts to create and sustain high-involvement innovation Use of a formal problem-solving process Use of participation Training in basic high-involvement innovation tools Structured idea management system Recognition system, often parallel system to operations Can extend to cross-functional work but on an *ad hoc* basis
3 = Strategic high-involvement innovation	Policy deployment links local and project-level activity to broader strategic goals Monitoring and measurement drives improvement on these issues, which can be measured in terms of impact on 'bottom line'—for example, cost reductions, quality improvements, time savings, etc.	All of the above, plus formal deployment of strategic goals Monitoring and measurement of high-involvement innovation against these goals In-line system

TABLE 4.3 *(continued)*

Level	Performance	Practice
4 = Autonomous innovation	Strategic benefits, including those from discontinuous, major innovations, as well as incremental problem solving	All of the above, plus responsibility for mechanisms, timing, etc., devolved to problem-solving unit High levels of experimentation
5 = Strong high-involvement innovation capability	Strategic innovation Ability to deploy competence base to competitive advantage	High-involvement innovation as the dominant way of life Automatic capture and sharing of learning Everyone actively involved in innovation process Incremental and radical innovation

Organizations move through the levels as the key behaviours (identified in Table 4.2) are adopted and reinforced, and as the form a behaviour takes becomes more highly evolved. For example, at Levels 2 and 3 staff may work effectively at solving problems allocated to them by management, but at Level 4 employees would take responsibility for discovering and prioritizing, as well as solving, problems for themselves. The model is evolutionary, as opposed to additive—all the key behaviours would be present at Level 2, although in a relatively immature form; for a firm to advance to a higher level the behaviours need to evolve further.

Classifying evolution of high-involvement innovation in these terms can help firms understand where they stand in relation to other companies and how they can develop a plan to expand their own abilities. But it is important to recognize that these represent generic 'archetypes'. Each organization's experience will be specific to the organization, but their development of a high-involvement innovation capability will have to pass through these common stages. Progression from one stage to the next involves both maturing of particular routines (and their constituent behaviours) and also adding new routines to the core set.

The idea of increasingly skilful practice of the basic HII behaviours, and the notion that improved results (in terms of business benefits) follow from higher levels of such practice, has much in common with other models for organizational development such as the Capability Maturity model of software development or the Business Excellence model (Paulk and Curtis 1993; Povey 1996).

BOX 4.3 Try it yourself.

The idea behind innovation auditing and the use of reference models is to provide firms with the opportunity to reflect in a structured way on what they have achieved and where they might go next. The model described here has been used in a variety of cases to help firms in this fashion, and to provide feedback and guidance for further development.

A simple version, developed as a short 'do-it-yourself' self-assessment for high-involvement innovation, appears on the website associated with this book. You can use this to think about your own organization or department and to reflect on where and how things could be taken further to involve more people and sustain their commitment to innovation.

The address for the website is http://www.wiley.co.uk/.

4.7 Enabling Development of High-Involvement Innovation

Thus far we have been looking at what is essentially a diagnostic map of the journey that firms make in trying to engage high involvement in innovation, but the core managerial question is not so much one of what as how? Given the desire to move between stages in the model described above, what actions might be necessary? The process is essentially one of organizational learning, in which what are often unfamiliar behaviour patterns are first articulated and then reinforced over time.

Moving along either of these dimensions is not an accident but comes from a determined effort sustained over time and supported within the organization. It is a bit like becoming a marathon runner—the idea is relatively simple and you may become motivated to try it whilst sitting in the armchair one afternoon watching a race on TV. However, the process of actually competing requires that you go through a process of gradual training, changing some of your behaviours (like diet) and trying new ones out, repeating and rehearsing, learning techniques from others, and so on. Your performance will gradually improve, from not being able to run further than the end of the road to the point when 2, 3, 5, 10 km become possible—and, if you can keep up the momentum, eventually you will be able to complete the first marathon. The learning does not stop there—there are new challenges in terms of competing in races and so on—and there is the ever-present danger that if you stop practising, there is a gradual slide back towards the armchair!

This is the problem facing any organization trying to implement HII—one of climbing up an escalator that is moving downhill! But our research has also identified patterns in the kinds of things that get in the way or slow down progress towards HII—and in the kinds of things which an organization can use (enablers) to deal with these obstacles and to maintain their momentum in HII.

Two themes are important here. First is the role of artefacts as both the product and as an enabler of changing behaviour. Following Schein (1992), we see organizational culture—'the way we do things around here'—as a set of embedded behavioural patterns that are underpinned by group norms, which in turn follow from individual values and assumptions. These ways of behaving create symbols and structures—for example organizational rules and procedures—which in turn reinforce and consolidate the behaviour patterns. So, for example, the reward and recognition system within an organization says much about what kinds of behaviours are valued and encouraged and about underlying values (Schein 1992).

The importance of this concept in our discussion of implementing high-involvement innovation is that it is possible to identify a number of enabling structures and systems, which can reinforce and support the desired behaviour change. Such enablers include training, structures and systems; in the following chapters we will give some examples of critical enablers in moving between stages in our model.

BOX 4.4 Applying the model to small and medium-sized enterprises (SMEs).

After reaching a licensing agreement with CENTRIM at Brighton University, the Confederation of Danish Industries (Dansk Industri A/S — DI) translated and modified the self-assessment tool for use in Danish SMEs. Piloting and further development of the Continuous Improvement Self-Assessment Tool (CISAT) occurred in co-operation between DI, managers from a number of leading Danish manufacturing companies, and researchers at the Center for Industrial Production at Aalborg University. Subsequently, the CISAT has been used to facilitate CI in several Danish organizations. In an effort to extend the applicability and accessibility of the CISAT, DI and researchers from the Center for Industrial Production created an Internet version of the CISAT, which includes a number of support tools for guiding the process of conducting self-assessment as well as supporting CI within the organization. With the Internet version of the CISAT, organizations can conduct a self-assessment, obtain their 'results', and gain practical suggestions for building and strengthening CI enablers.

In addition to providing an organization with an overview concerning its current status with CI and highlighting the areas in need of further improvement, the CISAT has been an invaluable tool for generating and facilitating dialogue among members of an organization. In a recent research study, the process of conducting the CISAT was instrumental in creating channels of communication and cross-functional co-operation at the shop-floor, middle-management, and top-management levels in a medium-sized Danish manufacturing company.

(I am grateful to Frances Joergensen, who researched the Danish Industries programme, for this.)

4.8 Contingency Issues

The second key point is that there is clearly a risk in the foregoing that implementing high-involvement innovation is seen as something for which there is a universal prescription. It is important to place this in context; our work suggests that the core behavioural routines—the abilities—are generic, but the ways in which they can be introduced and embedded within a particular organization will vary widely. For example, all firms need a behavioural routine around using a systematic problem finding and solving cycle, but which type of cycle and how it operates—in a formalized ritual, in a workshop format within a quality circle or as an informal mental checklist—will vary widely between organizations. Similarly, the ways in which ideas are managed or participation encouraged and rewarded will depend on particular local and national characteristics.

4.9 Summary

This chapter describes attempts that have been made to draw together a number of research strands to create a reference model for the development of high-involvement innovation capability. Having such a model is helpful because it allows firms to position themselves in terms of how far they have travelled and to identify where and how they might move forward. In the next five chapters we look in more detail at each stage in this model, at key blocks and barriers that make progress difficult and at enabling resources to help firms move forward on their journey towards high-involvement innovation.

References

Bessant, J. (1995) 'Networking as a mechanism for technology transfer; the case of continuous improvement,' in Kaplinsky, R., den Hertog, E. and Coriat, B. (eds), *Europe's Next Step*. Frank Cass, London.

Bessant, J., S. Caffyn and M. Gallagher (2001) 'An evolutionary model of continuous improvement behaviour,' *Technovation*, **21** (3), 67–77.

Bessant, J. and T. Rickards (1980) 'The Creativity Audit: introduction of a new research measure during programmes for facilitating organizational change,' *R&D Management*, **10** (2), 67–75.

Boer, H., A. Berger, R. Chapman and F. Gertsen (1999) *CI Changes: From Suggestion Box to the Learning Organization*. Ashgate, Aldershot.

Caffyn, S. (1998) *Continuous Improvement in the New Product Development Process*. PhD thesis, University of Brighton, Brighton.

Chiesa, V., P. Coughlan and C. Voss (1996) 'Development of a technical innovation audit,' *Journal of Product Innovation Management*, **13** (2), 105–136.

Cook, P. (1999) *Best Practice Creativity*. Gower, Aldershot.

Design Council (2002) *Living Innovation*. Design Council/Department of Trade and Industry, London, available at http://www.livinginnovation.org.uk.

DTI (1994) *Innovation—Your Move*. Department of Trade and Industry, London.

DTI (1997) *Competitiveness Through Partnerships with People*. Department of Trade and Industry, London.

Ekvall, G. (1990) 'The organizational culture of idea management,' in Henry, J. and Walker, D. (eds), *Managing Innovation*. London, Sage, pp. 73–80.

Francis, D. (2001) *Developing Innovative Capability*. University of Brighton, Brighton.

Kanter, R. (ed.) (1997) *Innovation: Breakthrough Thinking at 3M, DuPont, GE, Pfizer and Rubbermaid*. Harper Business, New York.

Leonard, D. and W. Swap (1999) *When Sparks Fly: Igniting Creativity in Groups*. Harvard Business School Press, Boston, MA.

Paulk, M. and B. Curtis (1993) *Capability Maturity Model for Software*. Software Engineering Institute, Carnegie-Mellon University, Pittsburgh, PA.

Povey, B. (1996) *Business Process Improvement*. MPhil thesis, CENTRIM, University of Brighton, Brighton.

Schein, E. (1992) *Organizational Culture and Leadership*. Jossey Bass, San Francisco, CA.

Chapter 5

GETTING THE INNOVATION HABIT

In the following chapters we will explore the different levels of the model presented in Chapter 4 and look at some of the issues involved in reaching these levels and moving on to the next level. This chapter looks at the first level—where organizations are exploring the potential in trying out high-involvement innovation and also at the limitations of such an approach. It gives an idea of the main barriers likely to emerge and some proven strategies for dealing with these challenges, and concludes by signposting the steps needed for the next stage in the high-involvement journey.

This early stage is typified by organizations for whom innovation has been a fairly random or *ad hoc* activity and by those who innovate more systematically but who place high reliance on small 'licensed' groups of innovators to do this. For various reasons there is a recognition that there may be benefits in involving a wider group of people on a more systematic basis—and so different attempts are made to develop high-involvement innovation.

These can be successful in the short term—not only in terms of direct project-related benefits, but also in improved morale and motivation amongst the workforce. However, there is also a high risk that the experiment will go sour and the resulting after-taste will make it more difficult to repeat at some stage in the future. For example, many organizations became involved with the 'quality revolution' in the last part of the 20th century, often spending significant sums of money in trying to establish a culture of high involvement in innovative problem solving focused on the target of trying to improve quality. For many the experience was less than satisfactory—whilst there was often early enthusiasm, this soon fell away and was replaced by a much more wary view of the motives and mechanisms underpinning involvement in innovation (EIU 1992).

5.1 Unlocking High-Involvement Innovation

'I used to think people were part of the problem—now I see them as part of the solution . . .'

It is one of the paradoxes of the 20th century—and one of the challenges of the 21st—that we do not make use of our most significant asset. Whilst everyone in an organization comes equipped with the capability to find and solve problems and to come up with creative new solutions to old difficulties and new issues, we fail to mobilize all but a small amount of this capacity. There are many reasons why this strange state of affairs has emerged (as we saw in Chapter 3), but the result is that the 'normal' state of affairs in most of our organizations is that the majority of people are not expected and not enabled to participate in creative activity. Making the change is not an easy matter, though, because there is such a history of non-involvement, and the whole way in which the organization is structured and behaves reinforces this view.

So the first step on the journey towards high-involvement innovation is going to be one of breaking loose from the old-established view and trying something new. Given the scale of the embeddedness of the old model and the potential risks of trying new things, we should not be surprised that much of what goes on here is really about playing around with new ideas rather than systematically trying to change the way the organization works.

BOX 5.1 Barriers to high-involvement innovation.

In principle, there is no reason why people can't become involved in innovation — the trouble is that a range of personal and organizational barriers seem to get in the way. For example:

- I don't know how to . . .
- Nobody asked me to . . .
- What's in it for me? — why should I bother?
- There's no point — no-one listens to us anyway
- We can't afford it so why bother suggesting it?
- No-one cares enough to say thank-you if you do put up an idea
- You post suggestions in the box — and that's the last you hear of them
- No-one ever tells us what's going on
- Keep your head down is the best way to get on here . . . don't put your head above the parapet!
- It's not my job to . . .
- They're not interested in our ideas — that's the job of the guys in white shirts

Faced with a list like this, we can begin to understand why it is that high-involvement innovation is such a rarity. Most organizations, most of the time, are composed of people who feel some or all of these blocks and barriers to their expressing and using their natural creative skills. It's much easier just to keep your head down and get on with the day job, leaving the other, creative self to your spare (and more interesting and emotionally rewarding) time.

It also explains why companies feel so frustrated when they try to unlock the creativity across their workforce. Of course, it takes more than just inspiring words or visions to make it happen, but even firms that have spent a great deal of time, money and energy trying to mobilize high involvement find themselves frustrated at the lack of progress or enthusiasm. After the initial honeymoon effect there is a real risk of falling back to the old model.

It's made harder by the fact that some of this can be managed directly—for example, managers can change the way the organization is structured; they can modify the reward system; they can allocate time and resources to innovative activities; they can invest in training and development.

However, they can't get inside people's heads and tinker with their emotions. They can't directly change what people believe simply by telling them—that road has been tried by many, not always scrupulous, leaders in the past. People have enormous resilience and will only believe what they are comfortable with and what they see as supported by the things they see around them. So building high-involvement innovation is going to need a long process of gradually convincing people to believe something different, to use that to shape their behaving in a different way and gradually reinforcing this with external elements until it becomes 'the way we do things around here'. In other words it's about culture change.

5.2 To Boldly Go . . .

The trigger for change can come from many directions. It may be reflection—a manager looking at his organization and deciding there might be a different way (Semler 1993; Lewis and Lytton 1994). It may be that a crisis pushes the organization to think about doing something differently—for example, when the Japanese copier maker Canon made its first ever loss, it responded by asking for ideas from the workforce. The subsequent acceleration of innovation set the growth path for the company (Japanese Management Association 1987). Sirkin and Stalk (1990) report in similar fashion on the turnaround at a troubled paper mill. Or it may involve following a widely publicized case example or copying what someone else has done (Joynson 1994).

Whatever the starting point, it is often the case that the decision to change is in the form of an experiment rather than a major policy decision. Typically, someone in the organization makes a suggestion along the lines of 'let's see if there is something we could do to tap into the brain power of our people' and things flow from there. The strength of this approach is that it opens up new possibilities—but the weakness is that it does not really deal with the issues of structure or support. Why should people contribute their ideas? What sort of ideas? What's in it for them? How can they do it?—Do they have the skills and the ability to think? How do we manage the flood of ideas which might result? Thinking about—and dealing with—questions like these is critical if the organization is going to make high-involvement innovation a sustainable part of 'the way we do things around here'.

Just as there are many triggers, so there are many ways of carrying out the experiment. It could be through some training or intervention work. It could be as part of a change—for example, the introduction of a new system or layout, during which employees are asked for their ideas and encouraged to implement them. It could be part of a campaign to try and improve some aspect of the business—for example, asking everyone for their ideas to help improve quality or reduce delivery time. And, of course, it could be part of the background structure—the suggestion scheme or box, which has been there for a long time as a way of encouraging people to put in their ideas for improvement.

5.3 Some Examples

Using the model framework developed in the previous chapter, we would call the innovation culture—'the way we do things around here'—a Level 1 capability. To get a feel for the kind of organizational behaviour we might expect to see in such an organization, take a look at the following examples.

Case (a)

Case (a) involves a motor components manufacturer involved in supplying various items of trim made from moulded plastics. It employs around 700 people on several sites and has recently been confronted with a strong challenge for performance improvement from major customers. Faced with the need to offer significantly higher and more consistent quality levels and a cost reduction of the order of 10%, it has begun looking at high-involvement innovation as one of several possible strategies for dealing with the emergent crisis. Whilst there is a general awareness that other firms have been able to obtain benefits through high-involvement innovation, the company is not clear how this is being done. Some improvements have been achieved through changes in layout and flow, and the shift to a 'pull' system, but these were instituted by a group of external consultants, whose brief did not extend to workforce involvement. Responsibility for a 'continuous improvement (CI)' programme has been given to the Human Resources director who has instituted a one-day training programme for all staff, which introduces the basic concept of CI and some simple tools. Results so far have been patchy; whilst there is enthusiasm amongst some staff, there is also scepticism from others, many of whom see this as 'one more initiative'. Benefits follow a similar pattern; in a few areas there have been useful and interesting ideas, which have led to tangible improvements, but in other areas little has changed.

Case (b)

Case (b) is a manufacturer of high-quality speakers and accessories for the consumer hi-fi market. It has a strong position in design, but has recently been paying close attention to improving its manufacturing operations. As part of a move towards cellular manufacturing and improved production flow, it is working to try and develop a teamwork approach. Higher involvement is seen as an important element in this, and the company has been heavily influenced by examples of problem-solving groups that it has seen in other firms as part of a programme of visits which it recently undertook. Implementation so far has consisted of some basic training in problem-solving tools and the introduction of an area on the shop floor where staff are encouraged to meet and suggest improvements during discussions around a white board.

5.4 Characterizing Level 1 Innovation Capability

Both of these companies are clearly interested in high-involvement innovation and have begun to try and change behaviour within the organization to deliver it. But these attempts are limited in scope and lack systematic application; they are typical of Level 1 in our innovation stage model. High-involvement innovation is not well understood and is being introduced in a piecemeal and random fashion, largely based on copying ideas that seem to work elsewhere, and on a generalized 'sheep dip' approach to training in basic continuous improvement (CI) tools. Whilst there is initial enthusiasm and support for the changes amongst the workforce, there is a risk that this 'honeymoon' period will be followed by one of disillusionment and a view that nothing has really changed—largely because nothing (in terms of structure, procedures, etc.) has. An attempt to put in place a new culture is undermined by the reversion to the old and long-established pattern. The challenge for organizations at this level is to move from what is essentially playing with the concept towards a more systematic design and implementation of a programme aimed at changing behaviour patterns.

Essentially these stories highlight the key features of Level 1—experimental, *ad hoc*, driven by positive motives and expectations, but lacking an underlying system or rationale. Not surprisingly, activity at this level yields a somewhat patchy experience—sometimes it works well, whilst at other times it falls on its face. Joynson describes a series of cases in which a carefully structured input can release creativity quickly and lead to major improvements in key productivity dimensions within a couple of days—a process that also provides a significant boost for employee motivation and morale. A similar positive experience has been reported by many of the participants in the UK's Industry Forum, an initiative run by the Society of Motor Manufacturers and Traders to help establish improvement capabilities in firms producing car components (Joynson 1994; Bateman and David 2002).

TABLE 5.1   Mapping Level 1 characteristics onto the model framework.

Key organizational abilities as they appear in the model	Level 1 characteristics—typical indicators of relatively low progress to developing these abilities
'Understanding'—the ability to articulate the basic values of high-involvement innovation	Little or no improvement behaviour, and a lack of focus to any which does take place
	Little/no motivation to improve
'Getting the habit'—the ability to generate sustained involvement in innovation	Problem solving—if it happens at all—is on a random and occasional basis
	Incomplete solutions or dealing with symptoms rather than root-cause problems
	Little/no learning, so 're-inventing the wheel' effect
	No formal participation—pockets of enthusiasm
	People get little or no feedback on ideas which they suggest—at times feedback may even be negative, discouraging the behaviour further
	Weak implementation—if people do suggest something it is for others to do something about it
'Focusing'—the ability to link high-involvement innovation activities to the strategic goals of the company	No targets, randomly directed, fire-fighting—fix problems as and when they crop up
	Local and often short-term focus
	Little benefit to firm

(continued overleaf)

TABLE 5.1 *(continued)*

Key organizational abilities as they appear in the model	Level 1 characteristics—typical indicators of relatively low progress to developing these abilities
'Leading'—the ability to lead, direct and support the creation and sustaining of high-involvement innovation behaviours	Often not at all—managers may even act to discourage it Little/no perceived support from the top Little/no motivation People do not believe in the idea even if management pay lip service to it 'No-one around here listens'—ideas are taken for granted or ignored No support for initiative—may even be punishment for stepping out of line 'Do as you are told' culture
'Aligning'—the ability to create consistency between high-involvement innovation values and behaviour and the organizational context (structures, procedures, etc.)	No-one has this responsibility and there is often considerable inconsistency between high-involvement innovation and the prevailing arrangements, which block or stifle it Conflict between values and high-involvement innovation—e.g. people are simply pairs of hands, people should do as they are told, etc. Little/no space or time for innovation—emphasis on activity and output No fertile ground for high involvement to develop Underlying inconsistencies stifle it at birth Systems and procedures discourage involvement
'Shared problem solving'—the ability to move innovative activity across organizational boundaries	No perspective outside the immediate workplace No or random sharing of information Little or no trust—adversarial relations between groups
'Continuous improvement of the system'—the ability to strategically manage the development of high-involvement innovation	No-one has this responsibility High-involvement innovation not recognized or developed as a formal concept
'The learning organization'—generating the ability to enable learning to take place and be captured at all levels	Little or no investment in training or development Little or no use of relevant concepts or tools to facilitate high-involvement innovation No use of formal cycle/no structure to problem solving Blame culture—mistakes are avoided, hidden or else punished No attempt to capture knowledge—projects treated as one-off events

We can briefly map the typical characteristics associated with Level 1 onto our model framework, given in Table 5.1.

5.5 What's the Problem?

Making the first moves in Level 1 is not difficult—the problem arises in terms of converting the initial enthusiasm around a good idea to something more substantial and sustainable. Amongst typical problem issues that emerge when trying to implement change at this level are:

- Lack of awareness—the idea of involvement in innovation is outside the 'normal' experience of people within the organization and there is an anxiety or suspicion about what is involved, the motives of management in bringing it in, the level of real commitment, etc. These are understandable reactions and underline the importance of clear communication of the key messages about the underlying values of high-involvement innovation
- Lack of skills/knowledge—it is one thing to ask people for ideas to solve problems or explore new opportunities, but this is unlikely to elicit a significant response unless people have the necessary tools and the skills to use them. Whilst most professionals are trained in some form of systematic approach to finding and solving problems, the same is not necessarily true of others in the workforce. Related to this difficulty of finding and solving problems is that of running out of problems—people are not skilled in separating out root causes from symptoms and important from less important problems—with the result that a lot of time and effort can go into dealing with irrelevant or unimportant issues
- Lack of space/time—a common problem is that whilst organizations become interested in the idea of high-involvement innovation, they are reluctant to commit resources to it—and particularly to change the 'way we do things around here' to accommodate it. Trying to force-fit a high-involvement approach into an environment that is still locked into a fire-fighting mode of operation and that does not allow some space and time for people to practise and explore high-involvement innovation is unlikely to make much progress. Very quickly people will pick up on the dissonance between what is being said and the actual availability of space and time to make something different happen—and the new behaviour patterns will be damped out
- Lack of real management commitment/paying 'lip service' to the idea of high involvement. Joynson (1994) describes a case at a white-goods manufacturer in the UK, which employed him to try and engender a higher level of participation. As the Managing Director is quoted, 'we want you to get across the message that we really mean it when we say we want everyone to be involved. You can help do that for us.' After a short training programme a number of teams began work on short-timescale, intensive improvement projects such as machine set-up time reduction, machine feeding and handling improvements, workplace layout improvements and so on. The experience—which was televised for a BBC series—proved successful in the short term, not only in terms of results (for example, the set-up time on a big press was cut from 53 to 25 minutes in a single session, whilst productivity in another machine was improved by 28% through changes in the handling system), but also in morale and motivation. But ten weeks later when the film crew returned, the situation had reverted to the old style and suggested a lack of real commitment amongst management to the changed approach. In the case of one set of improvements that had been suggested it transpired that it had taken weeks to have some small components made to fit to the presses and thereby increase their productivity. 'There was a general complaint that the design engineers, the cost department, and the production engineers were dragging their feet over the changes the team wanted to see. All these people represented middle levels of management—people in a position to stop things happening if they had a mind to' (Joynson 1994)

- Lack of recognition—it is easy to neglect the point that offering ideas is essentially a voluntary commitment on the part of individuals and groups in the organization. They don't *have* to do it and they can choose to participate or not according to how they feel about the process. For this reason it is critical that people feel that their ideas are valued and acknowledge, even if, objectively, they are not the most useful or practical in the world. In simple terms, people are making a gift of their ideas—and are likely to be annoyed and disappointed if their gift is ignored or brushed aside

- Beyond the basic issue of recognizing and reacting to the preferred suggestions, it is also important to recognize that, where those ideas do have a value, people are likely to want to know what is in it for them. The calculation is simple—if the idea saves money (or time, waste, defects, etc.), then some return ought to come back to the author of the idea. Research shows that this is not a simple financial transaction—people mainly look for other forms of recognition unless the benefit from the idea is of significant proportions, in which case they expect an equitable share of the benefits. But the principle is clear—lack of attention to recognizing what people offer as ideas is a fast way of turning them off. And, at the limit, trying to introduce high-involvement innovation ideas in a context in which people fear for their jobs is not likely to succeed—people can work out that improved productivity can result from fewer people and their suggestions may end up accelerating this process. As one employee of a company which tried just that put it, 'we're not stupid—no-one round here is going to work to improve themselves out of a job!'

- Lack of feedback—related to the recognition issue is that of feedback: what happens to an idea, once it has been suggested? Again people have expectations that something will happen—either their idea will be implemented straight away or, failing that, they will receive some feedback as to when and how it will be taken forward. Handling the problem of meeting this expectation with the reality of limited resources for implementation, and the possibility that many ideas will not really be practical, is not easy—but failing to address it is likely to mean that people stop suggesting things because they feel no-one really cares about or uses their ideas

- Lack of continuity—a high-risk factor is that any attempts to introduce high-involvement innovation are seen as simply another initiative, one to add to the many whose corpses litter the organization's recent memory. The reaction of many staff when faced with another apparent fashion-driven initiative is to keep their heads down and wait for it to pass—not helpful in trying to build and sustain a different culture in the organization

- Lack of leadership—here the risk is that people perceive the attempt at introducing high-involvement innovation as something to which management subscribes and pays lip service, but which does not fundamentally change their behaviour or the ways in which the organization actually operates. Although the words are there, managers do not themselves behave any differently and there are no resources or other expressions of commitment to underline the stated importance of high-involvement innovation

- Lack of implementation—linked to the feedback question, this refers to the risk that ideas, even good ones, are not seen to go anywhere because the organization lacks implementation capacity. Particularly where those ideas need specialist skills and resources to take forward, it may be the case that there are finite limits to the rate at which they can be progressed—but popular expectation is for ideas to be used. When this appears not to be happening, the reaction is often to hold back on suggesting further ones, and eventually the flow dries up

5.6 ... and How to Deal with it

Faced with issues of this kind, what can we do to keep the momentum and to make progress on the journey to high involvement? The following is a list of some useful enablers, organized around the key behaviour clusters that we are seeking to develop in an innovation culture.

Developing and Helping Awareness and Understanding

Much can be achieved through basic presentations of the company's position and the potential broader role which people can play in sharing their ideas to help move things forward. Figure 5.1 shows an example of such a presentation, which is given to all workers at an iron ore mine in Thabazimbi, South Africa. Significantly the bulk of the workforce at this mine are illiterate and amongst the rest there are a variety of dialects and languages so the company (Kumba Resources) chose to develop a presentation that is based on pictures and cartoon characters (De Jager *et al.* 2002).

FIGURE 5.1   Extract from Thabazimbi mine strategy presentation.

Simple training inputs can be powerful mechanisms for developing understanding and simultaneously sending a message about the value placed upon the employee. Joynson's book describes a number of such cases where 'Sid's heroes' (his term) quickly learn and deploy the basic skills of finding and solving problems (Joynson 1994). Imai (1997) reports on similar experiences in Japan.

Understanding of the principles underpinning high-involvement innovation can also be fostered by encouraging staff to talk to others—for example, through a programme of visits, or through attendance at workshops and conferences or through visiting suppliers and talking to them about difficulties that represent problem opportunities for improvements. A number of examples used in different companies can be found in Gallagher and Austin (1997).

Enabling Involvement and Participation in Problem Finding and Solving

Once people are prepared to try and share their ideas and understand why this process can be of value, the next hurdle lies in the basic skill set to accomplish something. At Level 1 a number of simple but robust tools are available which can yield surprisingly powerful results. These range from equipping staff with a basic problem-solving approach (often modelled on the Deming 'Plan–do–check–act' cycle) to using some specific tools and techniques such as cause and effect analysis (fishbone or Ishikawa diagrams), check sheets, process maps and brainstorming. Early use of these will require some level of facilitation, but groups quickly learn to take the techniques which they have been taught and use them unsupervised. Beyond the basic toolkit there is also scope for using structured approaches to common problems—for example, the 5-S technique (see Box 5.2) or set-up time reduction (see Box 5.3).

BOX 5.2 The 5-S approach.

The 5-S approach is widely used as a continuous improvement (CI) tool. It is designed to focus operator involvement on continuous improvement of their own local environment, and the power of the approach is that it develops skill in using simple problem finding and solving tools and motivates and encourages workers because they are able to affect their own workplaces in positive fashion. The term 5-S derives from the five areas that could provide ideas for improvement; in Japanese these all begin with the letter S:

- Seiri—organization and layout
- Seiton—orderliness
- Seiso—cleanliness
- Seiketsu—another word for cleanliness
- Shitsuke—discipline

In implementation it is simple—a team-based approach in which members discuss how to organize and tidy their environment and ensure that everything is in its place and available for use without wasting time looking for it. (The value of this can be seen in the area of set-up time reduction, for example (see next box), where a surprising amount of time can be wasted simply looking for relevant parts and tools.) 5-S is a powerful tool for starting high-involvement programmes because it is extremely simple, requires few skills, is local in orientation and can generate visible benefits very quickly. Good descriptions of the approach and its use can be found in Japanese Management Association (1987), Suzaki (1988) and Joynson (1994).

BOX 5.3 Set-up time reduction.

Reducing set-up times offers increases in flexibility, shorter lead times and reduced inventories. It also offers firms the chance to compete effectively in markets characterized by demands for greater product variety or more rapid product innovation.

Set-up time is made up of four basic components, which apply to all types of machine. These are:

- Preparation and finishing — getting parts, fixtures and tools ready, delivering them to the machine, and the reverse of the process, taking the old ones away (together with any necessary cleaning or maintenance). This component represents about 30% of set-up time
- Mounting and removal of tools and fittings. This component represents around 5% of set-up time
- Measuring, calibrating and adjustment so as to ensure that the correct positioning, speed, temperature, or other conditions are fulfilled. This component accounts for around 15% of set-up time
- Trial runs and adjustment, to ensure that the machine is now set up correctly. This accounts for around 50% of set-up time. Clearly the better the adjustment, the less time required for this stage

Reducing set-up times was one of the major breakthroughs of the original efforts within Toyota and owes much to the work of Shigeo Shingo. His approach, which has become known as the SMED (Single Minute Exchange of Die) system, led to massive reductions in set-up times on a range of equipment, not only in the large-press working machinery area but across the manufacturing board (Shingo 1983).

In essence Shingo's system evolved through a classical piece of work study, watching how changeovers were effected and constantly trying to improve on them. His observations took place in the 1950s in a variety of factories and the system was refined during the 1960s in his work with Toyota. The process made extensive use of the principles outlined above of involving all the workforce and never accepting that the problem had been solved, simply that it had been improved upon. Indeed, the momentum was maintained at times by senior management setting apparently impossible goals. For example, as Shingo comments, '... in 1969 Toyota wanted the set-up time of a 1000 tonne press — which had already been reduced from four hours to an hour and a half — further reduced to three minutes!'

The consequence of this is that the system is basically simple and can be applied to any changeover operation. It relies on observation, analysis and creative problem solving. There are four basic steps:

1. Separate out the work that has to be done while the machine is stopped (called internal set-up) from that which can be done away from the machine while it is still operating (external set-up). For example, typical external set-up activities include the preparation of dies and fixtures and the actual movement of dies in and out of stores and to and from the machine in question. Typical internal tasks are attaching/detaching dies, adjustment and testing. Shingo estimates that between 30% and 50% of set-up time can be saved by doing external set-ups rather than including these operations as part of internal set-up
2. Reduce the internal set-up time by doing more of the set-up externally. This can be done, for example, through the use of pre-set dies or special easy-fit fixtures holding the new dies. External set-up times can themselves be reduced by colour coding, easy-access stores of tools, special transport equipment, etc., all designed to minimize the time taken for moving and finding

3. Reduce the internal set-up time by simplifying adjustments, simplifying attachments, developing special easy-fit connections, devoting extra resources to it at the critical time (making it a team effort with several people leaving their 'normal' jobs to help out with the changeover, etc.). Adjustment of dies once in position often accounts for up to 50% of the total internal set-up time, so finding ways of reducing or eliminating the need for adjustment (for example, through the use of locator pins or grooves) is a rich source of opportunity. Another example, quoted in Suzaki (1988), is the pre-heating of dies for injection moulding machinery so that the machine is able to start running much earlier

   Another important way of reducing internal set-up time is the use of parallel operations, where extra assistance is provided at the critical time of changeover and the time is reduced by several people working in parallel. This not only improves things by having extra pairs of hands, but it also cuts time out which a single operator would spend moving around fetching carrying and fitting. Suzaki gives a useful illustration of a set-up done in parallel, where the simple addition of an assistant for some of the key stages in a changeover cut the internal set-up time for a press from 57 to 10 minutes

4. Reduce the total time for both internal and external set-up. Implicit in this is the concept of continuous improvement, of constantly monitoring, analysing and developing new attacks on the problem

Changing over set-up is thus a precision, team-based activity in which everything is to hand, special-purpose tools and fixtures are used and everyone knows what he/she has to do. A very close and effective analogy can be seen in motor racing when a car makes a pit-stop for tyres to be changed. This is also accomplished in seconds — as a result of a very similar process.

Set-up time reduction demonstrates a number of important principles of continuous improvement. Opportunities can be identified through 'watching with new eyes' — taking a closer look (perhaps with a video) and discussing ways of separating out activities. Analysis — using various techniques (e.g. PERT networks to determine critical paths) — and creative problem solving using the whole group through techniques like brainstorming can generate many potential improvements. Over time the pattern of experimenting and repeated attacks on the problem means that the set-up time gradually falls. Recording progress, e.g. on a downward sloping graph, so that all can see is an important way of continuing to motivate people in the process. There is the added bonus that ideas developed for one set-up time reduction may well be transferable to other operations or product areas and demonstrations of 'before and after' set-up time reductions can also motivate other groups of workers and help boost morale by sharing success.

Set-ups are not just a manufacturing problem

Although this technique evolved in manufacturing, it can be applied in any situation where there is a need to clear away and reset for a different activity — for example, changing and preparing rooms for occupancy in a hotel, setting up between operations in a hospital theatre or getting a table ready in a restaurant. One famous example of its application is by Southwest Airlines, who used the approach to great effect in minimizing turnaround times for planes at airports, in the process ensuring higher levels of productivity by reducing the time planes spend on the ground.

The aim here is to provide early impetus towards regular problem finding and solving and so the use of tools that have the potential for quick hits and for highly visible results is preferred. For example, 5-S leads to a visibly more ordered and clean workplace whilst set-up times can often be reduced dramatically in the first couple of sessions of group problem solving. Whilst it could be argued that this development of discipline is hardly significant innovation, we should remember that an important dimension of innovation relates to the context in which new practices are introduced. Things are innovative if they are new to the adopting unit, even if they are not 'new to the world' (Rogers 1984). As a simple mechanism encouraging people to suggest ways of *how* to carry out such cleaning up it provides a powerful building block for shared problem finding and solving behaviour, which can later be applied to more complex challenges.

Leadership

At Level 1 the risk is particularly strong that management will be seen to give out mixed or contradictory messages. Espousing the principles of high involvement is relatively easy, and communicating them to the workforce equally so. But, if the perception is that there is only lukewarm commitment or even hostility to the principle—see the Joynson example mentioned earlier—then the experiment can backfire and people will be more reluctant to take the risk in future. These is a need for consistency of message and an element of leadership by example.

This can be achieved in a number of ways—for example, by taking an active role in the training and facilitation, by appointing a senior-level manager to act as champion, by engaging in problem finding and solving behaviour directly, by laying down demanding challenges for a 'campaign' of improvements and rewarding/celebrating the achievement of those targets, etc. Simple acts of recognition are also valuable in establishing a climate supportive of high-involvement innovation—for example, one manager at Milliken Industries, a textile manufacturer, sent a personal note of thanks around to any employee who had made a suggestion.

Leading by example can take many forms—in one case a 5-S programme in a major Japanese car manufacturing plant was instigated by the plant manager ceremonially setting to work scrubbing and cleaning up what had been identified as the dirtiest machine in the factory, while the rest of the workforce watched! The process was then extended to the next dirtiest machines and the next most senior managers, and so on. Whilst this may sound like an engineered PR stunt, it had the desired effect, sending a clear message about an underlying value associated with high-involvement innovation. Everyone needs to get involved and the simple step of beginning the cleaning process highlights the basic process of looking to find improvements and then implementing them.

Another powerful mechanism for demonstrating leadership and support is through the commitment of resources—for example, in some firms each team that volunteers to try and find/solve problems is given a small operating budget of their own to spend as they think fit. The resulting sense of empowerment is strong and the gesture underlines a sense of management backing and commitment.

Ensuring a Good Fit Between the Way the Organization Works and High-Involvement Innovation

One of the most difficult steps in moving to high-involvement innovation is to integrate it within the day-to-day operations of the organization. In many cases it remains something to be done at the sidelines or in 'spare' time—in part because of its experimental nature and the consequent unwillingness of supervisors and managers to disrupt things too far. One of the most successful approaches to dealing with this problem is to try and ensure a regular but short session with high frequency—for example, establishing a pre-shift team meeting or a review session before handing over. This allows for reinforcement and practice of innovation behaviour without major impact on output. Another approach that is widely used is to focus on some local level project, such as 5-S or set-up time reduction in which there is a visible and useful benefit to offset against taking people off-line.

Another potential source of difficulties lies in the reward and recognition system or, rather, its absence. If the traditional pattern has been one in which it was not considered part of anyone's job to make suggestions, then simply saying that things have changed is unlikely to mean a new behaviour takes root. Instead some form of reinforcement will be helpful—and evidence suggests that token and symbolic rewards can help here. These can range from badges and pens through to more substantial rewards such as meal vouchers or cinema tickets. In each case, the emphasis is not placed on the monetary value of the reward so much as on reinforcing the behaviour that leads to suggesting ideas. As we have noted above, one particularly successful scheme donated a small amount to a nominated charity every time someone came up with an idea.

Enabling Learning

The risk with high-involvement innovation, especially at this level, is that improvement takes place but is not captured. This can lead to examples of repeatedly finding and solving the same problem, 're-inventing the wheel', or people in different areas coming up with the same solutions to the same problem. This places emphasis on the need for simple mechanisms to capture, document and share ideas—for example, via newsletters or display boards. Another variation on this theme is the use of group presentations to others—this has the dual benefit of increasing motivation as well as spreading knowledge about new ideas, which can be adopted and used by others.

There is also scope for involving people in revising and taking ownership of standard operating procedures (SOPs) etc. within their operating area. For example, making available a camera and encouraging people to document their proposed changes to the way in which they carry out their tasks can quickly be integrated into SOPs and can deal with some of the difficulties on ensuring compliance with safety and quality standards such as ISO 9000.

Enabling Focus and Direction in High-Involvement Innovation

Although Level 1 behaviour is essentially a set of short-term experiments, a tentative step in the direction of high-involvement innovation, there is scope for making sure it moves the organization in the right direction and can have an impact on its strategic goals. In particular by implementing a focused programme—for example, 5-S—there is an implied degree of targeting and focus on the resulting problem-solving behaviour.

Enabling Cross-Boundary High-Involvement Innovation Activities

In similar fashion, although Level 1 behaviour is not associated with high levels of problem solving and even less so with cross-boundary working, there are tools—such as process mapping—and arrangements—such as cross-functional teams—which can be used to develop a better awareness of the shared nature of many problems and the need to think in terms of wider solutions.

Supporting and Developing the High-Involvement Innovation System towards Higher Levels

If Level 1 behaviour is to persist and gradually move towards high levels of involvement and sustainability, then there is a need for an identifiable resource base amongst the organization's staff who can support and facilitate the process. In turn, these people are unlikely to have skills or experience in making this happen (unless they are external consultants brought in for the purpose—in which case the risk is that when they leave the capability may leave with them). This puts emphasis on the need for facilitator training and development and also for enabling them to connect with others—for example, in an experience-sharing network—with whom they can exchange ideas and review the difficulties involved in maintaining momentum.

5.7 Summary

Whatever the starting point, it is often the case that the decision to change is in the form of an experiment rather than a major policy decision. Let us see if there is something we could do to tap into the brain power of our people? The strength of this approach is it opens up new possibilities, but the weakness is that it does not really deal with the issues of structure or support. Why should people contribute their ideas? What sort of ideas? What's in it for them? How can they make an input?—do they have the skills and the ability to think? How do we manage the flood of ideas?

This is an important and sensitive stage—for many people it is the first time they will have been involved and the risk is that they can quickly become cynical about the whole idea. But, carefully nurtured, such extension of involvement can lay the foundations for a much more strategic capability.

For many firms, the experience of Level 1 is simply that of an interesting experiment, a diversion from the normal way of doing things. After the experiment things revert to the old pattern, and the level of involvement is low. But for some the experiment proves interesting enough to prompt further action—to begin to try and mobilize involvement and creativity on a more systematic basis. How they do this—and how they approach the challenges outlined above—is the subject of the next chapter.

5.8 An Extended Example – The Case of Friday Motors Ltd

This case looks at the experience of introducing Level 1 activity in a little more detail—and highlights the difficulties of moving beyond simply playing with the concepts of high-involvement innovation to actually making it happen in systematic fashion.

Friday Motors is a motor dealership involved in the high-value end of the market, selling and providing after-sales service for a well-known prestige brand of vehicles. Although the sales operation has been highly successful, the level of performance in the service and repair facility is less so, and in a recent customer service review across the whole group this operation scored badly. As a result, the management team decided to try and do something different, and recognized the potential for moving to more of a team-working approach to the problem of service and repair of cars.

The basic operations involved in service are not particularly complex, but there are many places within the process where errors and mistakes can enter. The effect of these is often that small problems can become compounded so that the impact on customer service is significant. For example, a typical issue arises when a customer leaves his/her car for service at 9 am expecting to be able to pick it up at 5 pm. The first step in the service process is a diagnosis, which may simply indicate that all the car needs is simple replacement of oil, adjustment of various systems and cleaning. However, it may also highlight particular problems requiring more work and specialist parts—something that will require the availability of parts and of specialist skilled labour to undertake the work. All being well, the car should be ready for collection, cleaned and polished, at 5 pm.

Unfortunately this apparently simple set of tasks can go wrong in many ways—all of which have the effect of delaying the process and possibly making it impossible to finish the job within one day. For example:

- Once the need for new parts has been diagnosed, these may not be available in the stores and may need to be ordered—possibly the special-delivery arrangements from the local parts warehouse do not run to getting these there on the same day or, if they do, the traffic conditions or something else make it impossible
- There are not enough skilled mechanics available to carry out the work because they are busy working on other cars
- The skilled mechanics are available but they do not have the specialist tools to work on the car. These tools are expensive, so the company only issues a small number of sets—but even these have a certain 'resale' value and are regularly stolen!
- Once the work has been completed, the cars are then parked outside in the yard to await collection. Unfortunately the lack of space means that they must be double or treble parked—and, when the customer arrives to collect, it may be impossible to extricate the car. This in turn could be through lack of drivers, or through the loss of the relevant keys

The point is that none of these are major problems, and most are predictable and likely to occur with regularity. They are also not difficult to solve, once identified. Many can be fixed in minutes—for example, the issue of where the keys are for a car can be resolved by the simple device of a 'keyboard' on the wall—if the keys aren't hanging up there is a name against the space to indicate who has got them. But not solving them has big implications for the customers—they are left waiting for their cars, or informed that their original estimate of same-day service is not possible (because of lack of parts, staff, etc.) and so they are without their car for a sustained period of time. In an attempt to patch up customer relations, the company may be forced to loan out cars and provide other forms of service—all costly—to placate the customer and cover up for the underlying problems.

The impact of all of this on the business should not be underestimated—it is costly in terms of customer relations (and amongst a group of highly vocal customers who have paid a high price and expect a high quality of service). It is costly in terms of the correction and placating costs to try and deal with the results of the problems. And it is costly in terms of some of the prevention approaches—for example, one way to avoid the problem of lack of availability of parts, tools or skilled staff is to carry more of them, but at a huge extra cost to the firm.

The company decided to try and use CI as an approach, having heard about the principles in a management seminar. They invited a consultant to explain the principles and decided to try a simple and low-level intervention based on trying to get staff to work on some of these problems. There was no strategic rationale nor any long-term view of this as a means of organizational development. Given that many staff in the business were unskilled and that labour turnover was high, they were not convinced that investing heavily in training would be the answer—and they were also concerned not to make their problems worse by involving staff in training instead of servicing cars!

The intervention involved taking two groups of staff and giving each a one-day training programme on some basic problem-solving tools. The groups were mixed, involving staff from the different areas (stores, mechanics, reception, etc.) and each comprised around eight people. The training involved simple exercises to demonstrate the principles of problem solving and to show that everyone had the capability to contribute to this kind of activity; brainstorming, fishbone charts and process maps were the three approaches introduced. Early in the session the groups were involved in identifying key problem issues and the emerging list was clustered into typical and recurrent issues—for example, the factors typically leading to customers not being able to drive away their cars at 5 pm after service.

By the end of the day the groups had worked on simple process mapping and identified a range of potential solutions, some of which were easy to implement and likely to bring benefits quickly, others which would require further work and some possible investment. The groups were then invited to spend the next two weeks working these up into a set of proposals for change which they would present to management for acceptance/implementation. The levels of enthusiasm at this stage were high and at the end of the day feedback to management was positive. The follow-up sessions were also successful, with some well-thought-through solutions to core problems and a programme of changes, which focused on several of the key problems affecting customer service levels.

Whilst this approach was successful in the short term (indeed, as a result of the changes implemented by these two pilot groups, the company performance improved enough to raise their position in the national customer service survey significantly) it did not represent a major change. It undoubtedly demonstrated the potential of involvement in problem solving and the use of some simple but powerful problem finding and solving tools. It also gave a sense of confidence to the staff that they could handle this kind of activity ('it's not rocket science') and that management were at least prepared to listen if not always totally enthusiastic about their ideas. But this initial enthusiasm and learning were not consolidated; there was no strategic commitment to extend the training to the rest of the staff or to develop it further to more sophisticated approaches aimed at tackling some of the bigger problems. It worked in 'fire-fighting' mode and undoubtedly helped in the short term—but then things got busier and other things came along to distract management attention, and the initiative sank below the surface.

This is in many ways a typical example of Level 1 behaviour. The basic ideas of CI are being explored, there is initial enthusiasm and there are some useful results emerging. To take things further, though, will require a much more systematic and committed approach.

References

Bateman, N. and A. David (2002) 'Process improvement programmes: a model for assessing sustainability,' *International Journal of Operations and Production Management*, **22** (5), 515–526.

De Jager, B., M. Welgemoed, J. De Jager, C. Minnie, J. Bessant and D. Francis (2002) 'Enabling continuous improvement—an implementation case study,' in Smeds, R. (ed.), *Continuous Innovation in Business Processes and Network*. HUT University Press, Helsinki University of Technology, Helsinki.

EIU (1992) *Making Quality Work; Lessons from Europe's Leading Companies*. The Economist Intelligence Unit, London.

Gallagher, M. and S. Austin (1997) *Continuous Improvement Casebook*. Kogan Page, London.

Imai, M. (1997) *Gemba Kaizen*. McGraw-Hill, New York.

Japanese Management Association (1987) *Canon Production System: Creative Involvement of the Total Workforce*. Productivity Press, Cambridge, MA.

Joynson, S. (1994) *Sid's Heroes: Uplifting Business Performance and the Human Spirit*. BBC Books, London.

Lewis, K. and S. Lytton (1994) *How to Transform Your Company*. Management Books 2000, London.

Rogers, E. (1984) *Diffusion of Innovation*. Free Press, New York.

Semler, R. (1993) *Maverick*. Century Books, London.

Shingo, S. (1983) *A Revolution in Manufacturing: The SMED System*. Productivity Press, Cambridge, MA.

Sirkin, H. and G. Stalk (1990) 'Fix the process, not the problem,' *Harvard Business Review*, July/August, 26–33.

Suzaki, K. (1988) *The New Manufacturing Challenge*. Free Press, New York.

Chapter 6

SYSTEMATIC HIGH-INVOLVEMENT INNOVATION CAPABILITY

This next stage in the model involves organizations trying in a formal and systematic way to extend participation in innovation. Many activities which organizations around the world are using in the direction of 'kaizen', lean teams or quality circles would come under this banner. In this chapter we explore the strengths and benefits of such an approach and look at some ways to help embed and sustain such initiatives.

At this level in our model firms can expect to obtain real benefits, but the majority of these will often be rather localized and limited in their impact. There is also a risk that activities at this level eventually run out of steam and fall away after the initial 'honeymoon' period. The chapter discusses some of these limitations in Level 2 development of innovation capability and explores the conditions under which organizations should seek to move to the next stage—of strategic innovation capability.

6.1 Taking High-Involvement Innovation Seriously

The previous chapter showed some examples of what can be achieved when people are enabled to contribute their ideas. The benefits highlighted in the cases described came not only in the opening up of new solutions to problems, but also in the motivation of people involved. However, although the sense of potential emerges from developing Level 1 innovation capability across the organization, so too does the challenge. If we think this is a good idea, then making it part of the way of life of the organization is going to need some systematic and sustained effort. This is the essence of Level 2 capability—making high-involvement innovation systematic across the organization.

At a minimum the questions in Table 6.1 need to be addressed if such behaviour is to have a chance to take root and have an impact on the business.

Experience shows that it is problems with one or more of these issues that make high-involvement innovation (HII) programmes run aground. It also becomes

TABLE 6.1   Typical issues in moving to Level 2 capability.

Question	Response required will include the need to try things like . . .
What's in it for people?	Putting in place some form of recognition/reward system that acknowledges their contribution
How to do it?	Training and skills development around problem finding and solving and related innovation capabilities
	Setting up suitable vehicles—problem-solving teams, quality circles or whatever—to carry through high-involvement innovation (HII) activities
Who is going to help support them?	Identification and training of suitable facilitators
	Commitment of senior management to support and champion the cause
How will this fit in?	Ensuring that organizational structures and systems support rather than block HII behaviour
	Making space and time available to carry out HII activities
How will the flow of ideas be managed?	Putting in place some form of idea management system
How to maintain momentum?	Ensuring this is more than another 'fashion statement' by the organization
	Planning for long-term strategic development of HII capability
	Linking HII to the organizational development strategy
Where and how to get started?	Identifying suitable pilot areas/teams/projects

clear from the list that moving to Level 2 is a significant commitment—it starts to cost real money and time and, although benefits start to flow (see below), the investment is not really going to pay back in a short timescale. An increasing number of organizations feel that it is worth making such a commitment and a variety of approaches to developing a systematic Level 2 capability can be found, often under the banner of total-quality or lean-thinking initiatives. Chapter 2 gave an overview of the evidence base, but it is worth reminding ourselves with a few 'snapshots':

- Case 1 is a small firm making carbon-based components, based in the north of England. High-involvement innovation (HII) was adopted as part of a general restructuring programme, which included moving to cellular production and introducing just-in-time manufacturing. In their first year of moving to systematic CI the firm had 12 'continuous improvement teams' (involving a total of 31 employees—around half of the workforce). Examples of their activities were:
  - Producing parts for major engineering customer—scrap levels were averaging 8.5%, and the team set a target of 5%. Thirteen possible solutions were generated; implementing the main ones brought the average scrap level to 0.9% and kept it there
  - Packing for carbon rings needed improvement to prevent damage in transit. A three-person team worked on this and reduced the number of damaged

rings from eight in the first six-month period to zero in the subsequent six-month period.

Overall total savings in the first full year of HII were around £212k (on a turnover of around £5m), but this underestimates the full benefits because many savings are not one-off but impact as recurring cost savings in subsequent years. In addition, improved internal efficiency means that failures and problems are being avoided and thus turnover and profit are boosted

- Case 2 is an electronics company, which grew rapidly in the mobile-phone accessories market. High-involvement innovation (HII) amongst their 600-strong workforce is seen as a key plank in their development, and has been running for 2 years now. Turnover is around £25m.

An initial round of pilot projects was carried out before spreading HII to the rest of the organization. Benefits from the pilot projects include:

  - On one surface mount line, efficiencies were raised from 30% in 1993 to 90% in 1994 and tangible savings estimated at £10k per month
  - In a stores project, shortage clearance times were cut to 19 minutes on average—this reduces the incidence of line stoppages, which cost about £5000/hour and so are significant

- Case 3 is a large bakery specializing in the production of a wide range of biscuits. This plant employs 700 across three shifts, and HII has been running for around a year, producing savings of about £250k
- Case 4 is a producer of domestic heating systems, who has managed to achieve savings running at around £1m per year (equivalent to 20% of profits on a turnover of around £70m)
- Case 5 is an IT services company, operating in a number of countries. In this example a secretary was working in one of their Eastern European sites and noticed some furniture requisitions coming across her desk en route to her boss. On her own initiative she investigated and found this was being sourced from overseas because local furniture was not of high enough quality. However, she also knew that several offices were being closed or re-organized in the UK and, in the process, various items of office equipment and furniture were being freed up. She chased up the inventory list and instead of making a purchase of around £5000 for new furniture was able to arrange a transfer. Following the success of this venture, the same was applied to stationery and other office equipment. What this underlines is the simplicity of the ideas, the culture which enabled both initiative and also cross-site communication—and the learning and extending of the basic principles. Savings were not huge compared to the company's turnover, but the example and the cumulative effect of many suggestions like these underline the extent to which this way of thinking had become part of 'the way we do things around here'.

Further case examples of this kind (including a number of service-sector cases, whose experience mirrors that of the manufacturing examples cited above) can be found, together with a detailed discussion of how they were achieved, in the following sources: Sirkin and Stalk (1990); Robinson (1991); Kaplinsky (1994); Westbrook and Barwise (1994); Kaplinsky et al. (1995); and Gallagher and Austin (1997).

6.2 Making High-Involvement Innovation a Part of the Culture

In addition to the direct problem issues indicated above, there is one more we should consider—the change in the way people think. This is at the heart of the problem of moving to Level 2 and it is worth us spending a little time looking at it. As we saw in Chapter 3, organizations (and the groups that they contain) behave in certain ways because of the things that people believe and that underpin shared patterns of behaviour. Simply saying something like 'everyone has a brain so they can contribute' is easy, but getting people to believe it throughout the organization is a different matter. This is a self-reinforcing cycle—believing something means we behave in a certain way, which in turn reinforces the belief. What emerges at the end is a shared set of beliefs that underpin a shared way of behaving—'the way we do things around here'.

It is relatively easy to introduce a new idea about how the organization is going to work—for example, let us imagine a Managing Director who has seen CI working somewhere else and wants to try it in his/her organization. The first steps are likely to involve talking about it and trying to make explicit the underlying ideas and beliefs. For example, 'everyone can be creative and can contribute their ideas—and we will value them, however small'. Or the even more difficult 'mistakes are opportunities for us to learn—so we'll move to a no-blame culture'. There is absolutely nothing wrong with these as beliefs—but getting people to share them and 'buy into them' to the extent that they make people behave in a different fashion to what has gone before is not easy. Still more difficult is doing so for long enough and reinforcing the message strongly enough that these do become new patterns of behaviour—'the way we do things around here'.

Consider how many ways these simple beliefs might be undermined. First, people are often somewhat sceptical of new ideas and increasingly so in a climate where new initiatives come through with great frequency but seem to involve no more than a flurry of activity before a return to the status quo. Why should this one be any different? Such caution is not confined to those employees whom the organization is trying to involve—it can also pervade the thinking of those charged with introducing it. Sadly, not every manager shares the view that people are willing and able to be creative and to contribute their ideas—and many suspect that trying to encourage this is a waste of time, which could be more valuably spent on other tasks. At best it might make people feel a bit happier—but such motivational improvements may prove costly if there is no impact on the bottom line.

Beyond these initial doubts there are the issues we have already mentioned—of individual and organizational resistance to the idea of high involvement. For many different reasons the belief that ideas count and the practice of actually offering them up can be quickly suppressed, especially if the various negative factors work in cumulative form. People find themselves hearing the words about the organization wanting their ideas, but they also think to themselves things like:

- 'My idea's no good—I'll look stupid if I say anything'
- 'Why should I bother—they won't do anything with it, they never do'
- 'It's just another case of them trying to get something more out of me—why should I?'

- 'I don't know how to do this'
- 'I haven't got the time'
- 'They never listen anyway'
- 'It won't last—I'll just keep my head down till this one goes away'

What this often means in practice is that attempts to move to Level 2 innovation capability run out of steam and the overall honeymoon effect gives rise to a return to the old beliefs and ways of doing things. For this reason, making the transition and sustaining Level 2 is a major challenge and needs commitment and maintenance of momentum. How can this be achieved?

Once again we can learn from experience of others and identify some typical and regularly occurring types of blocks and barriers—and look at some of the enabling approaches which help firms deal with the issues.

6.3 Characterizing Level 2 Innovation Capability

Once again we can use the model developed in Chapter 4 to explore Level 2 issues in more detail. As Table 6.2 shows, there is an attempt to deal systematically with many of the core behaviours, but typically these are not fully developed or embedded. The right-hand column draws on case examples of organizations trying to implement Level 2 high-involvement innovation.

TABLE 6.2 Putting Level 2 high-involvement innovation in place.

Key organizational abilities as they appear in the model	Level 2 characteristics—typical indicators of progress on the way to developing these abilities
'Understanding'—the ability to articulate the basic values of high-involvement innovation	The principle is generally broadcast and talked about but not everyone subscribes to it—high level of enthusiasm but also scepticism
	Some success stories open up possibilities of different way of working but persistence of old-style blame culture
'Getting the habit'—the ability to generate sustained involvement in innovation	There is a formal approach—PDCA* or equivalent—in which some people are trained. However, its use may be patchy and need support and reinforcement
	Problem finding and solving is primarily local level, short term and project focused. Emphasis is less on the outputs than on getting the habit of problem solving
	Local-level success stories, but little strategic advantage. No bottom-line benefits, so it becomes hard to justify continued efforts and investment
	'Honeymoon' effect with gradual fade—initial enthusiasm gives way to disillusionment. Runs out of steam when the 'slack' has been taken up
	Little link to formal daily routine. Usually special time/place set aside for the activity. Projects are often out of the mainstream
	Involvement is voluntary and patchy—high dependence on enthusiasm and champions and seen as something extra and needing extra support and resources. Considerable missionary efforts required to spread the word and establish the habit

(continued overleaf)

TABLE 6.2   (*continued*)

Key organizational abilities as they appear in the model	*Level 2 characteristics—typical indicators of progress on the way to developing these abilities*
	Not part of the formal expectations of people
	Feedback on suggestions via supervisors, team leaders, etc. Dependency on someone else to respond. May be negative if the interval between suggestion and feedback is long or if the answer is always no. Danger of depending too much on particular supervisors or team leaders, some of whom may not be good at giving feedback
	Some local-level implementation takes place but the dominant mode is still one of implementation by others with the skills, resources, etc.
	Measures, if used, may be seen as controls rather than drivers for HII. Costs of measurement may exceed benefits realized
	Mainly passive and local search for improvement opportunities, using existing problems and 'low hanging fruit' issues—the 'squeaking wheel' effect. May only treat symptoms rather than root causes and sometimes runs the risk of running out of targets once obvious problems have been found and addressed
'Focusing'—the ability to link high-involvement innovation activities to the strategic goals of the company	Some people are aware in broad terms of what the overall aims of the business are, but not aware of how their local contribution might fit in. Consequence is a lack of focus to improvement efforts and an overemphasis on local-level actions
	No link between improvement and the things which make the business succeed or fail—with the risk of improving the wrong or the irrelevant things
	Slogans and briefing sheets describing strategy on notice-boards, but little or no link to actual problem-solving activity
	Some local-level measurement activity or, when it does happen, measurement is often sporadic and infrequent. Little link between measures and actions because of lack of frequency etc.
'Leading'—the ability to lead, direct and support, the creation and sustaining of high-involvement innovation behaviours	Some champions and some patchy support, but also blockers and sceptics present
	If managers are perceived to listen, then the cycle of suggestion becomes a virtuous one. However, if they are perceived not to listen, then very quickly the behaviour declines
	Limited implementation depending on resource commitment. Tends to be 'low hanging fruit' and more difficult problems are shelved
	Limited decision making by those who are involved in making suggestions—typically implementation decisions are separated out from the suggestion process
	Direction is given but most emphasis is on getting the HII habit rather than on specific strategic targets
'Aligning'—the ability to create consistency between high-involvement innovation values and behaviour and the organizational context (structures, procedures, etc.)	Some attempts to adapt structures and procedures, but often blocked by lack of power on the part of an HII team and by the weight of existing structures—e.g. reward systems, team structures, work organization, etc., which cannot be changed
	HII is seen as something 'nice to have' but is essentially marginal—any major changes which it implies to structures or procedures would be 'rocking the boat'

TABLE 6.2   (*continued*)

Key organizational abilities as they appear in the model	Level 2 characteristics—typical indicators of progress on the way to developing these abilities
	Occasional low-frequency or possibly annual review. Often lacks structure for review and assessment
'Shared problem solving'—the ability to move innovative activity across organizational boundaries	Mainly local orientation with occasional inter-group linkages and awareness of wider problems
	Local level loyalty—some co-operation between near neighbours but largely inward looking
	May have some basic knowledge of external customers but in general terms only—not able to provide measurable indicators of what the customer wants
'Continuous improvement of the system'—the ability to strategically manage the development of high-involvement innovation	HII is managed by a steering group or individual champion but has a predominantly local focus, and the emphasis is on getting started
	Problems may emerge such as dependency—nothing happens without the drivers
	Problems in drawing attention of senior management because of lack of measurement or indicators to link HII with business results
	Planning is tactical in nature, concerned with operational fine-tuning of the current level of HII activity and with building up the system. Time frame is essentially short term
	High-level support is 'second-hand'—senior management commitment is assumed but their day-to-day involvement is slight
'The learning organization'—generating the ability to enable learning to take place and be captured at all levels	Training and development investment but mostly confined to job-related skills
	Application of basic continuous improvement tools but often needs facilitator or 'prompt' to enable this
	Formal problem finding and solving cycle espoused and taught, but used only with guidance and support
	Lip service paid to concept of 'mistakes as opportunities', but old culture of blame still dominates. Some attempts to capture learning help avoid repetition of mistakes

*PDCA = plan, do, check, act—a brief statement of the problem solving cycle originally proposed by the quality expert W. Edwards Deming and sometimes called the 'Deming Wheel' (Deming, 1986).

6.4 What Stops Us Getting There?

In many ways the move from Level 1 to Level 2 is one of the most difficult to make and sustain because it requires putting in place a comprehensive system, the purpose of which is to enable and reinforce a set of behaviours that are unfamiliar to the organization. As Table 6.2 indicates, there are many different barriers that can block or inhibit the development of capability at this level, ranging from specific and concrete issues (such as the lack of suitable skills, structures or facilitation) through to less tangible perceptions, such as a sense of missing commitment from senior management.

Box 6.1 gives some responses made by a group of facilitators across a wide range of organizations to the question 'what is the biggest barrier to implementing and sustaining systematic high-involvement innovation?'.

BOX 6.1 Problems in implementing and sustaining Level 2.

- A lack of commitment from the lower levels of the organization — the debate within (our company) is whether this is due to the fact that there is no remuneration for continuous improvement ideas ... There is also mistrust that the process (of making suggestions) will jeopardize their jobs

(Marine engineering firm)

- Quality initiatives have been seen as leading to job losses ... there is a degree of hostility and a cynical view that quality is a euphemism for more for less

(Insurance business)

- As my organization runs a three-shift system there is, occasionally, a tendency to forget that everybody at some stage or other is faced with exactly the same problems. So, instead of working together as one, there tends to be an inclination to lean towards a defensive and non-communicative nature ... I would say that this splintered approach and different conception at times have an adverse effect ...
- The concept of teamwork where team leaders and team members make decisions to shape the future of their team has been difficult for the 'empire builders' to embrace. They see their previous position of power being eroded and they cling on desperately to the remnants of their once mighty and influential departments ... our progress has undoubtedly been hampered by the unwillingness of certain people to 'let go'

(Paper manufacturer)

- Some staff feel the programme to be too prescriptive and bureaucratic; when it was launched it was felt at the time that the programme needed to be highly structured if it was to be successfully implemented but there's a paradox here — you need system at the start but then loosen up or you'll lose it!
- Quantification of benefits is proving difficult
- There is frustration at the top of the division as to what can be done to rejuvenate it
- Some staff feel that time devoted to continuous improvement activities is wasted effort
- Forms of recognition to acknowledge success tend not to be spontaneous due to a preoccupation with concepts such as setting precedents and equality of rewards

(Insurance company)

- The evolution of the policy (for high-involvement innovation, formally imposed from corporate HQ) has resulted in the activity being seen at operator level as a suggestion scheme. Often this means that 'improvements' are suggested which someone else is expected to turn into reality
- At Senior Management level continuous improvement is seen as an important tool but is not thought out. Some think that it should only relate to small improvements, almost at a personal level. Generally it is felt that it should be self-financing, i.e. there is no allowance in any budget for activity relating to high-involvement innovation
- Other senior managers feel that they have always practised it anyway before anyone gave it a name, and there is therefore no need to modify their management style or anything within their department. They therefore find it hard to go with the new programme

(Stationery products company)

- There is a degree of mistrust between management and unions, with its origins in the fact that the employees were not offered a share of the newly formed company. The union is reluctant to commit fully to any continuous improvement activity without some form of payment to members, and has employed tactics to slow progress down, e.g. filling teams with stewards

  (Auto components firm)

- Some department managers and the works managers seem to think 'now we have implemented it and all our people are motivated and understand the system, so we can continue with our normal work' . . . It is obvious that many busy managers, despite their espoused belief in it, do not take the time to make continuous improvement an integrated part of the daily work

  (Engineering company)

- Many ideas are implemented without being recorded
- Some ideas may be getting lost because individuals are 'too busy' to forward them or simply 'can't be bothered' to present them formally
- Similarly there is the conflict between those areas where the creativity of new ideas is seen as part of the individual's job description or department function (e.g. design, marketing)
- There is a formal system but it doesn't always work

  (Instrumentation company)

- Complaints of lack of time due to 3 × 3 12 hour shift pattern
- Staff reaction to jargon
- Bureaucracy, form filling, rigid approval mechanisms, rigid meetings
- Creating and communicating a strategy with hard measures
- Leadership style/ability
- Absence of mechanisms for identifying improvement opportunities
- The 'initiative' label attached to it and complaints of initiative overload

  (Chemicals producer)

- Like many other 'world class' companies XXX has been on the high-involvement journey for a number of years but unfortunately it has recently lost its way and momentum. This could be, in part, due to the introduction of self-directed teams approx. 12 months ago within manufacturing. These teams are expected to have continuous improvement (CI) as a key objective but have tended to focus on meeting production targets at the expense of CI . . . ownership of it has therefore to be re-established

  (Capital goods producer)

6.5 Barriers to High-Involvement Innovation and How to Overcome them

In this section we will look at some of the more commonly reported difficulties in trying to put Level 2/systematic high-involvement innovation in place—and at the ways in which different organizations have tried to overcome them.

Consistency Problems

This relates to the fit (or otherwise) between high-involvement innovation (HII) and the way the organization operates—its structures, procedures, etc. A common issue here is the difficulty of allowing sufficient time and space in the organization's daily operations to allow HII to happen. Other difficulties include a conflict between the way things happen and the new ways in which higher involvement is being encouraged—as Box 6.2, an example from a large pensions company, shows.

BOX 6.2 Example from a large pensions company.

One of the barriers to empowerment in our company is the system we use to improve our work processes. The system is called a Systems Query Request (SQR) and encourages staff to raise problems with the daily processes and possible solutions. The benefits to the company are reduction on costs and a happier member of staff. The barriers are:

1. Timescales — to raise an SQR the member of staff first completes an SQR form and then hears nothing about it for months. This can deter staff from raising SQRs in the future as there is no immediate impact
2. Recognition — the credit for the SQR on release often goes to the person who solves it and not to the person who originally requested it. Again this can deter people raising future SQRs as they see no personal gain and no recognition
3. Budget constraints — depending on the importance of the SQR or how much it can save the company, an SQR can be delayed. The company currently have a list of over 100 SQRs raised and these are now in a priority order but the company will only release 10 at a time. Again this proves disheartening if your particular SQR is near the bottom, even though it may be a regular problem. It can give the impression an SQR is of little importance. Also most SQRs save money long term, so quoting budget constraints as a reason for delay can appear strange
4. Management — if an SQR raised is seen as a quality success, a financial reward of £40 is paid to the individual responsible. This can appear pitiful if the management are quoting it as a great success which is saving the company thousands of pounds a year. Again this can make an individual feel all he is doing is benefiting others financially and not himself

---

Some ways of dealing with this problem of consistency include:

- Include in the business plan non-financial performance measures, such as the rate of innovation and the speed of internal processes, to give improvement a higher priority
- Allocate half an hour each week when employees across the company can legitimately take time out to discuss their work processes and how they could improve them. Once the practice of examining and improving processes, and the value of doing so, has become established, it will no longer be necessary to earmark time formally for this

- Make high-involvement innovation (HII) a part of everyday work (e.g. via regular process reviews, process measurement) so that it is not treated as a separate, optional activity
- If managers are having difficulty finding enough time to support HII, they might be helped by time management training
- Tactics used by some companies include: using overtime for HII training and getting it going; reducing the line speed in order to free up personnel; including time for meetings in the annual budget; and introducing a new management structure

Lack of Commitment from Managers

As we saw in Box 6.1, there is often a problem with lukewarm support or even direct hostility on the part of senior managers to high-involvement innovation (HII). They see it as a threat; there may be a challenge to their views on what motivates people; they may not subscribe to the company strategy, etc. Amongst ways of dealing with this are:

- Answer the question 'What's in it for me?' using the language managers speak (i.e. in terms of operating costs, margins etc.)
- Persuade managers to deliver HII training—teaching is a very effective way of getting managers to understand what HII is really about
- Involve middle managers in the development of HII rather than impose it from above. Identify and develop management champions who will energize and support HII
- Support managers as they try to adopt a more participative style, for example with training in leadership and facilitation skills
- Use promotion, appraisals and public recognition to reinforce the message that managers who actively support HII will get on in the company

Lack of Skills — and the Need for Training

Enabling participation in innovative activities for people who have not hitherto been a part of the process will require a significant investment in basic training around the concept and relevant tools, followed up with regular opportunities to practise using the skills. The early stages are all about acquiring the basic habits of high-involvement innovation (HII)—learning to find and solve problems systematically, using simple tools to help the process, and capturing some of the benefits in new ways of working. For example:

- In launching its HII programme, a major diesel engine manufacturer provided a minimum of three days' training for every one of its employees, to provide the basic platform for understanding HII and to establish the process in people's minds. Additional inputs—for example, for those with the responsibility for facilitating it—were also made, with periodic updates in such training. Its initial investment in training during the 18-month start-up period was of the order of 16 000 person days

- A large UK auto components maker, in building its Process Improvement Teams (involving around 700 people), provided three days of training for each team member, to establish the basic process and concepts of HII
- In a major pharmaceuticals company, Waste Elimination Teams (WETs) were launched simultaneously for all employees in the tablet packaging area. WETs were permanent improvement teams formed around dedicated line teams (operators and line leaders), guided by a WE facilitator. Originally, team improvement activities were preceded by a training course consisting of six half-day sessions over a six-month period, covering 'Just-in-Time' (JIT) (using a simulation exercise), tools and techniques of problem solving (and cycle) and team building. Later, only the JIT element of the training was kept as an up-front session; the remaining elements were incorporated as and when required by the teams

Once the basics have been mastered, the next stage involves focusing this problem-solving capability on suitable targets that make a difference to the business, and learning to monitor and measure progress towards meeting those targets. This requires clear communication of the overall business strategy and breaking it down—'policy deployment'—to local-level improvement targets with which people can identify. (This theme is picked up in detail in the following chapter.) For example:

- A small company manufacturing metering equipment has been using policy deployment to drive its HII programme for the past four years, and this has helped it achieve significant performance improvements across a range of measures. At the heart of this process is a training programme that invests in multi-skilling (most staff can carry out all of the manufacturing and many office tasks) and in the tools and process of HII. This includes linking their kaizen activities to strategic targets, which are regularly communicated and displayed

At the same time there is a need to learn to spread more widely—across different functions, into new areas (for example, in new product development) and even into dealings outside the firm—with customers or suppliers, for example, as in the following:

- When a large aerospace contractor launched a high-involvement innovation initiative across functional and departmental boundaries, they carried through an intensive training programme focusing on:
  - Interactive team building
  - Interpersonal skills (personal/group behaviour)
  - Facilitation (effective meetings, problem-solving process and tools)
  A separate module was also introduced on leadership skills (covering effective management, coaching). The training took place over several days off-site and involved working in groups on real organizational problems (Gallagher and Austin 1997)

At the same time emphasis shifts from the team being told what to work on to some degree of 'self-management'—deciding on projects, finding and implementing solutions and capturing and standardizing the lessons learned.

High-involvement innovation not only requires skills in finding and solving problems; it also poses new challenges in managing the process. Within teams there may well be a need for basic meeting and team-member skills, and certainly a requirement to develop facilitators to help the group function. An example is as follows:

- A south-coast electronics manufacturer has been running a programme for the past three years. In the early stages a critical element in establishing the process was the identification of a group of around ten people who were chosen to train as facilitators. In selecting these new facilitators, the engineers responsible for overall development of the HII programme looked for people who were enthusiastic, approachable, open-minded and knowledgeable about the company. In addition, all held some position of responsibility, although not necessarily one that involved supervising others. Where possible, these employees were included as participants in the pilot teams so that they could start to familiarize themselves with the HII process.

  Formal facilitator training was carried out in February 1995 as a three-day course off-site, with the assistance of external consultants. The first day of the training introduced the concepts of continuous improvement, put them within the strategic context of the firm and explained the role of the facilitator. The remaining two days focused on using the consultants' version of a formal Process Improvement Problem Solving (PIPS) cycle and the associated tools, using a number of interactive exercises to enable a more hands-on approach. The training also covered facilitator skills, including interpersonal skills.

  Whilst the facilitators were enthused by the training, there was a general agreement that they did not feel sufficiently confident to start facilitating teams. Consequently, it was decided to provide the facilitators with a further opportunity to practise the tools and process by allowing them to work together as an improvement team on a live project. The facilitators chose to investigate ways of improving the effectiveness of noticeboard communications, an issue that had arisen earlier in the training session

Another important set of skills required is that for steering the overall HII programme—recognizing when and where inputs of training or other enablers are needed and when the organization needs to make a step change to move to the next stage of HII development.

Put simply, training is essential to making high-involvement innovation happen—without it, there is a high risk that learning will not take place. But training also plays several other roles, beyond enabling the development of skills. It can act, for example, as a powerful motivator, something that is seen as a reward or a recognition of the employee's value to the firm. It is a truism to say that people are an organization's most valuable assets—but they certainly are when it comes to their creative problem-solving skills. Training not only develops and sharpens these, but also provides a strong reinforcing message about how much this contribution is valued:

- As one supervisor turned cell-leader explained, in discussing the changes following the introduction of high-involvement innovation into his engineering company, '... previously, the overriding aim was to push things through on time, and this was reinforced by the bonus scheme. Thinking for yourself was not encouraged (by the bosses)... training makes you look at things differently. Now cell members are encouraged to put ideas forward.' The results have been impressive, with a reduction of 35% in manufacturing lead time, a dramatic decline in rework and a cut in inventory of nearly 50%. Just as important, absenteeism is minimal and morale is high

A second key theme underpinning training for high-involvement innovation is the importance of moving beyond simply developing problem-solving skills—the 'know-how' component—towards understanding why and where these should be deployed. This 'know-why' component is often missing, but unless people understand how their particular contribution fits into the wider picture, high involvement is unlikely to find its way into the company culture and become part of 'the way we do things round here':

- A large aerospace manufacturer's HII programme has been characterized by a combination of continuing employee development punctuated by major change programmes. In the first, back in 1990, they introduced the Kawasaki Production System. This was based around the concept of Just-in-Time production, with an emphasis on waste elimination and continuous improvement. In addition to the introduction of Japanese-style production techniques, teamworking and problem-solving groups were started. Natural Work Teams (NWTs) were created around each manufacturing cell. Problem-solving activities were carried out within the teams who were trained in a seven-step process.

  This was followed later by the establishment of Integrated Production Teams, which met on a daily basis to discuss production schedules and any problems that arise. These provided a focus for cross-functional team-based HII activity around the redesign of manufacturing systems. To help bring about the necessary learning a team of company staff working with consultants developed and delivered a training programme for everyone in the Manufacturing Systems Department plus others who interfaced with the department. Around 150 people were trained in modules that included know-how elements (such as the tools and techniques of manufacturing systems design), know-why elements (including manufacturing strategy and simultaneous engineering) and cross-functional teamworking.

Lack of System for Handling Ideas

A major problem can arise in high-involvement innovation in part because of a success in getting people to come up with and offer ideas. Unless there are structures in place to manage the flow of ideas, the risk is that the organization will be overwhelmed and unable to use them all. Quite apart from the lost opportunities which this represents it poses an additional problem—that of turning people off the idea that their suggestions are valued. Without timely feedback and some form of action, even if it is only an explanation of why the idea cannot be taken further, people are likely to lose motivation. The concept of suggestion boxes is one that goes back a long way but has the major limitation that it is essentially a one-way system—people post their ideas in and may never get a response back. By contrast, suggestion schemes today are sophisticated multi-level systems, which include routes for processing ideas and giving feedback, reward and recognition components, display and sharing opportunities and other elements. For a good description and guidelines for how to design and implement a suggestion scheme, see the website of 'ideasUK', http://www.ideasuk.com, which was formerly the UK Association of Suggestion Schemes.

Idea management systems vary in implementation, but in general they operate on several levels—for example, a simple 'do-it-yourself' system for those ideas that people can put into practice themselves, a more detailed one in which extra resources may be needed and where the organization needs to take a decision to commit them, and major projects, which could have significant impact but which will take time to organize. Amongst points to consider in support of effective idea management systems are:

- The system should motivate people. Implementing someone's idea is one way to motivate that person. Some Japanese firms can claim that over 90% of all suggestions are implemented
- Implementation should be timely. By not responding to an idea in a suitable time frame, the company may miss out on the opportunities that led to the idea being suggested in the first place. Slow response can also discourage people
- Who is going to accept the ideas? Will senior managers be the only people who can make these decisions? Why not allow staff to participate in vetting ideas? They may not be in control of the budget, but there should be some degree of ownership of the idea suggestion/management process
- Who is going to implement the new idea? Again, why not let staff participate in the planning and implementing of new ideas?

Lack of or Inappropriate Reward/Recognition System

A significant component of a high-involvement innovation (HII) programme, and one that must be carefully planned and monitored, is the recognition or reward system. The objective of this system is to encourage and motivate staff participation in HII activities. Acknowledging the efforts and achievements of the people in the process can lead to further involvement. Rewards do not have to be large financial sums; in fact, it can sometimes be important not to use financial rewards as these mechanisms are difficult to break away from in later stages.

The whole issue of reward and recognition is fraught with difficulty. The trick is to find a means of acknowledging people's efforts in a way that makes them feel appreciated, but without involving large individual monetary rewards and bureaucracy, which undermine the concepts of HII and risk alienating those who do not qualify or feel they have been overlooked. Table 6.3 gives some examples of recognition mechanisms currently being used in the UK, at an individual level as well as for teams, and a suggestion for recognition across the company. Examples of recognition that proved unsuitable include: posters being given to people who did not have walls; mugs awarded to workers who were not permitted to carry drinks around; and poor-quality barbeque sets received by staff in recognition of a 'job well done'—many of whom had nowhere they could use a barbeque!

The nature of reward and recognition within a company may change over time, with token gifts or small sums of money being awarded in the early days in order

TABLE 6.3   Recognition mechanisms.

Examples of individual recognition
Token gifts, e.g. mug, chocolates
Certificates
£1 donated to the elected charity for each idea
One month's use of reserved parking space near entrance
Entry into monthly lottery
Verbal thanks from supervisor
Mention in company newsletter

Example of team recognition
Round of drinks
Meal out
Presentations to management group/rest of department etc.
Mention in company newsletter
Photograph on notice-board
Memo from Managing Director

Example of company-wide recognition
The equal division, among the entire workforce, of profit achieved *above* the annual profit target, the
 assumption being that the 'extra' profit results from improvement efforts made by people
 throughout the company

to motivate initial participation and to reinforce the message that the company values small-scale improvements; later these may be phased out as HII becomes ingrained in the company culture and naturally occurring. However, if the culture permits, it may be better from the start to avoid recognition in the form of financial rewards or gifts. In a variation of this, a company gave a box of chocolates or similar token gift for each first idea, no matter how small, to acknowledge initial participation; further ideas were recognized with verbal thanks. Just saying 'thank you' goes a long way—especially when it comes from the top of the organization. However, one of the most powerful motivators is for people to see their ideas implemented—that fact that *action* has been taken on *their* recommendation is often more effective than any token gift. One company gets round the problem of the demotivating effect that declining a suggestion may have by asking people to submit their ideas *after* they have implemented them, so management hear about only those ideas which are practical.

A potential pitfall of a formal system of recognition is the demotivating effect it can have if an individual or team gets overlooked. One company avoids this by inviting teams to put themselves forward if they want their improvement activity to be featured on a special notice-board in the canteen. There may also be a need to train managers and supervisors in how to recognize people appropriately. Intangible forms of recognition—writing a memo, discussing an idea with its originator, listening to a team's suggested course of action, and so on—may take up more management time, but this activity is very important and should be given the time it deserves.

The 'how' of recognition is only one of the issues. Other equally important questions to answer are:

- Who will be recognized—individuals, teams, everyone?
- Who will give recognition—managers, peers, participants?

- What will be recognized—end result, adherence to process, creativity, team working?

Lack of a Structured Approach for Finding and Solving Problems

Whilst many of the people responsible for innovation in low-involvement organizations have been trained in some form of scientific method or equally structured approach to thinking, the same cannot be assumed for others in the organization. If we want to develop higher levels of involvement there is a need to train and equip people with these skills and to encourage the use of structured frameworks until such problem finding and solving becomes second nature.

At its simplest, we can see the basic cycle of problem finding and solving as shown in Figure 6.1.

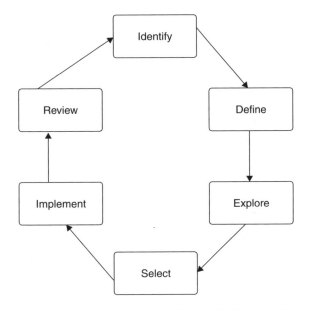

FIGURE 6.1   Basic problem finding/solving cycle.

In the first stage—identify—the organization recognizes that there is a problem to solve. This may be an emergency or it may be a minor difficulty that has been nagging away for some time; it may not even be a 'problem' but an experiment, an attempt to find out a new way of doing something.

Whatever the initial stimulus, finding a problem then triggers the next stage, which is to define it more clearly. Here the issue is often to separate out the apparent problem (which may only be a symptom) from the underlying problem to be solved. Defining it also puts some boundaries around the problem; it may be necessary to break a big problem down into smaller sub-problems which can be tackled—'eating the elephant a spoonful at a time'. It can also clarify who 'owns' the problem—and thus who ought to be involved in its solution, if the solution is to stick for the longer term.

Once the nature of the problem has been analysed, the next stage is to explore ways of solving it. There may be a single correct answer, as in crossword puzzles or simple arithmetic—but it is much more likely to be an open-ended problem for which there may be a number of possible solutions. The challenge at this stage is to explore as widely as possible—perhaps through the use of brainstorming or other group tools—to generate as many potential solutions as possible.

Next comes the selection of the most promising solutions to try out—essentially the reverse of the previous stage, since this involves trying to close down and focus from a wide range of options. The selected option is then put into practice—and the results, successful or otherwise, reviewed. On the basis of this evaluation, the problem may be solved, or it may need another trip around the loop. It may even be the case that solving one problem brings another to light.

In terms of learning, this is essentially a model for experimenting and evaluating. We gain knowledge at various steps in the process—for example, about the boundaries of the problem in defining it, or about potential solutions, in exploring it or about what works and what does not work in implementing it. The point is that, if we *capture* this learning, it puts us in a much better position to meet the next problem; if it is a repeat, we already know how to solve it. If it is similar, we have a set of possible solutions that would be worth trying. And if it is completely new, we still have the experience of a structured approach to problem solving.

Why use a *structured* approach? In theory, the model looks pretty useful for ensuring that we find and solve the right problems, and that we learn from the experience. In practice, things are often less successful—mainly because the cycle is not always followed in quite the way described. For example, we often jump over the stages in the cycle and, in taking short-cuts, miss out on alternative solutions, which might be better. We often fail to define the problem and instead assume that the initial 'presenting' problem is the one to be solved; a bit more analysis may reveal that this is a symptom or a by-product of the real one. Alternatively, it may be that defining the problem reveals that it is too big to be solved, or that it is owned by others who have good reasons for not wanting to solve it, or have already tried, and so on.

Table 6.4 lists some common limitations to effective problem solving, which restrict the learning possibilities.

For these reasons training and practice in using such a cycle are critical to building firm foundations for high-involvement innovation.

This process of problem finding and solving has been applied to many different types of problems and improvement opportunity—for example, reducing the set-up time on machinery, reducing defects in a particular area and reducing the time taken to respond to customer enquiries (Shingo 1983; 1986). It is often embedded in broader methodologies—for example, much training in TQM is based on what has come to be termed the 'Deming Wheel'—a simple version of the above model with four stages—Plan, Do, Check, Act.

Lack of Suitable Vehicles for Driving Forward High-Involvement Innovation

The issue here is how to mobilize the creativity of everyone in the organization and channel it into finding and solving problems and identifying improvement opportunities. A few ideas popping up at random are unlikely to have much of

TABLE 6.4   Limits to effective learning through problem solving.

Limitation	Effect on problem solving and learning
Failure to define the problem—missing out the definition stage	Solving the wrong problem, or treating symptoms rather than roots causes
Lack of exploration	Wasting time on solving problems to which a solution already exists
	Lack of focus in developing solutions—solving parts of other problems as well as the core problem
	Jumping to the first and most obvious solution—not necessarily the best
Repeating well-tried solutions	'We've always done it this way' may be useful, but there may be a better way. By failing to explore, new opportunities may be missed
Limited perspectives in exploration	Solutions reflect only one point of view—and may miss out on key information, experience or insight
Lack of evaluation	Time is wasted trying out too wide a range of solutions rather than focusing on a small number
Lack of review	No chance to learn from the experience and pass this knowledge on to others. Danger of re-inventing the wheel at some future date

an impact on the big strategic targets of the organization. Nor is there likely to be much effect if only a handful of people take part, even if they are creating new ideas like mad. There needs to be some way of mobilizing and involving people across the whole organization—and doing so on a regular basis.

What we need is a process and mechanisms to enable it to happen. And, whilst the basic process might be common, we should not lose sight of the fact that different situations need different mechanisms. All roads may lead to Rome, but there are lots of different ways of travelling down them. Enabling vehicles for high-involvement innovation (HII) come in a variety of shapes and sizes and each vehicle has its own strengths and weaknesses. Some large ones can have a great impact, but are relatively slow and consume a lot of fuel (resources). Others are smaller and therefore more manoeuvrable. Yet others are adapted to suit special terrain. The skill lies in picking the right vehicle for the job and to have a selection to choose from so that the HII programme does not stall or stop because one particular vehicle breaks down.

Different organizations use different vehicles and combinations for many different reasons, including the following:

- To spread involvement to more people—for example, moving from a group-based approach to an individual one
- To re-energize a flagging programme—for example, by launching a short-term sprint campaign in which everyone is involved
- To deal with different kinds of problem—for example, big complex multi-departmental problems are probably best tackled by task forces

- To meet different personal preferences—some people like to work in teams, others are natural 'loners' and prefer a more individual kind of HII vehicle

---

BOX 6.3 Getting in the driving seat.

The MD and Quality Manager of a medium-sized manufacturing company believed that continuous improvement would help the company survive the recession and provide an impetus for tackling several long-standing issues that had started to grow into serious problems and could no longer be ignored. They understood that high-involvement innovation (HII) is about involving everyone in the organization and ran a series of awareness seminars, attended by all employees over a three-month period, at which they explained the concept of HII and its underlying principles. The MD and Quality Manager identified a number of 'Champions' who they saw as being the main conduit for extending HII activity throughout the organization. The Champions were tasked with encouraging people to look for and implement improvements, and to give help where it was needed.

There was an initial burst of activity, especially on the shop floor, where the Production Manager was a very active Champion. Many staff were enthusiastic about the idea of HII and started to work on improvements, often in small workplace groups. Early successes started to be featured in the company newsletter.

However, after about six months there was a noticeable drop in improvement activity. The level of activity in any area depended largely on how active the local champion was and, in many cases, it was the same handful of people responsible for all the HII going on. By the end of the year there had only been a small amount of improvement in the big problem issues the company faced, though other problems had developed. In retrospect, this was attributed to the *ad hoc* nature of the improvement activity: people worked on whatever they wanted and this led in some cases to groups with conflicting objectives pulling in opposite directions to each other, and to the way the company wanted to go. In addition, the informality, while encouraging spontaneity, had also led to a lot of time being spent in meetings and discussions that led nowhere, duplication of effort and inconsistency. These factors combined to leave many people feeling disillusioned with HII and little inclined to continue to take part.

As a result of sharing this experience with his counterparts in other companies and finding out what they were doing, the Quality Manager drew up a proposal for some formal 'HII vehicles'. This was accepted and put into effect during the following year. The vehicles enabled people to participate in HII activity as individuals and as members of teams. The system was deliberately kept as unbureaucratic as possible, but the provision of these formal vehicles quickly brought significant benefits: a much wider range of people became involved in HII because there were company-wide mechanisms that they could use; and the increased control over team activity ensured that all the teams worked in the same direction, and in a way to help achieve the company's objectives. This stronger focus led to a much improved ratio of effort to benefits gained, which in turn increased motivation and stimulated repeated involvement in HII. There were still a few problems — in particular, pockets of little HII activity and some management resistance — which took time to resolve. Nevertheless, the introduction of these formal vehicles was a watershed in the development of HII in the company.

In another case, an automotive components company had been running team-oriented HII vehicles for three years. The vehicles worked well and had brought many benefits, including significant savings. However, there was a limit to the number of teams that could be up and running at any one time and so, although nearly 30% of the workforce had been in at least one team, that left over 70% who had not yet taken part in any formal HII activity. To enable everyone to become involved in HII the company introduced a second type of vehicle, aimed at individuals. This led to high levels of participation, with many good improvement ideas being suggested and implemented by people throughout the company.

Another company introduced a second type of vehicle for a different reason. It had no tradition of teamworking and, after HII was introduced, management found it difficult to get improvement teams running. They did not want to rush people into teamworking until they felt more comfortable about it. However, the staff were having lots of ideas and the managers were concerned that, unless they did something, these ideas would be lost and people would lose interest. So they decided to set up a second vehicle that would enable individuals to get on with implementing their smaller improvement ideas and that would also capture the more far-reaching ideas so that they could be worked on by teams in the future.

The point is that there is no single best way—each organization needs to decide which vehicles are the most appropriate at a particular moment in time. Successful high-involvement innovation organizations tend to run a fleet of different vehicles and use them all to further their continuous improvement activity.

The larger vehicles tend to:

- Be driven by senior management
- Take the form of company-wide initiatives
- Have relatively long timescales (often years)
- Have a greater impact on the organization than smaller vehicles
- Be resource intensive

The names and functions of these larger vehicles vary between organizations. Some companies use HII lorries to facilitate company-wide assessments from which improvement opportunities are identified; these assessments are often based on the criteria for awards like the European Foundation for Quality Management Award and the Malcolm Baldrige National Quality Award (Garvin 1991). Other companies have used HII lorries to co-ordinate improvement efforts that span the whole company, for example, reducing lead time and increasing customer satisfaction.

The medium-size vehicles tend to:

- Involve 4 to 10 people
- Be cross-functional
- Have medium timescales (months)
- Be of variable impact, though they can result in major improvements
- Have lower resource requirements than the larger vehicles

These are the most common types of vehicle and they come with many different labels: Process Improvement Groups, Corrective Action Teams, Quality Circles, Task Forces, to name a few. Such vehicles deal with all sorts of issues, including improvements to process, product, environment and the organizational infrastructure. For example, in one company a Task Force identified the need for an extra water valve to be used when bringing a generator on-line; this was put into effect and resulted in a significant reduction in water loss. In another company an Improvement Team was set up to investigate the more effective distribution of post and parcels around the site. The team, which comprised personnel from the post room together with some internal customers, made a number of changes leading to over £4000 savings in the first year—and greatly reduced the incidence of parcels being lost!

Small vehicles tend to:

- Be used by individuals
- Focus on local workplace improvements
- Operate on a short timescale (hours/days/weeks)
- Have a relatively small impact, but often bring benefits other than direct cost savings
- Have low or no resource requirements

Of all the vehicles, the small ones embody the core value of high-involvement innovation well by involving everyone and being available at all times. The bicycles, skateboards and scooters in a HII fleet are set in motion by individuals having ideas for smaller-scale improvements and, in many cases, implementing the improvement themselves. For example, one idea that came from a bicycle scheme was to replace the large coffee urns in the meeting room with small thermos jugs; this was done and resulted in a great reduction in the amount of undrunk coffee that had to be thrown away at the end of the morning.

BOX 6.4 Examples of operating guidelines.

These are the abbreviated operating guidelines followed by the HII vans (termed Process Improvement Teams) in one company:

1. Management agree the objectives of a Process Improvement Team (PIT)
2. Members of the PIT are trained in tools, a problem-solving process and teamworking
3. The PIT returns to the workplace and works on the problem/improvement opportunity during normal working hours. The Team Mentor has overall responsibility for steering the PIT
4. There are fortnightly progress reviews with the local manager
5. The PIT makes a formal presentation to the management team every six to eight weeks, reporting on progress, problems, etc.
6. Completion of the project is celebrated with a buffet lunch, at which each team member is presented with a certificate
7. The records of the PIT (minutes, data collected, graphs, calculations etc) are kept in a Project File for future reference. The Quality Manager is responsible for transferring the solution and other learning achieved by the PIT to other areas of the factory, as appropriate

The same company also has a much smaller vehicle—a HII bicycle. The guidelines for this reflect its objective of involving as many people as possible in implementing small workplace improvements:

1. Discuss your idea with your supervisor
2. Implement your idea—ask your colleagues or supervisor to help if necessary

3. When your idea has been implemented, record it in the notebook provided
4. At the end of each month, remove the records from your notebook and put them in the green box in the canteen for collection by the Quality Manager

Thank you for your idea!

BOX 6.5 How one organization introduced a 'bicycle' to help with high-involvement innovation.

A UK based multi-national organization employing around 25 000 people world-wide decided to introduce a HII bicycle. The intention was to have a mechanism that would encourage everyone to make process improvements, and would at the same time support previous quality initiatives.

After six months researching what other companies were doing, the company decided to design their own vehicle. Pilots lasting six weeks were run at several sites in the UK and mainland Europe. These resulted in modifications to the bicycle and the way it operated, which were tested in a second wave of pilots. Although some of the original problems had been eased, there was still a capacity problem — the system relied on local co-ordinators to monitor and chase up ideas, and after about 150 ideas they could not cope with any more. The company took the decision to invest in the development of an object-oriented computer system that could monitor and progress ideas electronically. After further trials, this electronic bicycle was introduced to areas within the organization as they became ready for it. Introduction was backed up with training for local co-ordinators, awareness raising and communication (including a video, posters and a newsletter), support in the form of a Help Desk and various promotional activities. The bicycle activity was monitored centrally, with particular attention paid to participation levels in different business areas, the number of ideas submitted and the percentage that were subsequently implemented.

In this instance, the electronic bicycle proved an appropriate solution for a high-tech company. However, the significance of this example is not the high-tech vehicle that resulted, but the process the company went through to develop and introduce a successful bicycle: a process that involved two years of research, pilots and learning, leading up to a carefully planned introduction backed up with training and other forms of support.

The idea of complementary vehicles addressing different aspects of innovation is an important part of developing high-involvement behaviour. For example, Kodak has seven different vehicles, ranging from simple 'bicycle'-type schemes, through a new product-idea suggestion scheme, through small-group activity, cross-functional teamworking and task forces. There is even an 'innovation office' for looking at crazy and 'off the wall' ideas, which may have potential for breaking new ground.

In the Japanese context efforts have been concentrated on three dominant mechanisms—task forces (and similar cross-functional project teams), small groups and shop-floor individual suggestion activity, known as *kaizen teian*

(KT; kaizen = unending little improvements; teian = suggestion schemes) systems. For example, Sony began their CI activity in 1946 and now operate three parallel systems—KT, 'borderless suggestions' (a mechanism for dealing with cross-functional improvement ideas) and patent proposals. More importantly, employees know where and when to use which system to take their ideas forward. There is a clear learning process that Japanese firms have gone through; for example, Isuzu now have a multi-vehicle system with KT linked to small-group activities and driven by policy deployment. This developed over a ten-year period of learning the basic CI habits and behaviours and continuously refining the system.

KT activity is very simple, usually individual based and loosely comparable to Western suggestion schemes. There are, however, major differences, not least in the nature of suggestions processed and the implementation and participation rates. By using what are essentially 'bicycle'-style vehicles, participation rates are reported as high as 70%, with the majority of suggestions actually adopted and put into practice (according to the Japanese Human Relations Association—JHRA). Individual company cases have been published in the West, drawing attention to firms like Toyota and Matsushita obtaining millions of suggestions every year. These are predominantly KT-type suggestions, and the JHRA data suggests that for an extended period of time this has been a key factor in contributing to competitive success.

KT has developed extensively across Japanese industry with most growth now coming from the service sector, at least in terms of number of suggestions. This is partly due to the relative lack of emphasis in earlier years in this area; the experience in manufacturing has been that volume precedes quality of ideas and that in more mature companies the numbers of suggestions are lower but their impact higher. For example, Hitachi were receiving suggestions at the level of 100/employee during 1986 but now only have 25; however, these are of significantly higher impact. Importantly, Japanese firms also use policy deployment to set targets in terms of both direction and number of suggestions.

KT systems have a number of important features:

- They are essentially for non-management employees
- They are designed to complement rather than replace small group and other vehicles for high-involvement innovation
- They have a powerful behaviour modifying effect because they involve short-cycle and frequent repetition of problem-solving behaviour. Typically this takes place linked to the daily workgroup meeting. In this way the culture—'the way we do things around here'—becomes altered
- The same frequent cycle linked to targeted problem solving means that there is a powerful vehicle for learning and for translating tacit knowledge into formal knowledge
- The suggestions encouraged and offered in KT schemes have very low impact and rely on accumulation for their effect. For this reason attempts to evaluate and measure against financial criteria are unlikely to succeed and may outweigh the benefit. For this reason reward systems are designed to reward the behaviour rather than the content of individual suggestions, and it is the behaviour that is of primary value to the company

- That said, it is possible to evaluate KT efforts, through the mechanisms of policy deployment (see the next chapter for a detailed explanation of this). Here, a broad target is set with clear and measurable objectives. Achieving this target can be equated to a bottom-line saving, which can often be of considerable value—for example, cost reductions of 15–20% over the year. These result from the accumulation of KT suggestions. To this 'external' measure can be added the internal evaluation process whereby ideas are ranked in a hierarchy of impact and where the more significant ones can be passed to a site evaluation committee, which will put a monetary value on their impact

The notion of reward is important in KT, but not in the strict monetary sense. The underlying principle is one of recognition and motivation, with money or goods being used as a symbolic 'thank-you' rather than a financial reflection of what the idea is worth. Many companies give no financial payments at all, whilst in others the awards are goods and services—for example, in Honda the top award is a trip to the USA. (In 1998 this was won by a suggestion to change the packing of bicycles, resulting in a simplification of the packing process and a time saving of 9 seconds per bicycle. The benefits were small, but significant when multiplied by the volume of bicycles shipped (300 000 per year); the result is equivalent to around four person years.)

The JHRA has been tracking the experience of KT in its 600 member firms, but it is important to put this in context; these are larger and more experienced and represent a fraction of the total 1.6m firms in Japan. So the overall experience of high-involvement innovation may be no different to other countries. JHRA uses a simple form to capture the experience of companies, and they in turn use forms to record suggestion levels (though not individual suggestions), which are filled out by team leaders.

In operation KT depends on a few simple principles:

- The need for a suitable structure in which it can happen—in Japan the work-group provides the context for this, allowing the team leader to facilitate and providing frequent review and feedback via the daily meeting
- The need for simple evaluation and report procedures to manage the process—most systems are operated by team leaders and involve a single sheet of paper which takes 3–5 minutes to fill in
- The need for simple on-the-job education and training, which reinforces and develops skills around problem finding and solving
- The need to develop recognition that kaizen activity is part of the normal job expectation
- The need to devolve responsibility and ownership of implementation to ensure motivation and commitment
- The need for high levels of participation
- Significantly the level of use of tools is low, and most groups rely on simple discussion and observation
- The need for repetition of key messages reinforced by the award system—about targets, about the problem-solving process, etc.
- The need to capture learning by storyboards and displays—in some companies there is even an annual book in which ideas are captured and shared across the

plant. For example, GlaxoSmithKline Japan publishes the best 200 ideas from the 10 000 plus it receives every year
- The need to capture learning into standard operating procedures (SOPs)—and to have a process that allows autonomous adjustment of SOPs without compromising standards

Lack of Suitable Tools to Enable Innovation

The basic toolkit to support high-involvement innovation does not have to be extensive, though it may need customizing to suit particular applications. Some tools, such as problem-solving ones like Pareto analysis and fishbone diagrams, seem to work in all vehicles. The experiences of a range of organizations suggest that the most widely used tools include:

- Brainstorming
- Cause and effect analysis (using the 'fishbone' or Ishikawa diagram)
- Flowcharts
- Check sheets
- Run charts
- Graphs
- Pareto analysis

However, there are many other simple yet effective tools that have been extensively written about—for example, see Atkinson (1990); Oakland (1989); Owen and Morgan (2000); Shiba *et al.* (1993). Reference is often made to the 'basic seven' tools of quality control and the 'new seven' more advanced ones, but these are only components of a much wider set of techniques, which can be used under different circumstances. A well-balanced toolkit will have tools to assist with a range of activities such as data collection, data analysis, idea generation, planning and implementation, and control.

Many organizations have an official toolkit, often in the form of a booklet or loose-leaf binder. This is probably best made available to staff in conjunction with tools training given to people as they become in a position to use such tools, for example when about to join an Improvement Team. The toolkit can be added to by modifying existing tools or even developing new ones. It is recommended that someone is designated 'Toolkit Manager' and given responsibility for maintaining the toolkit and co-ordinating the addition of new or amended tools.

The ability to match the most appropriate tools to a particular task is an important one, which is probably best acquired through 'learning by doing'. This means that people need to have freedom to experiment with different tools, to learn what works best in a particular situation, and to gradually develop their competence in using the tools effectively. In this context the facilitator's role is to offer guidance and support in using the tools, rather than spoon feeding people and telling them which ones to use. For example, in one company the facilitator introduced tools to a continuous improvement team as and when he considered necessary. The team members had not been given even the most basic tools and process training and remained dependent on the facilitator throughout. The result was a passive team who did not understand the significance of particular tools and why some were more appropriate than others for certain tasks; they had also been deprived of the opportunity to learn for themselves by experimenting with different tools.

Communications and Information Flow

Within the context of high-involvement innovation (HII) communication needs to be multi-directional to be most effective. Our research supports earlier findings that, although most companies have a variety of mechanisms for top-down communication, in many organizations there are fewer channels for communicating laterally or from the bottom upwards (Gallagher and Austin 1997). Examples of the latter include, for example, suggestion schemes and team briefings at which interaction is encouraged.

Instances of effective lateral communications are typically based on some version of cross-functional teams. For example, a company that employs around 400 people making control and instrumentation equipment has set up teams based on the workplace—the members of a manufacturing cell would be a team, or people performing different functions but working in the same geographical location. These teams generate and implement improvements related to their own work area, but in addition the 29 team leaders meet each month to share improvements of interest to other teams, and to make decisions on the overall HII process in the factory. Another example of a channel for lateral communications comes from a manufacturer of diesel engines. Here, the manager responsible for the 4 litre engine area began a newsletter for everyone in his assembly and machining areas. The newsletter continues to be produced by and for the 4 litre workers and aids communication between shifts and between the assembly and machining areas.

On a practical level, while learning is taking place, good communications can prevent duplication of effort or enhance parallel activities. For example, in one case a process plant operates 24 hours a day on a shift system; the workforce is divided into four shifts, each of which works 12 hours at a stretch, and there are two shifts running in parallel night and day. A 20 minute hand over between successive shifts ensures that people know what has been going on in their area over the previous 12 hours. However, there is no means of communicating between parallel shifts. It was only after a team had spent a lot of time and effort on an improvement that it came to light that another team, on the parallel shift, was working on exactly the same issue. Although members of both teams benefited by going through the learning process, there was considerable duplication of effort; effective lateral communications would have enabled representatives from both teams to work on the problem together, pooling ideas and experience, not only saving time but also possibly coming up with a better or more imaginative solution.

Feedback and Idea Implementation   Within a high-involvement innovation organization this is especially important when it comes to ideas put forward by individuals; in this situation, ill-conceived feedback (e.g. comments that are negative or reveal lack of understanding of, or interest in, the proposal) can be as demotivating as no feedback. So when an employee of a large IT organization suggested to his manager that the company should move its headquarters to Paris, rather than disregard the idea out of hand, the manager requested him to work out the costings involved; two weeks later the staff member reported back to the manager that, having made some calculations, relocating to Paris would not be such a good idea after all. Had the manager, knowing from the start that the idea was completely impractical, automatically rejected it, this would probably have left the employee, who had made the suggestion in good faith, feeling deflated and less likely to put forward further ideas.

Speed of response is often as important as the nature of that response. Some organizations in our research specify that all idea givers should receive initial feedback within a certain time frame, often 24 or 48 hours. In one example, a food producer, any suggestion that costs less than £100 was guaranteed to be on line the next day—or at least in the process of being installed (Bessant *et al.* 2001).

Capturing and Sharing Knowledge   A key feature in successful high-involvement innovation is the sharing of knowledge acquired in one area or project with others—in part to stimulate new ideas and in part to avoid the problems of 're-inventing the wheel'. This places considerable emphasis on display and documentation within the communication system—and examples of effective mechanisms range from creative use of notice-boards, photographs, newsletters, inter-group briefings and workshops through to more extended techniques such as 'storyboarding'.

Storyboards are most commonly used by teams to communicate to colleagues and management the steps they have taken while working on an improvement project. The format of storyboards varies between companies but in general is a mixture of words, diagrams and graphs, and sometimes photographs, arranged logically, often according to the stages of the organization's problem-solving process or improvement cycle.

In addition to communicating the steps a team has gone through and the outcome achieved, storyboards are a means of:

- Capturing the learning that has taken place, not just about the 'solution', but also the process the team has experienced
- Spreading ideas (methodologies as well as end solutions) to other parts of the business
- Giving a high profile to improvements and helping to convince sceptics of the value of HII
- Recognizing the achievement of the team, especially if the team presents the storyboard to an audience that includes senior managers

For example, a medium-sized manufacturer of measurement equipment initiated high-involvement innovation (HII) activity at shop-floor level by setting up three teams of volunteers to work on specific areas that needed improvement. Storyboarding was included in the training the teams received as they began working on the projects. In this case, each team made two storyboard presentations—one after about three months, the second at the close of the projects (10–12 months). Both times the presentations were made to an audience comprising the other two teams, the Manufacturing Director, who had introduced HII into the company, and several other managers. All the storyboards were impressive: the teams made effective use of graphics (including flowcharts, graphs and bar charts) to present the data, as well as colour, cartoons and even gimmicks like 'footsteps' linking different stages of the process and fairy lights to attract attention. After the presentations the storyboards were displayed at prominent locations around the site so that other members of staff could see what the teams had been doing. The facilitators reported that the team members had enjoyed constructing the storyboards and that doing so after three months had helped to remotivate the teams, whose enthusiasm had started to tail off at that point.

In the case just described the teams were free to choose their own format for the storyboards. Another company uses a standard, pre-printed sheet, A1 in size. This is divided into boxes for specific types of information (e.g. names of team members, title of project, etc.) and for each of the steps in the company's improvement process. Although a standard format is often less visually attractive and there is less scope for creativity, it does have the advantage of ensuring that each step in the process is followed, and anyone looking at the storyboard knows exactly where to look to find out what the team did at a particular stage. These storyboards are displayed throughout the site, both on the shop floor and in the offices. Representatives from several other companies, impressed by the storyboard sheet, have taken the idea and adapted it for their own organizations; one company, for example, decided to make the storyboard more visually attractive by replacing process step 'boxes' with hot-air balloons encircling the globe.

A structured variation on the storyboard approach is the CEDAC system developed during the 1970s by Dr Ryuji Fukada. CEDAC (Cause and Effect Diagram with the Addition of Cards) is a problem solving methodology that expands on the basic fishbone diagram. The CEDAC chart, which includes a variant of the fishbone diagram, as well as details of the problem and solutions tried or under test, is a powerful communication tool; it provides an ongoing record of an improvement team's progress for all to see, and allows other people to give input in an orderly manner (Fukada 1990).

BOX 6.6 Communications as a key foundation for high-involvement innovation.

An auto component manufacturer in the east of England provides a good example of a company with a fairly well-integrated communications framework. This company is part of a large plc organization. In early 1980s the parent company, faced with declining competitiveness and profitability, launched a comprehensive programme of corporate-wide organizational, technological and institutional change. Business units were told to achieve targets 5–10% above their best competitors; some subsidiaries were subsequently closed down or sold off. The site in question underwent a massive change over several years, moving from a complex structure and organization to a simple one. The factory was transformed from process-oriented manufacturing to product-oriented manufacturing. Natural teams were formed, with people dedicated to a particular line; the structure was flattened; and lead times came down from months to days. The company then moved from this task-force approach to process improvement teams (PITs), and more recently to an implemented improvement scheme aimed at involving every employee.

During the restructuring and ensuing development of high-involvement innovation (HII), a variety of communication channels have been put in place to support these initiatives and encourage the emergence of an open, trusting environment. The communications framework in the company is not static; it is regularly reviewed and amended as necessary; for example, mechanisms that were in place have been redesigned to make them more effective (e.g. notice-boards, the company magazine), and additional ones have been added from time to time to reinforce teamwork and the HII culture. The company tries to make all communications 'as short and sweet as possible', but initial fears that stopping the lines for communications on a regular basis would lead to a drop in output proved groundless.

Every six months the Plant Manager publishes a brochure and holds a 'face-to-face' meeting with the entire workforce at which he discusses company performance (both good and bad). Questions are encouraged, in line with the company's policy of trying to make all communications two-way. There is a regular newsletter every month as well as *ad hoc* newsletters dealing with specific issues or improvements. The company magazine, which is produced quarterly, aims to provide a shared source of information and a forum for all employees and covers both social and operational issues. Its popularity has grown since it was redesigned to encourage communication at all levels and in all directions — whereas 'the old magazine used to go straight in the bin' now 'you see people reading it and taking it home to show the wife and kids'.

A relatively recent addition to the communications armoury are computer-scrolling notice-boards. These provide real-time feedback on factory performance giving data on, for example, output rates, quality levels and productivity. Response to the boards has been mixed, with some employees appreciating the 'real-time' nature of the messages and the fact that the information is made available to everyone, while others feel that they are unnecessary and intrusive.

There are a whole series of different types of meetings: for example, unit managers meet with their product managers every day to consider quality and output issues; each product manager has weekly production meetings with his craftsmen and -women; there are monthly meetings between union shop stewards and unit managers. Lateral communication is helped by weekly meetings of product managers within the same unit and, in a recent development, by meetings held every two weeks attended by all the product managers in the plant, at which they discuss problems between the areas. The cross-functional Process Improvement Teams (PITs) make presentations to the management team, regularly during the course of their project and on its conclusion, at which the PIT members relate their progress and senior managers provide constructive feedback.

Mechanisms for bottom-up communication include weekly team meetings, a suggestion scheme, an implemented improvement scheme and the 'help system'. The latter is based around paper Help Forms. These enable individuals to get feedback on any issue of concern, problem or query that they feel has not been effectively or satisfactorily dealt with through other communication channels. Several staff act as confidential intermediaries, passing the Help Form to the relevant individual(s), who are required to reply within a specified time. The transaction is complete only when the original user of the system is satisfied and signs off the Help Form to that effect. This system is used less frequently now as communications generally have improved and many conflicts or problems are solved informally. Indeed, face-to-face informal communication within the company has increased significantly since the major reorganization and there is much more 'management by walking about'.

The company has a co-ordinated system of notice-boards: there are separate boards for different types of information — performance/technology, social, trade union, suggestion scheme, training, general etc. — and they are colour-coded so that, regardless of where they happen to be in the factory, people know where to look for specific information. To help ensure that the information displayed is regularly updated, individuals are made responsible for a particular board. There are also static displays. For example, after a PIT has made its end-of-project presentation the storyboard is left on show for about a week. The factory's foyer area is also used for company displays on health and safety themes, history, new products, etc.

The direction the company has taken over the last decade, moving away from a traditional organization, through rationalization of the workforce and restructuring, and culminating in the adoption of continuous improvement and new integrated technologies, is reflected in its approach to communications: here it has shifted away from rather formal, bureaucracy-based mechanisms to more informal and open channels. Significantly, there is a steering committee, made up of people from all levels of the organization, which proactively addresses communication issues — evidence of board-level recognition of the importance of communication within the company.

6.6 Some Case Examples of Level 2 Capability

The following examples, drawn from a wide range of organizations, show the kind of systematic ways in which the issues in moving to and sustaining Level 2 innovation capability have been dealt with.

Terrific Telephones & Accessories

This is an example of an organization that has moved to a more systematic approach. It involves a medium-sized (750 employees) organization in the telecommunications equipment market, which experienced a period of radical change during the early 1990s. It faces a continuing need for improvements in quality, cost and delivery performance in what is a highly volatile and competitive market place; one of its responses has been to try and instil a culture of high-involvement innovation (HII). Although a number of efforts in this direction had already been made, the experience was similar to that in the two cases described above; limited and short-lived interest and success. By contrast, its new programme involved extensive planning through a steering group made up of representatives from different levels in the company. Two full-time HII facilitators were appointed and over a six-month period a systematic and structured approach to implementation was developed. Components included:

- A basic training module designed to introduce problem-solving skills and then to practise these skills, first on 'classroom' projects and then on small-scale workplace problems
- Identification and training of shop-floor problem-solving teams
- Facilitator training for HII team co-ordinators
- Development of an 'idea management system', which identified the ways in which employee suggestions could be recognized, evaluated and implemented with minimum delay
- Development of a reward system that offered simple ways of recognizing and thanking employees for suggestions and reinforcing the behaviour, whilst also allowing for an equitable share of any major benefits that followed implementation of a particular idea

The project was targeted first at a pilot area and then reviewed; those involved in the pilot then acted as 'missionaries' to take the approach to the other groups so that the diffusion of HII took place in a gradual and 'home-grown' fashion. During the pilot and subsequent roll-out the HII facilitators were actively involved in continuous adaptation and improvement of the basic HII process and supporting mechanisms and the whole programme was reviewed on a monthly basis by the steering committee.

This example shows a much more structured approach, which contains mechanisms designed to establish and reinforce some key behavioural routines. There is considerable scope for fine-tuning within this framework, but it has already established a discernible pattern of local-level improvements. It is typical of Level 2 capability in the model.

Although this case represents a more structured approach and can demonstrate sustained benefits, these are mainly concentrated at a local level and there is a longer-term risk of running out of steam. The main weakness in this approach is a lack of targeting of improvement activity and, associated with this, a lack of monitoring and measuring of key variables to guide and shape this HII behaviour.

Perfect Pipes

This is a company employing 80+ people in the design, production and marketing of pipeline products for use worldwide. The business was founded in 1904 and was acquired by a larger conglomerate in 1989. It has been pursuing total quality management and other approaches to developing high-involvement innovation since this point and this case study relates to its developments to Level 2 capability which characterized much of its experience in the 1990s.

This case is based on research carried out within the CIRCA programme. The basic assessment details are as observed but details of the company identity and operations have been disguised.

The company's approach was catalysed by an interest in 'total quality management' and a pressing need to support the implementation of a major new computer system using the MRPII (Manufacturing Resources Planning) philosophy. The vision for the future was characterized as 'Company of the future' and a key theme was the recognition that a more people-oriented approach was required, alongside the software development, to implementing the major computer innovation. In 1992 the BEAT (Business Excellence At The company) programme was launched at a half-day session attended by everyone. After that, Business Improvement Teams (BITs) began to be set up to tackle particular issues, but during the period of transition to the new computer little attention was paid to high-involvement innovation (HII), although there were a few BITs in operation.

In this case study the research team collected supporting data (from interviews, observations, company materials and other artefacts) to help establish the position of the firm against the reference model outlined in Chapter 4. The results are presented in Table 6.5 which provides an indication of the difficulties in achieving and sustaining this level of capability across the organization.

TABLE 6.5   Indicators of Level 2 innovation capability development.

Key organizational abilities as they appear in the model	Indicative observations about the extent to which these abilities have been established and embedded
'Understanding'—the ability to articulate the basic values of high-involvement innovation	The company has started to articulate values supportive of HII (e.g. in its mission statement) and has told customers and suppliers about its commitment. The 'Company of the future' scenario, which the company aspires to, includes involving everyone, moving to continuous improvement and adopting teamworking at all levels. There is a clear attempt to put this into practice—for example, in the provision of a fleet of vehicles and the fact that the suggestion scheme committee, which is chaired by the engineering manager, includes seven other people from anywhere and any level in the company However, in general the management style probably does *not* reflect HII values, with the exception of one or two managers (e.g. the Quality Manager and the Finance Director). Most managers operate in 'fire-fighting' mode and do not have much time for broader issues Managerial reaction to mistakes is mixed; for example, in the design department the reaction to failure is constructive: ideas put forward by individuals are adopted by the group, which then takes collective responsibility. But in other areas people feel that they will be blamed if they make a mistake. The attempt is there to try and create a culture where, as one of the HII supporting senior managers put it, 'once you have identified who was involved, you work on stopping the problem recurring, i.e. prevention rather than blame'—although he added that 'there is still a lot more work to be done about this'
'Getting the habit'—the ability to generate sustained involvement in innovation	There are some formal enablers (BITs, suggestion schemes), but these seem to generate a fairly low level of HII activity. In the case of the Bright Ideas scheme, this is not surprising since it excludes ideas about the suggestor's own work (on the grounds that they should be doing that anyway). On the other hand, the new production improvement scheme is designed to encourage operators to submit ideas about the processes they work with (one suggestion in the two or three months it has been going) Many people interviewed said that they make improvements as part of the job (i.e. not via a formal vehicle); as one clerk put it, 'that's part of the goals and targets: continual improvement within your own dept' The only problem-solving methodology available is the Corrective Action process, which is covered in BIT training (which would not be appropriate in many cases) and those interviewed who have participated in a BIT do not seem to have followed any process Tools are not widely used to support problem-finding and solving although there is some basic tools training in the BIT programme

(*continued overleaf*)

TABLE 6.5 (*continued*)

Key organizational abilities as they appear in the model	Indicative observations about the extent to which these abilities have been established and embedded
	Teams are not empowered to decide on and implement solutions on their own judgement—they have to gain approval of the Steering Committee
'Focusing'—the ability to link high-involvement innovation activities to the strategic goals of the company	At Perfect Pipes there is no clear link between the corporate objectives and the functional objectives. Company-level objectives are all financial and do not link to the non-financial objectives given to the functions. However, if some key non-financial objectives can be identified from company strategy, then the mechanism already exists for deploying them down: managers' goals and targets are linked into those of their Executive, and the staff's are linked into those of their manager. There are goals and targets for all office-based jobs (including secretaries) but not for shop-floor employees
'Leading'—the ability to lead, direct and support the creation and sustaining of high-involvement innovation behaviours	In general, it seems that most of the managers are lukewarm or neutral towards HII. Even those that think it is a good idea, with one or two notable exceptions, are not very active in promoting and demonstrating it. Senior management are not strongly involved in terms of personal sponsorship, but they demonstrate commitment by (a) adopting the 'Company of the future' model, and (b) offering no resistance in terms of cash or budget allocation for BEAT for training and developing the process
'Aligning'—the ability to create consistency between high-involvement innovation values and behaviour and the organizational context (structures, procedures, etc.)	Senior management have made sufficient financial resources available for BEAT in general, though to date these seem to have been directed largely at the MRPII element of BEAT, rather than at the high-involvement innovation component. Likewise other resources (time, personnel) seem to have been lacking because they were occupied in the MRPII implementation There is no evidence of ongoing assessment to ensure congruency. However, designing and working towards 'Company of the future' (which is what BEAT is all about) involves changes to systems and structures to bring them in line with the desired 'culture'
'Shared problem-solving'—the ability to move innovative activity across organizational boundaries	Working across internal boundaries is not as effective as it could be; one of the elements identified for 'Company of the future' is 'fewer organizational boundaries'. It is not clear what the situation is with regard to working across external boundaries, though the proportion of suppliers with 'preferred' status has increased and some of the BITs dealt with issues involving suppliers Where there is cross-boundary working, it appears to be directed (by management processes or the requirements of MRPII) and reactive rather than natural and proactive
'Continuous improvement of the system'—the ability to strategically manage the development of high-involvement innovation	Various groups are tasked with monitoring aspects of CI activity (rather than the 'whole CI system'), but the effectiveness of this is unclear

TABLE 6.5   *(continued)*

Key organizational abilities as they appear in the model	Indicative observations about the extent to which these abilities have been established and embedded
'The learning organization'—generating the ability to enable learning to take place and be captured at all levels	There is evidence that the company values and supports training, which can be (but is not necessarily) an enabler for learning. However, much of the training appears to be either sheep-dip or general awareness, or reliant on individuals requesting it, with several interviewees claiming that people were 'thrown in at the deep end'
	The anecdotal evidence is that most people will learn from their mistakes, but there is no substantiated evidence of individuals building on their learning experiences, sharing it, etc.
	There are no mechanisms for capturing and deploying learning unless the output from a BIT leads to a written procedure. The results of the BITs who have finished have not been communicated. Any documentation related to BITs the Quality Manager keeps in a file

Drug Delivery Systems Ltd — the Waste Elimination Programme

This case involved a medium-sized manufacturer of pharmaceutical products who had embarked upon several initiatives around the theme of 'world class manufacturing' (WCM). After initial successes the company realized that the WCM label was giving the wrong message—implying that it was really about change in manufacturing. They started thinking about what they were actually asking people to do, which was to look at their processes and improve them by systematically eliminating waste. A Steering Committee for the programme involving the Human Resources Director, the Finance Director, two dedicated Waste Elimination Managers, two Manufacturing Centre Managers and heads of some of the support units was set up. The role of the committee was to monitor activities and to publicize and promote waste elimination.

To support the programme, a generic problem-solving cycle, the WEP wheel, was developed. A number of facilitators were appointed to train employees and to stimulate waste elimination activities. Since the success of the WE activities was dependent upon effective teamwork, team building was incorporated into the WE training.

In terms of stimulating improvement activity, a flexible approach was adopted whereby WE facilitators were able to design high-involvement innovation (HII) to suit the individual needs of a particular work area. Waste Elimination Teams (WETs) were launched simultaneously for all employees in key areas—these were permanent improvement teams formed around dedicated line teams (operators and line leaders), guided by a WE facilitator. Originally, team improvement activities were preceded by a training course consisting of six half-day sessions over a six-month period, covering Just-in-Time (JIT) (using a simulation exercise), tools and techniques of problem solving (and cycle) and team building. Later, only the JIT element of the training was kept as an up-front session; the remaining elements were incorporated as and when required by the teams.

The teams met once a week off the shop floor. Section leaders had an input in helping to identify problems for the teams to work on, thereby assisting in targeting and focusing efforts, but would largely leave the team to tackle the problem by themselves (to ensure that they took on ownership of the problem). Each week the team would bring a list of actions and measures and monitors to the meeting. In the early days, virtually all of the work would be done inside the meetings. As the team became more familiar with the problem-solving process and with collecting statistics, more and more of the activities were progressed outside of the meetings, with the meetings being used to feed back results.

The tangible benefits arising from the WE activities were tracked and the company was able to save around £10 m in reduced waste, although it is difficult to say how much this came directly from HII projects and how much from other WCM work at the time. However, the main benefits came in facilitating cultural change and improving the working environment. People had generally taken greater responsibility for their work and for things that went wrong, rather than seeing this as someone else's job. Thus employees had developed a sense of ownership of their work and were more willing to take on other roles, for example in setting up the machines and checking quality (rather than waiting around and relying on other people). From the operator's viewpoint, the greater involvement in eliminating waste made their work more interesting and people had become far more used to creating their own ideas and following them through.

Initial problems in implementing the WEP were largely concerned with the need to overcome scepticism and convince people that the company was making a serious commitment to change. Early attitudes were largely negative as people had seen a lot of failed initiatives within the company and saw the WEP as another one that would soon die away. As one manager commented:

> 'There was a lot of trust to build up. In the past a lot has been said but not much has happened. Most of the promises that had been made in the past, they have failed to keep.'

They were successful, however, in overcoming most of the resistance. In general, people became less cynical and felt that they were empowered to make changes (although there was still a long way to go). Publicizing the benefits and successes played a key role in changing people's attitudes. Earlier lessons highlighted the need to avoid forcing change on people. Instead, it was important to try and create a demand for improvement activity and then support people in going about improvement in their own way, rather than imposing a standard, company-wide approach. It was felt the latter approach ran the risk of destroying people's energy and enthusiasm for improvement. Consequently, apart from introducing teams to the WEP problem-solving wheel, they tried to avoid being too over-prescriptive in telling people which tools they should use. One manager described the approach as providing a menu, from which people could pick and choose according to what suits them.

Although the WETs were initially supported by a facilitator, the eventual aim was to gradually transfer ownership of the WEP to the teams, with the facilitation role passing on to the line leaders. In some areas it proved difficult to get the line leaders to take on this additional responsibility. Although they were supportive and made a useful input, they did not actually feel that they 'owned it'. The company was attempting to overcome this by giving facilitator training to line leaders and co-ordinators, as well as refresher tools training for the teams, to better equip them to run their own WEP meetings.

Despite the fact that teams had made significant achievements under the WEP, there were limited mechanisms for recognizing contributions and sharing learning. The main mechanism for doing this was through publicizing achievements in the company newsletter. To facilitate greater recognition and sharing of experiences, a number of new mechanisms were introduced. For example, a monthly, lunchtime Continuous Improvement Forum was introduced, open to section leaders and above. This was also attended by the Directors when they were on site. Average attendance was around 30–50 people. At each forum teams gave presentations of their improvement activities. Giving people an opportunity to show managers what they have done proved to be an important form of recognition and provided a morale boost for the presenters. Conversely, it helped to demonstrate and raise the visibility of senior management commitment. Although people were often reluctant to put themselves forward for a presentation, most actually enjoyed the experience.

Internal HII networks were also introduced at both sites on a monthly basis. External speakers were invited to these and attendees were largely at the section leader level. Finally, informal monthly meetings were initiated between the HII manager and site facilitators to share experiences and discuss any problems. As a further resource, various publications were collated in a file to illustrate examples of what people/companies had undertaken and achieved.

Despite the benefits of these new mechanisms, they did little to promote sharing of learning between lower-level employees. For example, one complaint from employees was that they did not get the opportunity to see their colleagues presenting their work at the Continuous Improvement forum.

6.7 Summary — Reaching the Limits of Level 2

This chapter has explored the challenge of putting in place and sustaining a high degree of involvement in the innovation process. Achieving such capability has much to offer the organization in terms of improved performance and also in less tangible areas like motivation and morale. But to realize this potential requires a systematic effort across a broad front to try and change the established 'default' pattern of working—the culture of the organization.

Components of Level 2 systems for securing high-involvement innovation include embedding a problem finding and solving capacity, understanding and facility in using a basic innovation toolkit, systems for ensuring that ideas are managed and implemented, systems for ensuring appropriate reward and recognition, consistency between the values and operation of high-involvement behaviour and the rest of the organization's structures and procedures—and so on.

Putting these changes in place and then fine-tuning them to ensure sustainability is a major task and explains why organizations trying to establish Level 2 usually spend a long time and extensive resource here. The cases cited in the chapter and wider experience internationally lend strong support to the view that this investment is worth while and will repay itself. But even when some stability has been reached, it is important to recognize that we are still only at a relatively early stage on our journey towards high-involvement innovation. There is much more that could be achieved—and even staying at Level 2 for a long period brings with it the risk of gradual decline. Concerns can include scepticism about the impact on the bottom line, an overdependence on champions, a focus on local-level projects to the exclusion of broader, cross-boundary ones, a sense of 'moving the deckchairs on the *Titanic*', rather than tackling important strategic issues, etc.

When these symptoms start to appear, it is probably time to think about gearing up for the jump to the next level—that of strategic high-involvement innovation. That is the focus of the next chapter.

References

Atkinson, P. (1990) *Total Quality Management: Creating Culture Change.* IFS Publications, Kempston.

Bessant, J., S. Caffyn and M. Gallagher (2001) 'An evolutionary model of continuous improvement behaviour,' *Technovation*, **21** (3), 67–77.

Deming, W.E. (1986) *Out of the Crisis.* MIT Press, Cambridge, MA.

Fukada, R. (1990) *CEDAC—A Tool for Continuous Systematic Improvement.* Productivity Press, Cambridge, MA.

Gallagher, M. and S. Austin (1997) *Continuous Improvement Casebook.* Kogan Page, London.

Garvin, D. (1991) 'How the Baldrige award really works,' *Harvard Business Review*, November/December, 80–93.

Kaplinsky, R. (1994) *Easternization: The Spread of Japanese Management Techniques to Developing Countries.* Frank Cass, London.

Kaplinsky, R., F. den Hertog and B. Coriat (1995) *Europe's Next Step.* Frank Cass, London.

Oakland, J. (1989) *Total Quality Management.* Pitman, London.

Owen, M. and J. Morgan (2000) *Statistical Process Control in the Office.* Greenfield Publishing, Kenilworth.

Robinson, A. (1991) *Continuous Improvement in Operations.* Productivity Press, Cambridge, MA.

Shiba, S., A. Graham and G. Walden (1993) *A New American TQM: Four Practical Revolutions in Management.* Productivity Press, Portland, OR.

Shingo, S. (1983) *A Revolution in Manufacturing: The SMED System.* Productivity Press, Cambridge, MA.

Shingo, S. (1986) *Zero Quality Control: Source Inspection and the Poke Yoke System.* Productivity Press, Cambridge, MA.

Sirkin, H. and G. Stalk (1990) 'Fix the process, not the problem,' *Harvard Business Review*, July/August, 26–33.

Westbrook, R. and P. Barwise (1994) *Continuous Improvement in Leading FMCG Companies.* London Business School, London.

Chapter 7

STRATEGIC INNOVATION

The problem of fade-out mentioned in the previous chapter reflects a lack of connection between the bottom-up capability of high-involvement innovation and the top-down focus and direction of such activity. This next stage in the model involves providing a clear strategic focus linked to the needs of the business—and deploying it successfully throughout the organization. It also brings to the surface the importance of measurement as a key tool for ensuring that progress is made on a continuing basis.

Firms that are able to build and sustain strategic innovation systems can point to significant 'bottom line' benefits on a sustained basis—for example, year-on-year cost reductions or quality improvements. Whilst this is of considerable value, the limitation here is that innovation is by definition 'doing what we do better'—and, whilst there is enormous scope for driving out waste and for continuous improvement, the possibilities for doing different things are not well covered.

7.1 'Pretty in Pink'

Walking thorough the plant belonging to Ace Trucks (a major producer of forklift trucks) in Japan, the first thing that strikes you is the colour scheme. In fact, you would need to be blind not to notice it—amongst the usual rather dull greys and greens of machine tools and other equipment there are flashes of pink. Not just a quiet pastel tone, but a full-blooded, shocking pink that would do credit to even the most image-conscious flamingo. Closer inspection shows that these flashes and splashes of pink are not random but associated with particular sections and parts of machines—and the eye-catching effect comes in part from the sheer number of pink-painted bits, distributed right across the factory floor and all over the different machines.

What is going on here is not a bizarre attempt to redecorate the factory or a failed piece of interior design. The effect of catching the eye is quite deliberate—the colour is there to draw attention to the machines and other equipment which has been modified. Every pink splash is the result of a kaizen project to improve some aspect of the equipment, much of it in support of the drive towards 'total productive maintenance' (TPM), in which every item of plant is available and ready for use 100% of the time. This is a goal like 'zero defects' in total quality—certainly ambitious, possibly an impossibility in the statistical sense, but one which focuses the minds of everyone involved and leads to extensive and impressive problem finding and solving. TPM programmes have accounted for year-on-year cost savings of 10–15% in many Japanese firms and these savings are being ground out of a system that is already renowned for its lean characteristics.

Painting the improvements pink plays an important role in drawing attention to the underlying activity in this factory, in which systematic problem finding and solving is part of 'the way we do things around here'. The visual cues remind everyone of the continuing search for new ideas and improvements, and often provide stimulus for other ideas or for places to which the displayed pink idea can be transferred. Closer inspection around the plant shows other forms of display—less visually striking but powerful nonetheless—charts and graphs of all shapes and sizes, which focus attention on trends and problems, as well as celebrating successful improvements. There are photographs and graphics that pose problems or offer suggested improvements in methods or working practices, and flipcharts and whiteboards covered with symbols and shapes of fish bones and other tools being used to drive the improvement process forward.

This is an example of a factory in which systematic involvement in innovation—Level 2 in our model framework—has become the norm and is widely practised by most employees most of the time. There are reward systems, idea management systems, tools and techniques, etc. to underpin the system, and it works! But perhaps the key feature is that this bottom-up capability for finding and solving problems has been linked with a clear and shared sense of strategic direction and focus—people here do not just know how to find and solve problems; they also know *which* problems to work on and why and when. Linking the engine of employee involvement to such strategic targets is the challenge of Level 3 and the focus of this chapter.

7.2 What Is the Problem with Level 2?

We saw in the last chapter how difficult it can be to create the conditions in which people can participate in the innovation process in a regular and systematic fashion. Anyone can have bright ideas, but to turn this spark of creativity into a full-scale bonfire—and to keep it burning—takes a lot more than wishful thinking. The trouble is that, even after putting together systems and procedures that provide a structure for high-involvement innovation, the result may be a gradual fading out of interest and enthusiasm. So does this mean that the underlying idea of getting people involved is flawed? Or is the problem more one of 'all dressed up and nowhere to go'—the fact that people run out of things to improve and begin to lose a sense of purpose?

Evidence suggests that the experience of the 'honeymoon effect' is widespread. Firms begin some form of employee involvement programme with a significant degree of flourish and are often pleasantly surprised by the enthusiasm with which people respond. In the early days there is a noticeable lift in morale and motivation and a high level of participation. Measures of the effectiveness of the programme show plenty of suggestions being offered, and some notable 'big hits' amongst the many ideas being implemented. There is a sense of positive energy and a commitment to the idea, which has an infectious quality so that involvement across the organization increases.

But the down side of this is the gradual slowing down in the rate of suggestion and a falling off in enthusiasm and participation. There are fewer 'big hits' and, whilst a hard core of committed enthusiasts continue to meet and come up with ideas, there is a growing sense of 'so what'—one that is often reinforced by senior managers beginning to query the costs of such an exercise against the actual emerging benefits. In some cases there is a high-level champion who can put personal energy into the programme and maintain momentum, but often the original high-level support dwindles as the attention of those managers is taken up with other pressing concerns. Gradually a sense that the process was 'just another initiative' begins to emerge and accelerates the withdrawal of involvement—and a vicious cycle develops. Low involvement and enthusiasm produce fewer ideas, which reinforces the overall sense that there is no long-term future for the process. Eventually all we are left with is a structure and procedures, which few people use—like the suggestion box; it becomes a piece of organizational furniture without much use or purpose.

This is a somewhat gloomy distillation of the experiences of many different firms but it does underline the risks attached to high involvement and the problems of maintaining momentum. Getting serious about mobilizing people's creativity requires investment, but the return on that can fall off sharply after the initial enthusiasm. So what can we do to keep the process going and continue to grow a positive innovation culture across the organization?

7.3 Moving to Level 3 – Strategic Innovation

Of course, things are never simple and there is not a single explanation for why high-involvement innovation programmes falter and fail. However, it does appear as if a major problem is that they are just that—specific initiatives or programmes designed to make something happen. In the short term they receive attention and commitment from all sides—backed by senior management's energy and more importantly with resources that they sanction, supported by facilitators whose career development is linked to making a success of it and involving people for whom this is an exciting novelty and an opportunity to make a difference and get involved, rather than being simply spectators whilst others do the improvement work or else frustrated participants in a system they cannot change.

Like any project, initiatives have a life cycle—and the problem with high-involvement innovation initiatives is that, once the structures have been built and the processes put in place, the project is nearly finished. Running the system takes a different kind of approach, less dependent on short-term bursts of energy and resources and more dependent on becoming a part of the 'normal' structure of things. In other words, the move needs to be from an 'off-line' special activity to an 'in-line' part of the way we do things around here. Innovation has to move from being something that others do to being a central component of everyone's job. Looking for problems to solve and opportunities to exploit needs to become the norm.

Many things militate against this happening. As we saw in the previous chapter, if there is no consistency between the structures for innovation and for day-to-day operations, the initiative will quickly fall away. Unless time and space are available for people to stop and think about how to do things better, there is little chance that improvements will or can emerge. Unless there is a clear route to implementation—either directly or through others with special skills—there is little chance that improvements will actually happen.

But beyond this issue of consistency lies the more significant challenge of direction. If Level 2 systems are all about developing the skills and familiarity—getting the innovation habit—then Level 3 is all about pointing that capability in a particular direction and enabling people to use the targets to drive their own improvement activities.

7.4 Level 3 in Practice — A Brief Example

Perfect Plastics is an illustration of a company in which such targeting behaviour is in place. It is a medium-sized (300 employees) manufacturer of plastic films and packaging materials. High-involvement innovation (in the form of a continuous improvement (CI) programme) has been in place for seven years and during the past three years a systematic programme of policy deployment has been used to link CI behaviour to the strategic goals of the business. The company articulates a top-level strategic plan—its three-year review—and then breaks down the component elements in a systematic fashion to generate a set of improvement targets for every area and level of the business. The process through which this is achieved is essentially a 'consultative cascade', in which people get a chance to discuss and explore the strategy as it relates to their area, and to set goals that they are clear about. The mechanisms form part of what is sometimes termed the 'Hoshin Kanri' approach (Shiba *et al.* 1993).

Day-to-day operation of CI is similar to other Level 2 examples (mentioned in the previous chapter) in terms of group and individual activities, use of problem-solving approaches, idea management, reward and recognition, etc. The main differences are in the selection and targeting of improvement objectives and in the regular monitoring and measurement pattern (in this case via a daily pre-production meeting, which reviews progress and sets up new targets). The benefits are clear and now feed directly into the strategic performance of the company—because they were designed to do so. Over the five years in which this approach has been operating they have cut what they term 'cost of maintenance' (analogous to cost of quality, and including the real costs of poor maintenance etc. as well as the prevention and cure costs) by 25%, although some of this is clearly due to process and equipment change as well as CI. At the same time, productivity, measured as tonnes per employee, rose from 680 in 1993 to around 1000 in 1996.

This pattern of development of high-involvement innovation is typical of Level 3 in the model, and is characterized by a strategic focus and by monitoring and measurement behaviour being used to drive the improvement process.

7.5 Two Keys to Level 3 — Strategy Deployment and Measurement

This example highlights two key themes that are central to making progress to Level 3—strategy deployment and monitoring and measuring behaviour. If we see achieving Level 2 capability as something that spreads the capacity for finding and solving problems across the workforce, then Level 3 involves connecting that to some focused and meaningful targets for the organization. To do that requires that the organization knows (or works out!) what its strategy is and then finds ways of communicating this to the whole of the workforce. They need to be able to discuss, explore and challenge it and to derive from the broad organizational-level targets some specific projects on which they can work. The idea is to deploy the strategy, breaking it down into 'bite-sized' chunks, rather than looking for a single big-hit innovation that will help reach the target.

For example, if the strategic target is 'improve quality by $x\%$ in the next three months', then it is unlikely that a single solution is available to achieve this. But by asking the question 'how?' a number of possible directions can be identified—improve the quality of incoming goods and services, improve handling, improve processing at different stages, improve the quality management tools that people use, etc. Each of these represents a fruitful area for finding and solving problems, but each also lends itself to further breakdown—for example, if the chosen project area is improving quality in one of the processing stages, the question 'how?' can be asked again and used to generate further avenues to explore—improvements in equipment, in fixtures, in handling, in worker training, in operating procedures, and so on. Figure 7.1 shows this process of policy deployment in graphical terms, as explained in Box 7.1.

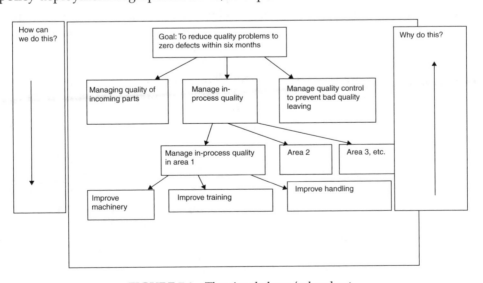

FIGURE 7.1   The simple how/why chart.

BOX 7.1 Simple how/why chart.

The basis of this approach is to begin with a high-level goal—for example, reducing defect levels to zero within a short time frame. By asking the question 'how?' we can identify several potential areas, all of which would contribute to the goal. By asking 'how?' again we can generate a lower order of options, and so on, driving down and down until we reach a series of specific projects which could contribute; see Figure 7.1.

To ensure that these represent useful projects and not simply improvements for their own sake we can reverse the logic and ask 'why?' going up the tree. If the projects are to make a useful contribution, it should be possible to trace a route up to the overall goal of improving quality.

So in this case:

- Using the 'How' logic to drive down:
  - How to reduce defects?—work on in-process quality
  - How?—work on area 1
  - How?—improve machinery
  - How?—check adjustments more frequently
  - How?—allocate 5 minutes each morning for each operator to carry out the check
- And using the 'Why' logic:
  - Improving machines (for example, adjusting them more frequently)—Why?—because this helps improve quality in area 1
  - Why is this important—because it improves in-process quality
  - Why?—because that helps reach the overall goal of zero defects within six months

---

The principle is essentially one of breaking down the big themes into small enough elements that they can connect with the innovation capability across the organization. (This differs from the 'conventional' approach where a few innovation specialists aim for big-hit projects which deal with the strategic challenge at high level.) However, it depends on being able to provide a reasonably small number of objectives and some specific—though challenging—targets. Simply saying 'this organization needs to improve its quality or its delivery or its costs' is not helpful since these are vague statements. There needs to be a tight focus—what must be done by when in order to gain strategic advantage? Examples might be 'reduce the percentage of late deliveries by 50% within the next three months', 'get to zero defects in the next year for our top five customers', or 'reduce costs by 15% over the next year'.

The power of having specific targets is that these can be broken down into equally specific targets for individual projects using the deployment approach outlined above. So it becomes possible to provide concrete measures of whether or not improvement has taken place—have things really got better? In this way measurement can become a powerful driver for continuous change. Instead of innovative behaviour relying on an *ad hoc* selection process—'what can we do to improve things here?'—there are now clear targets, which we know will make a difference because they are aligned with the overall strategy of the organization. They will make a contribution in the right direction—and even if each increment of change is small, their cumulative value can be significant. And we will know whether or not we have reached the target—and whether we need to keep on working on this problem or to move on to the next one, because we are able to use measurement to drive the process.

The result is an improvement cycle that harnesses the innovation capability to key strategic targets and uses measurement to keep it turning. In the process it moves innovation from being an occasional and random activity (Level 1) or one that concentrates on developing the capability without worrying too much about the direction (Level 2) to one that is directly linked to where the organization is trying to get to. As the world changes and the organization needs to set new strategic targets to keep up, so the innovation capability can be deployed in a new direction but using the same basic cycle. Perhaps most importantly, this stage makes innovation a central part of day-to-day work rather than a parallel, occasional or 'bolt-on' extra.

BOX 7.2 Hoshin Kanri at Hewlett-Packard.

HP is recognized as having been one of the pioneers in the use of policy deployment (Hoshin Kanri) in the UK and the following are key elements in this approach:

- Deployment of key breakthrough objectives (only 1–3 per year)
- Rigorous methodology requiring a succession of linked Planning Tables completed across multiple levels of the company
- At each level an objective is decomposed into a series of SMART (specific, measurable, achievable, realistic, targeted) strategies, each of which becomes an objective for the next (lower) level
- Top-down aspirations are matched with bottom-up operational capabilities and constraints through a series of 'catch-ball' negotiations
- When the cascades have been completed, a tightly inter-linked set of actions, necessary and sufficient to assure achievement of the object, is established
- Progress is monitored through an upward (reverse) cascade of reviews starting at operational level and progressively summarizing to Mission objective level
- After each review the Hoshin tables may be updated and modified to ensure continued alignment

This is based on a presentation given to CIRCA Network in 1999.

7.6 Characterizing Level 3 Innovation Capability

We can use the model developed in Chapter 4 to explore Level 3 issues in more detail. As Table 7.1 shows, there is a well-founded systematic approach to finding and solving problems and looking for improvement opportunities and some experience in using it. In addition to enabling the capability, the organization is now able to focus the efforts of its workforce towards tackling innovation questions related to achieving the strategic goals of the business—and to track and measure what it has changed and how far it still has to go. The right-hand column draws on case examples of organizations trying to implement Level 3 high-involvement innovation.

TABLE 7.1   Putting Level 3 high-involvement innovation in place.

Key organizational abilities as they appear in the model	*Typical indicators of Level 3 development of these abilities*
'Understanding'—the ability to articulate the basic values of high-involvement innovation	*On the positive side*: • Policy deployment framework provides a reference point for people to see where and how their contribution fits in • Some experience of Level 2 success available as reference for less experienced areas and as demonstration sites *But on the negative side*: • Risk of cynical view that 'this is just another initiative'—strategic emphasis can raise profile too high and risk of failure increases • Persistence of blame culture means that people stick to 'safe' projects and may not stretch for more ambitious and innovative targets
'Getting the habit'—the ability to generate sustained involvement in innovation	*On the positive side*: • Use of a formal process—PDCA* or equivalent—in which people are trained • People are encouraged and guided towards particular targets • People are skilled in the use of basic tool set—fishbones, check sheets, etc. and methodologies like set-up time reduction and 5-S—and can deploy these in different projects and areas • Vehicles for CI are clearly identified—often based on work teams—and time and space allocated for them since CI is seen as 'in-line', part of the job and not an 'optional extra' • Reward and recognition are more systematic, often with a direct financial component such as bonus scheme related to strategic improvements • Mechanisms exist for processing ideas, from simple and direct implementation through to more resource-intensive approaches, which require the support of other specialist functions • Feedback via supervisors, team leaders, etc. Relatively regular and relatively fast response—ideas get listened to and people get a response *But on the negative side*: • Use of problem solving approach may be patchy and need support and reinforcement • Problem finding and solving are primarily local level, short term and project focused. Emphasis is less on the outputs than on getting the habit of problem solving • Persistence of local-level success stories, but little strategic advantage identified—the loop back into bottom line is not closed • People have skill set but problem finding + solving (PFS) behaviour still needs energizing and facilitating—does not happen naturally and is seen as an extra and a special thing

TABLE 7.1   (*continued*)

Key organizational abilities as they appear in the model	*Typical indicators of Level 3 development of these abilities*
'Focusing'—the ability to link high-involvement innovation activities to the strategic goals of the company	*On the positive side*: • Most people are aware in broad terms of what the overall aims of the business are—and are aware of how their local contribution might fit in • Use of policy deployment helps workgroups identify and prioritize their CI actions • Use of measurement frameworks to guide and shape innovation activity and to assess progress • Ownership of measurement approaches is taken up by the workgroup rather than seen as someone else's responsibility • Measurement is seen as an enabler for continuous improvement, not a control mechanism • Innovation is seen as an integral part of the daily routine, built into the structure and procedures and linked to reward and appraisal systems *But on the negative side*: • Top-down commitment can be seen as lip service rather than a real strategic challenge • Lack of clarity at top level about what the strategy is prevents effective focus on high-involvement innovation targets • Lack of communication of strategy—and/or opportunity to explore and question and build understanding and ownership of strategic goals • Lack of skills or experience in measurement limits this to very simple charts rather than more powerful tools such as statistical process control • Measurement is seen as a chore not a coherent driver of improvement
'Leading'—the ability to lead, direct and support the creation and sustaining of high-involvement innovation behaviours	*On the positive side*: • Perceived systematic support for high-involvement innovation since this is a strategically driven process and one on which managers are themselves targeted and measured • Policy deployment framework (especially with measurement emphasis) enables formal links into reward and recognition—for example, through bonus schemes linked to achieved improvements, through individual or group performance appraisal, etc. *But on the negative side*: • Success or failure still depends on local enthusiasm (or otherwise) of individual managers and supervisors—effect can be patchy • Some champions and some patchy support but also blockers and sceptics present • Short-term scepticism—people aren't really sure. If support persists then change in attitudes is possible

(*continued overleaf*)

TABLE 7.1 (*continued*)

Key organizational abilities as they appear in the model	*Typical indicators of Level 3 development of these abilities*
'Aligning'—the ability to create consistency between high-involvement innovation values and behaviour and the organizational context (structures, procedures, etc.)	*On the positive side*: • High-involvement innovation is part of the strategy of the organization, resources are allocated to support it and its fit with procedures and structures is assessed and acted upon • Structures and procedures support and enable HII activity—for example, through allocating time and space, linking implementation capability, offering appropriate reward and recognition, etc. • Regular review to enable and ensure alignment *But on the negative side*: • Some attempts to adapt structures and procedures can be blocked by lack of power on the part of HII implementation team and by the weight of existing structures—e.g. reward systems, team structures, work organization, etc.—which cannot be changed
'Shared problem solving'—the ability to move innovative activity across organizational boundaries	*On the positive side*: • Policy deployment helps identify where cross-boundary issues are located and mobilizes shared problem solving • Use of measurement frameworks such as process mapping and process-level performance measures help identify where cross-boundary problems are located • Awareness of customer—both external and internal—helps encourage shared and cross-boundary problem solving • Beginnings of inter-organizational HII activity—joint projects with suppliers, customers, etc. • Use of cross-functional and other boundary-spanning teams as HII vehicles • Use of training and tools to help deal with cross-boundary problems *But on the negative side*: • Can still involve mainly local orientation with occasional inter-group linkages and awareness of wider problems • Local-level communications mainly focused within the group, with minor cross-functional links • Local-level loyalty—some co-operation between near neighbours but largely inward looking • May have some basic knowledge of external customers but in general terms only—not able to provide measurable indicators of what the customer wants
'Continuous improvement of the system'—the ability to strategically manage the development of high-involvement innovation	*On the positive side*: • HII is owned and managed by an identified group, which provides the focus for development • Regular monitoring and measurement—often using externally validated frameworks (see Chapter 4 for examples)—of HII development. Intervention and fine-tuning result from this assessment activity

TABLE 7.1   (*continued*)

Key organizational abilities as they appear in the model	*Typical indicators of Level 3 development of these abilities*
	• Continuing support at senior-management level, expressed in terms of resource allocation, active interest and involvement, willingness to explore structural changes, etc.
	But on the negative side: • HII steering group or individual champion lacks real organizational power to influence resource allocation or structural/procedural change • HII appears to need the steering group to have a hands-on approach to succeed—little happens without them • General sense of progress, but potential problems because of a lack of understanding of the dimensions along which to measure progress or the actions to take
'The learning organization'—generating the ability to enable learning to take place and be captured at all levels	*On the positive side*: • High-frequency and structured process means that learning cycle can be carried through regularly and often and the results captured and codified • Tacit knowledge is made explicit through a systematic high-involvement attack on key areas such as set-up time reduction, quality improvement or time saving[†]
	But on the negative side: • Training and development investment is mostly confined to job-related skills • Lip service paid to concept but old culture of blame still dominates • Little or no experimentation or opportunity seeking—dominant mode is corrective action, 'doing what we do better'

[*]PDCA = plan, do, check, act—a brief statement of the problem solving cycle originally proposed by the quality expert W. Edwards Deming and sometimes called the 'Deming Wheel' (Deming 1986).

[†]This theme of converting tacit to codified knowledge is at the centre of much of the work of Nonaka and a more detailed description can be found in Nonaka (1991).

7.7 Some Detailed Examples

It may be helpful to look at some examples of Level 3 innovative capabilities to highlight some of the themes outlined above. In particular, these cases clarify the key roles which the two key elements—strategy deployment and monitoring/measurement—play in successful and sustained performance. Many of these examples are of Japanese organizations because they demonstrate the significant performance 'dividend' that can arise from a sustained effort at developing and sustaining Level 3 capability. They have been involved in this activity for decades, going through an extended learning process around developing high-involvement capability to the point where they can rely upon a steady flow of ideas focused on key strategic targets. (Data for this section is drawn particularly from a study visit funded by the Engineering and Physical Sciences Research Council and facilitated through the EU-Japan Co-operation Centre.)

Case 1. Chemico

This is a plant belonging to a major chemical company, which was set up in 1962 and produces a range of around 100 adhesive tapes and packaging foams with a staff of nearly 300 people.

They have a strong foundation in high-involvement innovation, having won the coveted Deming Prize and numerous other awards for high performance achievements in fields like total productive maintenance. They make use of such national competitive award schemes as a means of focusing attention on the key strategic goals of the business. Their strategic Level 3 process is driven by a three-year 'mid-term plan' (MTP), which translates broad corporate objectives into focused missions at a plant level. The MTP for the plant is further devolved into broad aims for achieving this; here these are '. . . production which is flexible, trouble-free and stockless . . .'. And in turn these devolve into the specific objectives for the TPM programme.

This policy deployment process can be seen in the recent history of MTPs at the plant, as shown in Table 7.2. Characteristic of this is the use of the metaphor of 'pillars' supporting the construction of their success. In this case nine pillars are seen as contributing to the stretch goals of cost reduction etc.; these include things like 'no adjustment production', 'no supervision system' and so on. Each of these is in turn a target, but relevant for each production area, and is used to drive a systematic process of problem finding and solving. For example, achieving 'no supervision system' requires that the equipment is 100% available and reliable, and this can only happen if the causes of breakdown are carefully analysed and preventive measures taken to ensure that this type of breakdown does not happen. It uses simple techniques like fishbone analysis, but applies them with great

TABLE 7.2   The recent history of MTPs at Chemico.

MTP and date	Key objectives	Key elements
1986 TPM 1	'Increase competitiveness through FTS'. Develop 'Muda' (waste)-less plant—mainly worked on facilities and on developing a visual control 'open workshop' concept. Sprint target was winning the 'Excellent plant award'	Building up foundations for TPM by working on equipment ('eliminate Muda') and people ('form active groups')
1990 TPM 2	'Increase customer satisfaction' through market-focused cellular production, aiming at speed and quality delivery. Develop a 'good showing' FTS plant, with the aim of producing a showpiece factory. Sprint target was the 'TPM award'	Innovation in products and organization structure, and moving to a 'focused factory' approach
1994 TPM 3	10% expansion of business and improved customer satisfaction. Develop I-TPM (Ideas and innovation) programme, aiming to complete the FTS factory. Sprint target is the 'Special award' for TPM	25% reduction in direct labour input, 23% cost reduction in products, zero accidents and other stretch goals set

discipline and system to create a series of linked projects, each of which is suitable for individual or small-group kaizen activity.

This approach is backed up by extensive use of visual imagery and display—in part reflecting the pictographic nature of the language, but also to get away from words and down towards the underlying concepts in such 'mission' statements. One of the main charts shown is a pictorial representation of the MTP with a 'rich picture' capturing the key features, targets and challenges. Language is also developed around the programme so that there is a vocabulary of key words and phrases that people use in working on the programme.

An example of the operation of this approach was given. One of the nine pillars is 'no adjustment equipment'; in other words, in the ideal case, equipment that needs no adjustment. In practice, the argument is that on a large piece of process plant, 4–60m in length, they do not want to have operators constantly running up and down to make adjustments since this represents wasted time and energy. More important, such monitoring and adjustment adds no value—their picture to represent this stage was of a man standing with arms folded in front of a machine. The challenge is how to eliminate the need for supervision and checking of equipment without compromising safety. This provided the focus for small-group discussion and the use of simple kaizen tools. It led to a detailed seven-step programme for gradually chipping away at the problem via a series of small kaizen projects. These were:

- Initial cleaning up of machines and area
- Measures against contamination sources and difficult areas
- Preparation of a cleaning and lubrication manual and procedures
- Development of *jishu-hozen*—thorough self-inspection of plant by the oper-ators themselves rather than maintenance staff—this involves a five-stage training programme
- Voluntary inspection by operators
- Thorough quality inspection
- Adjustment-free operation

Working up through this agenda becomes the operator-level contribution to building one of the seven pillars. The first task was essentially cleaning up the floor—not a simple task since the production of adhesive meant that spills were often hard to remove and attracted other dirt. Importantly, the process of cleaning up involved *all* staff, led by the section manager who, symbolically, picked up the first brush and took on the dirtiest of jobs. One effect of this 'spring cleaning' was a very visual change in the way the plant looked—important as a motivator and also as an enabler of subsequent work.

Next came the process of identifying problem areas where contaminants arrived or where inspection was difficult to achieve. Amongst the simple kaizen ideas extensively deployed in response to this was the idea of 'museum cases'—putting a glass or plastic cover over key parts of the machine so that it was easy to see it in operation and, more importantly, to see where there was leakage. This meant that an operator could see where there was a problem at a glance—rather than having to wait for a maintenance craftsman to inspect the machine. In some cases, this principle of making it visible and accessible meant minor re-design or re-arrangement of machines. This is a key feature of TPM—amongst examples are simple U-tubes to show lubricant levels, the use of children's windmills to indicate motor function, and painting alignment marks on bolts to ensure that they are tightened to the correct tolerances.

The third step involved the thinking through and preparation of simple standard check sheets to define and capture learning about what has to be cleaned and lubricated. An important component of these sheets (which are displayed prominently next to each machine) is that they include not only what has to be done but an explanation of why doing it is important. The sheets are written by the operators themselves and make extensive use of photographs, diagrams and other visual images to help simplify and standardize the process.

Step 4 involves the development of self-inspection skills amongst operators and this is achieved by a systematic training programme accompanying further check sheets to institutionalize a procedure. Significantly operators have to attain 94% pass marks or repeat the training!

Step 5 involves implementing the self-inspection approach, using the procedure check sheets but also encouraging their systematic revision and updating.

Step 6 is a more systematic approach to improving quality, by building in measurements for what would have to be under control in a perfect system. This involves constructing a large matrix, which lists criteria down one side and desired values along the other axis. The list of potential criteria is huge, so this is simplified into key categories—for example, ease of set-up or stability level. The measurement scale is based on simple scales—for example, gauging ease of set-up on a notional 1–5 scale, where 1 is a set-up needing full support and 5 is 'touchless set-up'. The purpose of this is to set up, in the cells of the matrix, a series of projects that can first be addressed and then systematically improved. Using red and green dots provides a quick visual display—where there is a red dot there is a potential improvement project. Importantly this builds in a driver for *continuous* improvement, rather than a one-off fix of the problem.

Importantly, the categories, scales and the subsequent projects are all discussed and developed by the small group responsible for the area.

High-involvement innovation takes the form of continuous improvement (CI) activities and operates in the following fashion. Direct employees are grouped into teams of around eight and expected to work on CI directly and also to suggest projects that can be taken up by the engineers. There are daily meetings of each work team, together with occasional meetings for specific CI projects of the larger variety. All employees are required to contribute suggestions as part of their contract (the underlying theme being that their success is bound up with that of the company, so this is their duty). The current target is 10 ideas per employee per month, but they are only counted if actually implemented. The team leader (with reference to others if necessary) evaluates and grades the suggestions according to a simple scale:

- A grade suggestions are simple improvements, which are rewarded with a payment of Y300 (equivalent to the price of a pint of beer)
- B grade suggestions are larger scale and rewarded with a percentage of savings

In addition, employees who make their quota of suggestions per month receive a book token.

With roughly 150 direct employees out of a total of 300 this equates to around 1500 suggestions per month in production. Clearly there are problems in managing this volume of ideas, but this is simplified by using a single sheet of paper for each team on which each individual contributions can be recorded by the team leader. If there is a high-earning suggestion, then the team leader evaluates it and puts it forward to the site committee, which only looks at significant suggestions.

Case 2. Carco Vehicles

This car plant produces around 900 vehicles per day with a staff of around 2000, usually working two shifts. As with many Japanese firms, the high value of the Yen has hit exports hard, to the point that the company made a loss in 1990. They have responded to this crisis by systematic deployment of continuous targeted improvement, with three core themes:

- Development of new, attractive products
- Maintaining productivity levels
- Reconstruction of the company from within

Workforce involvement has been critical to this development, especially as there has been a continuing reduction in labour with a consequent loss of production knowledge. Their efforts at TPM began in 1992, partly as a way of increasing utilization and efficiency of existing plant instead of introducing new capital investment. The long-term programme includes simultaneous attack on quality improvement, cost reduction, employee motivation and increased education and training, and the specific 'stretch' targets are:

- Zero defects
- Zero accidents
- Zero breakdown
- 20% increase in labour productivity

The pillars on which these are to be achieved are:

- *Jishu hozen*—voluntary operator inspection and maintenance
- *Kaizen teian*—individual improvement activities
- Education and training
- Planned maintenance
- Development management
- Quality maintenance activities, including ISO 9000
- Tool/mould/die maintenance management aimed at zero defects and breakdowns

They began by setting up separate task forces to deal with each area, and developed a formal structure aimed at promoting TPM. The results undoubtedly helped in their recovery from losses by the end of 1995; examples of gains during the 1992–1996 period include:

- Breakdowns per month across the site: 5252 in May 1992 reduced to 194 in November 1996 (=96%) and targeted to fall further
- Reduction in warranty claims between 1992 and 1994 of 50% in the domestic market
- Accident rates cut—some areas have zero accidents recorded for the past two years
- Increases in total plant efficiency (calculated as an index) across various lines and units running at 55–80%
- Overall machine losses—damage due to machine problems is down from an index value of 100 to 60%
- Inventory is down by 50%
- Man hours per vehicle has gone down from 14 to 11

These have not been due solely to TPM, but the company believes it has made a major strategic contribution. Their view is that the biggest single impact of TPM was the speeding up and smooth introduction of the new model car, which meant that high levels of production performance were attained from day 1 and maintained.

In financial terms, they estimate a saving of 17.9bn Yen (based on an exercise similar to cost-of-quality accounting) over the period 1992–1994.

As with other companies, the three-year mid-term plan is the key mechanism for focusing and refocusing attention in CI. Recent plans have involved three main themes over the past decade:

- TQM was aimed at increasing productivity and quality
- TPS (Toyota Production System) was aimed at waste reduction
- TPM was aimed at obtaining high machine efficiency and availability and at increasing production rates through more reliable plant

Visualization of this is important; the dominant image is one of 'equipment and operator upgrading'. There are storyboards and display boards throughout the factory, including a master chart, which is a giant Gantt chart tracking progress to date and plans for the future. Each workgroup meets daily and this take place around their own storyboard.

The implementation of TPM includes a number of components:

- Daily review and improvement cycle—i.e. high frequency of small innovations
- Small and regular inputs of training—'one point lesson system'
- Motivation events
- Individual kaizen teian activities
- Small-group kaizen (successors to quality circles)
- 5-S activities to ensure workplace cleanliness and order
- Preventive maintenance analysis
- Design for maintenance
- 'Zero orientation'—no tolerance of waste, defects, stoppages, etc. as the target
- Step-by-step approach
- Voluntary participation and high commitment

The implementation of TPM involved a five-year programme spanning two mid-term planning periods. Part 1 ran from 1992 to 1995 and was designed to introduce the basic TPM mechanisms; activities included awareness and training and practice to embed the behavioural routines. Part 2—the current phase—involves aiming for the JPIM's Special Award for TPM. Significantly, the company is using very clear behaviour modelling approaches—articulating the desired behaviours and systematically reinforcing them to the point where they become routines.

Policy deployment is the link between these broad objectives and the specific improvement activities at shop-floor level. For each of the eight pillars of TPM there are specific targets, which can be decomposed into improvement projects. For example, 'maintain your machine by yourself', 'increase efficiency of machine to the limit' or 'reduce start-up times'. These vague signposts are quantified and analysed in terms of how they can be achieved and the problems that would have to be solved to make this happen—using simple tools such as five whys and fishbone charts. Diagnosis is top down in terms of setting the actual numerical targets or the extent to which operators can maintain their own machines; a team of specialist engineers carries this out.

As with other plants there is a step-by-step process for increasing capability in TPM, and this is linked to training inputs. For example:

Step 1. Clean up your machine
Step 2. Learn to detect different sensitive points
Step 3. Develop a procedure for lubrication and cleaning work
Step 4. Total inspection and check of different key points
Step 5. Autonomous inspection
Step 6. Adjustment and ordering
Step 7. Execution of this in self-management (unsupervised) mode

The company places strong emphasis on mechanisms for embedding these behaviours in the culture so that they become the way things are done and taught to others. An important aspect of phase 2—the current mid-term plan—is to find mechanisms for doing this. These include extensive use of training and development—for example, each employee receives 10 hours' initial training in TPM and then three hours/month of additional training on the job. They are also allocated 30 minutes per day to carry out their individual maintenance and to learn and improve this.

In addition to this operator development and individual improvement, there are also CI projects in particular areas on which groups work in team mode—for example, projects on sputterless welding or cleaning engine coolant, which involve consistent attack on problem areas over a period of weeks or months. Activities of this kind have led to, for example, major set-up time reductions; the 1000 tonne presses take less than 10 minutes to change and are changed four to five times per shift. Projects of this kind tend to take around three months.

There are some 30 odd groups working—10–15 in trim, 12 in body and assembly and 6–8 in the press shop. Group leaders spend half their time with the groups, facilitating, training etc., and the remainder acting as a floating resource to cover sickness, holidays, etc.

The evolution of kaizen has been through early team activities going back 20 or more years. Individual kaizen teian ideas did not come through at first, so a campaign was launched with the theme of 'what makes your job easier?'; prior to that the focus was outside the individual operator's own job area. The evolution of suggestions can be seen in data collected by the JHRMA, which suggest that on the site there is now 100% participation of the 'eligible employees' (around 85% of the total workforce). Of their suggestions around 88% are implemented, giving a 1995–1996 saving of around Y3.2bn.

At present the company is receiving around 20 suggestions per employee per month. One of the difficulties raised by the generation of some 40 000 suggestions per month is how to process them; this is primarily the responsibility of the group leader. Many of the ideas are minor changes to standard operating procedures and foremen/team leaders are authorized to make these. Ideas are judged against four levels as shown in Table 7.3.

TABLE 7.3   Judgement levels for suggestions at Carco vehicles.

Level	Reward	Volume
1. High level, considerable potential benefits and judged by senior management team	Y150 000 upwards	Only 4–5 per year
2. Again reviewed by senior team	medium—Y10 000 plus	20 per year
3. Basic, handled by team leader	Y300	
4. Minor—recognized to encourage continuous improvement activity	Y50	

The importance of recognizing and rewarding the low-level simple ideas was expressed by one manager: 'if we don't encourage fertile soil at the bottom, we'll never get the high-grade ideas later'. Motivation is also secured by strong top-level commitment. When the TPM programme was launched, the first stage built on 5-S principles and involved cleaning up machinery and plant. The plant director held a site briefing explaining his concern and the ideas behind TPM and then led the setting up of a 'section chief's model line', which was a line cleaned up and improved by all the senior managers as a demonstration. Symbolically, the plant director was the first to pick up a broom and begin the process. The line was followed by an 'assistant chief's model line', again to reinforce the commitment top down.

Case 3. Electro Products

This plant employs around 1700 full-time staff, plus 250 part-time staff, plus 550 sub-contractors; and unlike the preceding cases has not yet implemented a TPM approach—partly because its products still involve a high proportion of complex manual assembly. Once again, the approach of 'policy deployment' is central; the company first decides on business priorities and then identifies key broad themes which form the targets for three-year mid-term plans (MTPs). These MTPs are then systematically broken down into specific activities linked to stretching targets for each area of the plant, and these targets are in turn broken down into projects and targets for small-group and individual improvement work. So, in the case of this company, the seventh MTP expressed its overall objective as '... to strengthen quality assurance based on customer satisfaction ...' and this has led to a set of specific activities around building a customer-focused quality system, which identifies responsibilities for quality improvement projects within this structure. (A significant feature of this is the extent to which sales and marketing are now extensively involved in QA.)

In terms of the mechanisms for quality improvement, each strategic business unit within the corporation holds monthly quality meetings and these in turn make a three-monthly meeting with the central QA staff at company headquarters. There is also an annual quality conference at which all quality staff meet. Within the plant there is a monthly review of quality-related data—complaints, defect rates, etc.—and a report on the improvement activities going on within the various workgroups. In addition there are several special efforts to promote and maintain attention on quality matters—such as the 'President's tour' and the Quality Innovation Contest.

The quality system is driven by a 'cost of quality' approach, which is used to monitor quality and drive improvement activities. They estimate that this cost was around 1–2% of turnover when they began the present campaign in the MTP.

Improvement activities take several forms; first, there are individual activities based around the operators' personal responsibility for quality. There is then a system of small-group activities where time is allocated to problem finding and solving using various tools and approaches, in which all operators receive training. In 1996 there were 75 such groups, each meeting for about 1–2 hours per week, focusing on quality issues related to their area. These groups are given targets for improvement expressed in terms of a points system, and progress towards achieving these targets is displayed on the notice-boards in their area by means of green dots. In the first six months of 1996 they received 4873 suggestions in this fashion, which, when annualized, contributed an effect estimated by the company's panel as Y262m—equivalent to around Y53 000 per employee. The company pay for such suggestions is based on a points system—for example, if a team achieved the (high) target of 500 points, they could receive as much as Y2m; these suggestions are all recorded and assessed by a committee and points awarded according to their judgement. Using this system, the company paid the equivalent (again annualized) of Y7.6m to the 75 groups for 1996.

Data from the JHRMA suggests that for 1996 the company implemented 6.9 suggestions per employee per year (but this figure is low because of the high levels of employment). Participation rate in kaizen teian activity was 100% and 96.7% of suggested ideas were implemented. This contributed an economic benefit of Y15.5bn.

Case 4. Airco Machinery

This plant employs around 1800 people making a wide range of industrial equipment. Their approach is driven by a sequence of Mid-Term Plans with particular focus. In 1987, partly as a response to the *endaka* (problems of the high yen), they targeted TPM and in 1990 received the national TPM award. Prior to this, their target had been the development of their version of flexible JIT for high-variety production, which is still being used to drive a move towards mass customization.

The period 1990 to 1994 was characterized by the acquisition of ISO 9001 and the current mid-term plan is to achieve the TPM Excellence Award and ISO 14001 certification.

The motives for TPM relate to an increasing emphasis on automation and the preoccupation with ensuring minimal breakdown and machine attendance requirement. The five pillars supporting their TPM programme are:

- Autonomous maintenance
- Small-group improvement activities
- Early equipment management
- Planned maintenance
- Upgrading of employees via education and training

Each of these has a step-by-step sequence associated—as with other plants. For example, developing autonomous maintenance involves:

Step 1. Initial cleaning
Step 2. Countermeasures at the source of problems
Step 3. Cleaning and lubrication standards and procedures
Step 4. General inspection by operator
Step 5. Autonomous inspection
Step 6. Organization and tidiness
Step 7. Full autonomous maintenance

For each of these there is a check sheet, with details of what has to be checked for and a column for evaluation as shown in Table 7.4. Evaluation is carried out by section managers, each auditing an area other than their own. All operators are required to participate in this process.

TABLE 7.4   Countermeasures at source of problems at Airco machinery.

Item	Checks and actions (PDCA)	Key check points	Evaluation (0 = bad; 10 = good)
Initial cleaning			
Sources	Check	Did you find evidence of oil leaks, air leaks, etc.?	
	Plan	Do you really understand the trouble?	
	Carry out measures to avoid troubles	Are these measures being carried out as you planned?	
etc.	etc.	etc.	

Small-group improvement activities take place in addition to the individual operator work. These are made up of workgroups (average size is seven to eight people, but in some areas larger groups, up to 30 strong, operate) responsible for identifying and solving problems in their areas, towards the general target of 'no trouble' manufacturing. There are 41 workgroups across the site. Typical kaizen projects include development of simple turntables to improve access for assembly, moving tool storage racks, which accompany operators as they move with the moving assembly line, and an assembly table that tilts and has a transparent cover to permit easier inspection. These groups make extensive use of storyboards and other tools in their rest areas, which are integrated with the line. Storyboards use 'before and after' photographs and descriptions to remind existing workers and to train new ones in the rationale behind changes and to encourage further ideas.

Groups meet formally for 30 minutes twice per month but there is extensive informal activity, including the daily briefings and team meetings. The working day runs from 0800 until 1700, with a 10 minute daily meeting at the start of each day or shift.

The company receives around 1000 suggestions per month, and these are evaluated through a hierarchical system, with the first cut taking place at work-group level. High-grade ideas (of which there are around 3300 per year, equivalent to 10 per person per year) move up to the company committee responsible for evaluation and these are rewarded with larger sums. An important feature of the idea management system is that changes are captured and incorporated into the standard operating procedures such that ISO 9001 is not compromised; the company has a documented process for assuring this.

TPM is supported by a dedicated organization structure with several staff seconded to manage the promotion and implementation. The approach is simultaneously top down and bottom up, with policy deployment as the key tool for ensuring linkage. The broad objectives of TPM are broken down into specific projects and target activities, towards which continuous improvement can be focused. The specific targets for TPM 2—the current mid-term plan—are again stretching and include two overall objectives—productivity increase of 50% and an achievement of break-even point of 80% or less. (The break-even point is based on the ratio of fixed costs to added value. If this is 1:1, there is no profit, but at 0.8:1 or less the profitability is significant. To achieve this requires significant efforts at fixed cost reduction which they see as achievable through TPM.) The time targets in turn set up other targets:

- 1.5 times increase in new product introductions
- Productivity increase by 40%
- Cost of after-sales service reduction of 50%
- Improvement in method productivity of 10%
- Percentage of malfunctions down to 300 parts per million in process
- Enhanced maintenance competence to equivalent of one licensed person per group minimum

We can see this deployment through the plan to achieve one of these targets—the 'Perfect No-Stop Line PNS', which will have less than 300 ppm process malfunctions and a mean time between touches (i.e. operator intervention) of more than four hours. (They calculate MTBT on the basis of a moving average over 10 shifts.) In order to achieve this ambitious target they need to work on several sub-projects, covering both ergonomics and man–machine interfaces and also the level and type of plant and equipment.

In turn, this translates to a detailed series of tasks, which have to be dealt with in step-by-step fashion, as described in Table 7.5. In turn each of these ambitious

TABLE 7.5   Steps in achieving the 'Perfect No-Stop Line PNS' at Airco Machinery.

Step	Title	Aims
1	Total inspection on facility and product	No malfunctions No accidents No faults
2	Model plan	Prepare for no touch 100% good product No stopping No adjusting
3	Trial practice	Model of no-touch operation MTBT of four hours
4	First and subsequent development	Expansion and fixing of no touch system
5	Full autonomous maintenance	MTBT of eight hours or more

targets becomes a set of projects for training, experimentation and problem solving. Importantly the actual achievement is less significant than the journey itself, with all that it implies for building a deep understanding of the key barriers to TPM. Significantly, the company reports that the momentum within this project dropped off during the step 3–4 transition and they re-energized the project with major training inputs.

Training is a key feature of this company, with a systematic progression plan for upgrading all employees, aimed at levelling up and increasing skills in various maintenance and related skills. Significantly these training inputs include a component of 'know why' as well as know how, and cover issues outside the workgroup context—for example, the overall functioning of the PDS approach. Their approach is to use operators for most activities, supported by specialists—so that in maintenance there are only 10 formal specialists, but a further 100 plus with qualifications in basic maintenance skills. This equates to the target of at least one licensed maintenance worker in each workgroup.

Case 5. Industrial Trucks Ltd

This is a major producer of forklift trucks and related machinery and at this particular plant they employ around 900 staff producing three main product lines—industrial trucks, construction equipment and other new products.

Strategy is now focused on the 'Aggressive 30' programme, reflecting the 30 years since the plant was set up, and TPM and indirect cost reduction are the key themes. Previous mid-term plans have focused on TQC (1975–1992) but TPM has dominated since 1992. Current targets within the plan are:

- 1.5 times increase in overall productivity
- Breakdown reduced to 10% of current levels
- Streamline production flow by 30%
- Reduction in NPD introduction time of 50%

To deliver these they have a nine-pillar structure to the programme, which is deployed as in the other examples. Results from the first phase were encouraging; during 1993–1996 they reduced the costs of waste from an estimated Y7.8bn (=26% of total production value) to Y4.2bn; they plan to cut this further in the current plan. The total cost of waste is calculated and broken down into 46 areas, each of which becomes the target for improvement activity.

Kaizen operates in both top-down and bottom-up modes. Each workgroup studies its 'waste map' and identifies a series of projects, which are led by section managers. Each section has specific targets to achieve—for example, increase machine availability from 49% to 86% or cut work in progress from 100 to 20 vehicles.

The number of themes has grown, both for individual kaizen teian and for small-group activities as shown in Table 7.6. Each waste theme is plotted on a matrix, with the other axis being a detailed description of the types and nature of waste arising. This matrix gives a picture of the project targets, which are then indicated by a red (= unsolved) or a green (=solved) dot. Importantly, projects completed in one year can be revisited and the targets increased in subsequent years to drive through continuous improvement. For example, in the case of set-up time for changeover to new products the figures are as shown in Table 7.7 and in reducing the number of short (less than 5 minute) stoppages on a welding robot line as shown in Table 7.8. The tools and mechanisms used for this are classic SMED—video analysis, group discussion on waste identification and potential solutions, etc. (Shingo 1983).

TABLE 7.6 The number of themes at Industrial Trucks Ltd.

Year	Number of themes for small-group projects	Number for individual actions
1993	14	136
1994	28	230
1995	40	290
1996	46	360

In another area, machining of units increased from 206 per shift in 1994 to 221 in 1995, 238 in 1996, with a planned 255 in 1997. Much of this was a result of projects designed to increase the length of time that machines could operate unmanned, moving from 40 minutes in 1994 to 420 in 1996.

Overall results of the first phase TPM include:

- Plant lead time average 11 days down to 4
- WIP down from 340 units to 90
- Number of short stoppages reduced from 8160 to 1706
- Total productivity increased to 154% of the 1994 level

A significant element in the new MTP is the focus on administrative productivity. Targets here focus on two areas—material reduction (through better purchasing,

TABLE 7.7 Changeover to new products at Industrial Trucks Ltd.

Year	Number of changeovers	Time to effect each changeover in seconds
1993	255	2903
1994	285	3216
1995	298	2824
1996	304	1716
1997 plan	350	1100

TABLE 7.8 Reducing the number of short stoppages on a welding line at Industrial Trucks Ltd.

Year	Number of stoppages
1993	7 133
1994	10 179
1995	7 494
1996	2 671
1997 plan	700

etc.) and human efficiency improvement. The latter makes use of a Work Breakdown Structure approach, and analysis of this kind identified 160 kaizen project areas, which have contributed a 28.8% improvement in indirect labour productivity. The development of work on these themes is indicated in Table 7.9.

TABLE 7.9 Themes in the Work Breakdown Structure approach at Industrial Trucks Ltd.

Year	Number of themes worked on
1992	28
1993	21
1994	41
1995	38
1996	32

The basic model involves a kind of business process re-engineering (BPR) approach in listing the ideal and actual ways in which work could be carried out and then addressing projects to close the gap. For example, in one area the staff required reduced from seven to two via elimination of unnecessary work and increases in autonomy.

Much of the 'technology' for effecting such improvement has come from transferring concepts used in production—e.g. focus on high-value-added work and 'make contribution visible'. A version of cellular manufacturing is also in use in the main office where a kind of 'hot desking' approach (called 'free location') is in use. This has the advantage not only of reducing space requirements but also of breaking down many of the barriers between functional areas on the administrative side; the use of multiple copies of documents is also dramatically reduced. It is being backed up by training to develop multi-skilled workers able to move freely between jobs.

CI activities are grouped into small-group and kaizen teian activities. Where a kaizen target is identified, a label is stuck on and when the project is complete the label is removed. Over the past two years 6000 labels have been removed. Small groups meet for an average of 10 hours/month approximately four times per month. There are roughly 14 groups of 7–12 people.

Reward and recognition for ideas vary with the level of suggestion. For small kaizen it is assumed to be part of the job, but additional rewards can be given. There is a bimonthly boardroom presentation for the most effective suggestions. For simple teian suggestions the company uses the standard suggestion scheme and pays for these on a scale ranging from Y100 to Y20 000; some employees contribute over 200 suggestions per year. They are ranked in terms of their potential contribution to profit and a big idea would need to contribute Y1m upwards. The ranking is carried out by a panel and is generally perceived to be fair; in part this may result from the differences in overall payment systems (based on seniority) in which workers become accustomed to different levels of pay for the same basic work. There is also a redeployment programme so that staff are not worried about losing their jobs as a result of suggestions; for example, in the administrative area overall staff numbers have been cut from 217 to 139, but the other 78 people have been redeployed into sales, into new business ventures or to headquarters.

Once again, much is done to reinforce the behavioural messages and to lead by example. In the training workshop, where all workers go for repeated injections of training, there is a display of completed improvement projects, with some good ideas that can be applied to other equipment. For example, the use of little windmills on all outlets gives a simple visual indicator of whether or not a cooling fan is running. Another gauge mounted a simple needle on a bearing with a piece of white card behind it. This gave a clear visual representation of whether or not there was heavy vibration in the bearing—an idea that could be widely distributed.

Making things visible is a key theme—the use of the matrix charts with their red and green dots everywhere is a constant reminder of the overall CI programme. Furthermore, each project, as it is completed, is painted a shocking pink colour so that it is clear on walking through the factory where and what has been done—often sparking interest and application elsewhere, but at least reminding on a continuing basis.

7.8 It Is not just Japan

Before we leave the case examples, it will be worth emphasizing that the experience described in detail here is not confined to Japanese firms. There are widespread examples from around the world that demonstrate the significant potential of sustained Level 3 capability. A number of writers have reported such cases in detail, including Kaplinsky (1994), Gallagher and Austin (1997), Witcher and Butterworth (1997), Humphrey *et al.* (1998), Owen and Morgan (2000) and De Jager *et al.* (2002). The two cases that follow highlight both the benefits and the considerable efforts needed to build and retain such capability.

Case 6. Better Boilers Ltd

This company, an old family business, specializes in the manufacture of domestic heating systems for the UK market. It employs around 700 people and has a tradition of enlightened human resource policies with an emphasis on participation. However, it was a period of turbulent environmental change that pushed its thinking towards an emphasis on high-involvement innovation—in particular:

- Slowdown in growth as markets became saturated
- Consolidation of players in the sector led to an increase in price competition
- Changes among customers/distribution channels: as builders' merchants restructured from regional to national companies, this led to an increase in their purchasing power, which put pressure on
- Environmental pressures: increasing demands for more energy-efficient boilers put more pressure on R&D expenditure
- A rise in the company's cost base in both direct and indirect areas
- Expansion in the product range in terms of both volume and mix led to pressures on becoming more flexible (there were up to two dozen variants of some products)
- Failure to meet customer demand for specific models despite high overall stocks (stock turn was around nine), an indication of problems in production layout and management
- Quality problems: although the company had a reputation for high quality and was well respected, this was achieved only by high inspection and rework costs

The management recognized the need for fundamental change if the company was to survive and maintain its competitive position. The outcome was the formulation of a Company Improvement Plan (CIP), based on the introduction of Just-in-Time techniques. The plan incorporated the following aims:

- Support business growth plans
- Improve customer service and market opportunity
- Reduce business operating costs of stock, cost of quality and space requirements
- Reduce lead times
- Enable quicker response for new product introductions
- Strengthen competitive position

It identified seven specific areas on which improvement activities would focus:

- Quality improvement
- Balanced production
- Lead-time reduction

- Set-up reduction
- Pull systems
- Supplier networks
- Housekeeping

Four task groups were set up to manage change in key areas. The first was tasked with setting up a pilot production cell; the second focused on planning and the implementation of a revised approach to planning and scheduling; the third was based around human resource issues and communication, education and training to support CIP; the fourth task group was charged with the implementation of a Quality Improvement Programme.

Pilot Cell   One of the first activities under the new CIP was to pilot the JIT principles by setting up a new production cell for boiler production, which ran ten different models. This ran for four months on a pilot basis and proved to be a tremendous success, generating significant improvements in a range of areas:

- Product cycle time reduced from average of seven weeks to one day
- Throughput reduced from days or weeks to two hours
- Some set-ups reduced from 30 minutes to a few seconds
- 50% saving in floor space (30 000 to 15 000 square feet)
- 60% reduction in distance travelled (2200 to under 1000 feet)
- Significant reduction in scrap and rework
- All ten models could be made in a day

The improvement was also reflected by higher levels of morale. Although some employees were wary that it was still early days, comments from workers indicated clear signs of improvement:

> 'Anything we don't like or doesn't seem practical they are modifying for us. We have had some say in what we're doing. The commitment throughout and the attitude of management has been good. We have seen a different attitude. It's been better than before.'

> 'Everything is a lot more compact, it's a cleaner and neater area and everyone knows what everyone else is doing. I think it is a friendlier atmosphere. The new job has made the job easier and there is not as much carrying to do around the place.'

Due to the success of the pilot, the changes were adopted across the company.

Developing Continuous Improvement Capability   The next stage in developing capability came after a restructuring into focused business units (SBUs) and involved group-based voluntary teams called CITs—continuous improvement teams. These differed from SBU work teams in that they were voluntary and sometimes operated cross-SBU and cross-company. All teams were formally registered so participation could be monitored and appropriate support/facilitation made available.

Before teams set up, team leaders and team members were trained. All members participated in one-day awareness sessions (over a period of two years). Managers at all levels, from directors to team leaders, attended a two-week team-leader training programme (spread over six months) covering team-leading, problem-solving, enabling and coaching skills.

Everyone was given CIP handbooks explaining the principles of continuous improvement (CI), its role in the company, the mission statement, CIP principles, the problem-solving process and tools.

Recognition was addressed in a number of ways. For example, there were lunchtime recognition sessions at which each team had to make a presentation of their progress twice a year in front of an invited audience and attended by at least one director, other managers and guests.

A target was set of 25% participation by the end of the first 12 months of operation (actual was 28%). In the second year, the target of 57% was reached by mid-year and by end of that 12-month period 75% of the workforce had participated.

During this period the teams were given the authority to spend any amount if they could show a return in improved performance.

20 Keys Programme   Later, as the CIT activities appeared to be plateauing, the '*20 Keys*' *initiative* was introduced. Twenty corporate-wide objectives were identified, covering things such as housekeeping, stock control, etc., and each was described at five levels of achievement. CITs assess the current status of each key and set targets for improvement.

The keys act as a prompt for ideas for improvement and provide a supporting measurement system to monitor progress. The company's annual report highlighted the importance of this approach:

> 'This new system for measuring process performance against world class standards offers team members a valuable opportunity to progressive assessment. The package, which is applied to every aspect of the working environment, is proving invaluable in the identification and weeding out of methods which do not make a contribution to quality and profitability. This incremental approach not only creates a sense of shared control over the company's processes but also enables unnecessary costs to be traced and eliminated.'

This policy deployment approach operates in the following way. The team reaches consensus as to what the current performance is in each of the keys. It then constructs the radar chart and formulates an action plan. Targets are set between team leaders and general managers. Team leaders then discuss with their teams and reach consensus on improvement targets; identify which keys are most in need of improvement (high-profile keys); establish the work programme and monitor. Since targets are set through team consensus, the team has ownership of the targets. The team leader will monitor general progress. Teams meet regularly to discuss improvement opportunities. These opportunities are listed and prioritized through team discussion and consensus. The CIT Improvement Ideas Sheet is used to record the identified opportunity and progress it through to actioning the solution.

Following the success of the continuous improvement programme, the company embarked on a number of complementary activities, including an inter-firm CI programme with its suppliers, based on vendor rating and analysis of strategic challenges for policy deployment.

Case 7. Extending High Involvement in Drug Delivery Systems

This case details the development of high involvement within a company (originally described in Chapter 6) where Level 2 patterns had been established, but where there was a clear sense of 'running out of steam'. The original Level 2 work was based on a team-based set of activities under the banner of the Waste Elimination Programme (WEP).

Although the introduction of the WEP had led to significant improvements, the activity was largely internally focused, requiring people to eliminate waste from their own processes. This limited progress in two main ways. First, there was little direct link between these internal activities and the external customer, for example in prioritizing issues for action. Second, improvement was predominantly concentrated within individual areas (and predominantly within production) rather than across functions and work areas. The new business plan aimed to address both these problems.

The new business plan provided a clear direction for the business, through which individual improvement efforts could be linked to meeting the needs of the external customer. It provided the rationale, and therefore a boost, for improvement activity with clear guidance from the top, rather than encouraging improvement as an introverted activity. By combining the objectives of the business plan with self-assessments (based on the Business Excellence Model (Hendricks and Singhal 2002)), the company had an effective tool for identifying key areas for improvement and focusing efforts.

Seventeen steps were identified in the order fulfilment process. By bringing together the people responsible for all these steps under the co-ordination of the Product Stream Leader, this opened up the potential to extend CI beyond production and other isolated areas, to across the whole Product Stream. Bringing people together would enable them to share ideas and improvements and ensure that they are working to common objectives. Also, having made improvements within individual areas, they were now in a better position to do this. As the CI Manager stated:

> 'The focus of continuous improvement up to now has been very much looking at one of these steps and looking at, say, set up reduction or improvement on the packaging line and that's still important to us, reducing the size of each little box. But there's a more fundamental process which is saying you need all of the boxes.'

Targets were set around which innovation activities could focus—for example:

- Delivery to the customer: 93% ± 5 days
- Customer lead time: 10 weeks
- Product cost: equivalent 7% reduction

Another powerful target was improving Overall Equipment Effectiveness (OEE), which was partly triggered by the shift in the order profile toward smaller batches. This led to the increased importance of reducing set-up time, as the number of changeovers rose, and of being effective when the line was running.

The CI facilitator designed and implemented a system for utilizing OEE figures. People were also given training to ensure that they understood what the numbers meant. Operators recorded OEE information on a daily basis and this was then entered into and analysed by computer. The resulting data was used to generate actions at improvement meetings. Typically each meeting covered review of OEE figures, review of actions that were ongoing and new actions and obstacles. In this way measurement became a central part of the innovation culture at the plant.

Set-up reduction became increasingly important as batch sizes decreased. The introduction of OEEs had revealed the extent of the problem in highlighting downtime. Further, using Pareto analysis, it became clear that many of the issues affecting OEE were not operational issues but concerned set-up reduction. Consequently, a number of set-up reduction programmes were introduced to complement the OEE activities.

For example, on some of the tablet packaging lines, people were brought together for half a day to look at the data and generate ideas. People were asked to identify exactly what they currently did, using an activity chart, and how they could make improvements. These were put into an action plan, with the teams themselves having responsibility for completing most the activities. Reduction targets were agreed for the following three-month period—which all the teams achieved. This initial set-up reduction activity removed many of the more simple problems. The next stage was to tackle some of the more difficult problems, which were likely to be more engineering related and require more resources.

7.9 Making it Happen

These extensive cases highlight a number of points, which it is worth while summarizing here. First, getting to Level 3 is not a matter of 'more of the same' behaviour development and support of the Level 2 variety. It involves a step change, essentially bringing high involvement in from being an off-line activity to being a mainstream strategic one. And, in the process, it requires significant input of new resources—a focused strategy, effective policy deployment, efforts to ensure ownership and buy-in to that strategy, alignment of structures and systems to enable regular high-involvement innovation activity and underlying top-management support and active facilitation. Putting these in place—and maintaining the level of involvement through adapting and fine-tuning them—is no easy task and explains why many firms spend years yet fail to make the jump, whilst those that do so have engaged in an extended learning process.

If we retain the metaphor of making the journey to high-involvement innovation, there are a number of identifiable rocks, potholes and other obstacles to progress at this level. The good news is that experience suggests a number of proven enabling resources that can help people with many of these obstacles. Importantly, the growing knowledge and experience base around enablers means that firms can talk to others about what they have done and what they have been able to achieve. They can read case studies and see examples in practice. Such networking and experience sharing form a powerful resource (and a source of comfort and support!) in trying to enable the development of high-involvement innovation (Bessant 1995; Semlinger 1995; Bessant and Francis 1999).

For example, the cases above demonstrate the potential of mechanisms like training in and deployment of structured and focused programmes like 5-S, set-up time reduction and more advanced versions like Six Sigma.

Bringing high-involvement innovation into mainstream activity has the advantage of forcing the issue on putting many of the key building blocks in place. When there is clear strategic rationale for high-involvement innovation and people are able to measure their progress towards meeting improvement targets, it becomes difficult to mask the benefits that the organization obtains. So, trying to avoid the question of reward and recognition would quickly stall the high-involvement innovation engine—people are, not unreasonably, unlikely to offer ideas for improvement unless there is some attempt to share the gains. (And even less likely to do so if improved productivity appears to link to their losing their jobs!) Equally, deploying strategy into multiple projects for groups to work on is pretty pointless unless those groups are given time and space to work on them. There needs to be a system for using them—either directly (by empowering them to make changes) or by passing them to others in rapid response mode.

7.10 Monitoring and Developing High Involvement

Making the move from Level 2 to Level 3 implies a capability to look objectively at the extent to which high-involvement innovation culture has begun to emerge. It requires understanding of where and how to fine-tune and adapt the enabling mechanisms to help embed key behaviours. It also requires an awareness of when the limits to what can be achieved and sustained at that level have been reached. This ability—to monitor the development of high-involvement innovation—is a core feature of the model we have been using, and represents something whose strategic importance increases as we move to higher levels.

To borrow a piece of learning theory, we conceive of the evolution of high-involvement innovation capability in terms of establishing and reinforcing a learning loop. This can be represented by the model attributed to David Kolb, in which the organization's experience of high-involvement innovation is reflected upon, checked against an underlying theory and knowledge base, from which relevant interventions are designed and implemented to try and improve and enhance learning. Figure 7.2 shows this in diagrammatical form.

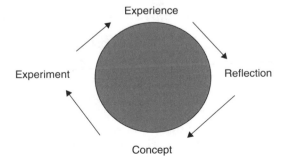

FIGURE 7.2   The learning loop.

In this model there needs to be someone—an individual or a group—who carries out the reflection using a theory base of the kind that this book represents. They have to assess where and how things might be changed to enhance and embed the pattern of behaviour that the organization wishes to create. However, there is also need for them to review where and when it is necessary to make a step change, to reprogram the entire learning cycle and move up to a higher level. (We can make use of the analogy of the central heating or air-conditioning system, where the main activity is about keeping things under control around the desired temperature. But periodically there is the need to reset the system.) Learning theory calls these types of learning cycle single loop and double loop, or adaptive and generative. The labels matter less than the important implications for the organization—it needs both if it is to move forward.

One important enabling resource in this connection is the availability of reference frameworks for looking at and measuring progress in developing high-involvement innovation. These often provide underpinning or complementary resources for major strategic change programmes that move the organization to Level 3—for example, the use of total quality management or total productive maintenance programmes.

This theme is picked up in more detail in Chapter 10, where we will look at the question of designing and implementing change programmes around high-involvement innovation.

Just as Level 2 capability takes a long time to spread and become embedded across the organization, so moving to Level 3 is an organization-wide strategic project whose real advantages emerge in the long term. (We can see the reality of this in the experience of many Japanese firms, which have endured both economic growth and recession and which labour under a high relative cost base. Despite these difficulties, many have been able to sustain a continuing reduction in costs and an increase in value through systematic deployment of high-involvement innovation over an extended period.) There is plenty of scope not only for fine-tuning and adapting the system but also for extending it across the enterprise—especially picking up on cross-boundary problems and opportunities.

7.11 Inter-Firm Implications

One of the most fertile areas for such development is at the inter-firm level, where much value is lost through problems occurring at the interface between organizations. For many organizations the late 20th century was a time for trying to put their own house in order and catch up with levels of 'world-class' performance. It is only fairly recently that attention has shifted to the inter-firm agenda, but there is clearly considerable scope for applying the same principles of joint problem solving as are used within enterprises along a supply chain or between players involved in developing a new product.

The scope for such inter-firm innovation is seen in a number of studies (Lamming 1993; Hines 1994; Hines *et al.* 1999; Dyer and Nobeoka 2000). For example, much of the 'lean thinking' agenda has moved to considering strategic management of the whole value stream, and engaging experienced and successful practitioners of the philosophy in-house in the extension of their tools and techniques to inter-firm issues (Womack and Jones 1997). We will explore this theme in more detail in Chapter 11.

7.12 Summary — The Limits of Level 3

Experience with Level 3 innovation capability suggest that firms are able to extract considerable benefits and gain traction on key strategic drivers. More importantly, if they can sustain this level of involvement, there is a real and measurable dividend available from a continuous stream of improvements. Figures such as 10% year-on-year cost savings are not uncommon, and the extension into supply chains opens up the scope for obtaining regular competitive advantage.

Faced with this consistent level of strategic benefit, why would firms want to travel further on their journey towards high-involvement innovation? Given the increasing difficulties of enabling and sustaining a more innovative culture, why not stay on the shallow part of the hill and leave the rocky and steep next steps alone? Leaving the metaphor aside, this is a decision that many organizations appear to have made—retaining an effective balance between relatively small groups of specialists working on high-impact innovation and the Level 3 deployment of 'do better/improvement' capability.

The limits to Level 3 lie at this interface between 'do better' and 'do different' innovation. For as long as the major strategic challenge is one of catching up, Level 3 capability is a great asset. But, whilst its strength lies in focused and targeted engagement of a high proportion of staff on incremental problem solving, there too lies its weakness. The Level 3 capability is good at 'do what we do better' innovation carried out in a controlled 'do as you are told' manner, but the scope for individual experimentation is limited and emphasis is often on error correction and improvement. For a capability that offers more and particularly offers more in the direction of open-ended problem solving, opportunity finding and more radical innovation, we need to look at the challenge of moving to Level 4. This is the focus of the next chapter.

References

Bessant, J. (1995) 'Networking as a mechanism for technology transfer; the case of continuous improvement,' in Kaplinsky, R., den Hertog, F. and Coriat, B. (eds), *Europe's Next Step*. Frank Cass, London.

Bessant, J. and D. Francis (1999) 'Using learning networks to help improve manufacturing competitiveness,' *Technovation*, **19** (6/7), 373–381.

De Jager, B., M. Welgemoed, C. De Jager, C. Minnie, J. Bessant and D. Francis (2002) *Enabling Continuous Improvement—An Implementation Case Study. Continuous Innovation in Business Processes and Networks*. HUT University Press, Helsinki University of Technology.

Deming, W.E. (1986) *Out of the Crisis*. MIT Press, Cambridge, MA.

Dyer, J. and K. Nobeoka (2000) 'Creating and managing a high-performance knowledge-sharing network: the Toyota case,' *Strategic Management Journal*, **21** (3), 345–367.

Gallagher, M. and S. Austin (1997) *Continuous Improvement Casebook*. Kogan Page, London.

Hendricks, K. and V. Singhal (2002) *The Impact of Total Quality Management on Financial Performance: Evidence from Quality Award Winners*. European Foundation for Quality Management, Brussels.

Hines, P. (1994) *Creating World Class Suppliers: Unlocking Mutual Competitive Advantage*. Pitman, London.

Hines, P., P. Cousins, D. Jones, R. Lamming and N. Rich (1999) *Value Stream Management: The Development of Lean Supply Chains*. Financial Times Management, London.

Humphrey, J., R. Kaplinsky and P. Saraph (1998) *Corporate Restructuring: Crompton Greaves and the Challenge of Globalisation*. Sage Publications, New Delhi.

Kaplinsky, R. (1994) *Easternization: The Spread of Japanese Management Techniques to Developing Countries*. Frank Cass, London.

Lamming, R. (1993) *Beyond Partnership*. Prentice Hall, London.

Nonaka, I. (1991) 'The knowledge creating company,' *Harvard Business Review*, November/December, 96–104.

Owen, M. and J. Morgan (2000) *Statistical Process Control in the Office*. Greenfield Publishing, Kenilworth.

Semlinger, K. (1995) 'Public support for firm networking in Baden-Wurttemburg,' in Kaplinsky, R., Coriat, B., den Hertog F. and Andreason, L. (eds), *Europe's Next Step*. Frank Cass, London.

Shiba, S., A. Graham and G. Walden (1993) *A New American TQM: Four Practical Resolutions in Management*. Productivity Press, Portland, OR.

Shingo, S. (1983) *A Revolution in Manufacturing: The SMED System*. Productivity Press, Cambridge, MA.

Witcher, B. and S. Butterworth (1997) 'The Hoshin Kanri method,' 2nd World Congress for Total Quality Management, Sheffield, UK. Available at http://www.mgt.uea.ac.uk/research/hoshin/.

Womack, J. and D. Jones (1997) *Lean Thinking*. Simon and Schuster, New York.

Chapter 8

AUTONOMOUS INNOVATION

The next—and very advanced—stage in the development of high-involvement innovation is where the organization is confident enough to 'let go' and allow people to experiment with their own ideas with a high degree of autonomy. It is attractive in that it opens up the possibility of radical innovation—doing something different—but it also carries risks since experimentation of this kind will inevitably involve making mistakes. In many ways, it is the kind of culture that one might expect to find in an R&D laboratory, but not as a part of the general 'way we do things round here' in the organization as a whole.

Creating the conditions under which people can act autonomously is not easy and in many cases firms have solved this by creating separate units or 'skunk works', where people are encouraged to be 'intrapreneurs' and to challenge the status quo without the need to leave the organization in order to follow up their ideas.

8.1 The Limits of Continuous Improvement

The great thing about achieving strategic innovation capability is that it provides for *continuous* improvement. As long as people feel supported and enabled and they buy into a shared sense of direction, they will generate projects and solutions that keep driving the numbers on quality, time, availability, cost etc. in the right direction. This has certainly been true of many Japanese firms and is increasingly seen as part of a much wider international experience. Strategic innovation capability provides for a repeatable dividend, a long-term recurring stream of competitive advantage.

So why move on from this position? Why not concentrate all your attention on sustaining effective policy deployment and maintaining a system that encourages and rewards people for making continuous improvement a part of their daily work round? Surely the whole point of the exercise is to build exactly this—the set of routines around finding and solving problems, which becomes 'the way we do things around here'.

The answer to this question is challenging. At one level such high involvement in strategic innovation is of enormous value to the organization, not just in terms of the significant and consistent, quantifiable savings that it enables. The ability to mobilize such a culture means that there is an engine for improvement which can be hooked up to various different strategic targets—and can help a firm keep pace with a turbulent and uncertain environment. If the pressure is on time, that becomes the driver. If it is on quality, then the engine can be connected to deal with this problem. The same is true for all the strategic drivers the firm faces—whether the driver is environmental improvements or variety or increasing customization—they are all legitimate targets for continuous improvement.

But there is an inbuilt limitation to this model of continuous *improvement*—it is all about mobilizing many people to help with the challenge of *doing what we do better*. We should not underestimate the huge scope that this gives us for using creative resources—as total quality management, lean production, total productive maintenance, business process improvement and a host of other experiences show, there is an awful lot of slack to take up and waste to drive out in most of our working systems. We can benchmark our products, services and processes and set challenging targets to bring them up to the frontier of 'world-class'. We can install new equipment or launch new products and then quickly accelerate our way up the learning curve, improving, modifying, getting the bugs out of the system and becoming the best in class. In a wide variety of ways we can explore the envelope and get closer to doing what we do as well as possible—zero defects, minimum process time, lowest waste, etc.

In the end there is a limit to continuous *improvement* activity. Eventually we reach the boundaries of what is physically possible—and our ability to obtain strategic advantage from 'do better' innovation begins to decline. For example, when everyone is able to offer the same low prices, then price ceases to act as an order-winning factor and emphasis shifts to non-price factors like quality, design, speed of delivery, variety of choice, customization, etc. Each of these opens up new space within which firms can compete—but this is not infinite space and other firms will seek to colonize the same territory. The result is that concepts like 'world-class manufacturing' become a two-edged sword. On the one hand, they are powerful ways of focusing attention on gaps that need to be closed, targets for 'do better' innovation activities. However, on the other hand, when the world-class frontier is approached, then it becomes increasingly difficult to gain an advantage over others; when you have closed the gap with the best, who do you benchmark against in order to find new areas to improve?

It is at this point that the other complementary component of innovation becomes significant. Rather than seeking to do things better, organizations also need to look for new things to do or new ways to create and deliver them—'breakthrough' product or process innovation. Once a new 'envelope' has been defined, there is enormous scope for 'do better' innovation to iron out the bugs, stretch the limits and otherwise develop and explore the space.

This is the conundrum that the innovation process poses—although there is huge scope for improvement innovation, there will always be the need to look to do things differently—to create new products or services and develop completely new processes, to open up completely new markets or even to rethink the entire business model. History tells us clearly that there is a driving force, which Schumpeter (1950) called 'creative destruction'. There will always be someone, somewhere trying to create innovations that make what you offer or do redundant. Maybe a motor car to replace the horse-drawn carriage? Or a continuous process to replace a batch-based one? Or Internet-based shopping instead of travelling down to the high street?

In this way variety gets into the 'innovation gene pool'—and fragmenting markets and the explosion of knowledge generation means that this is happening with increasing frequency. But breakthrough innovation of this kind does not emerge fully formed. Once someone has shown the possibility of something radically new, there is a long period of wide variation and experimentation around the new idea—not all first attempts necessarily work! But eventually a 'dominant design' emerges and people start to focus on it. Efforts then become focused on improvements and modifications—first to make a better product or service offering, but later on the attention shifts to improving the process that creates and delivers it.

We can see a pattern here of occasional bursts of activity that open up a new frontier, followed by an extended period of improvement. This is what biologists call 'punctuated equilibrium'—long periods of 'do what we do better' broken up by occasional 'do different' innovation.

8.2 Patterns of Innovation

This pattern comes through in many different examples. For example, think about the production of iron and steel. In the earliest days of cave life people identified the possibilities in making things out of iron and began to develop the basic technology to do so using simple fire, ore and other elements. Practice and a great deal of trial and error enabled a process of continuous improvement—yields rose, quality improved, the process became more reliable. Although most documentation took place by word of mouth rather than via blueprints and chemical equations, the technology of iron production became stable and subject to continuous improvement. The limits of this were in volume, quality and the downstream processing into different shapes and sizes—problems that were addressed by continuous improvement over several centuries. However, the rise in scientific understanding of what was taking place in the underlying chemistry, allied to the availability of new materials, meant that it became possible to produce iron much more efficiently via blast-furnace technology as opposed to slow charcoal-burning furnaces. Much of the Industrial Revolution was enabled by the widespread availability of cast iron—and the continuous improvements in its production—coupled with similar patterns of breakthrough and follow-up in downstream processing in foundries and forges.

The advent of steelmaking via the Bessemer process led to much more widespread use of steel as a construction material and emphasis on continuous improvement in its production and use. The 20th century was characterized by occasional radical process steps—basic oxygen reduction, electric arc-furnace technology, continuous casting, etc., coupled with long periods of productivity- and quality-improving continuous improvement.

In the early days of any new technology there is enormous potential for application. No one knows quite what to do with it—and they may try things that turn out to be impossible. This phase is characterized by lots of experimenting around the technology and its applications. People take risks because the stakes are low—no one knows quite what the future will hold, and the markets for the new applications do not exist—they are just made up of people who are interested in the new thing.

But gradually these experiments begin to converge around what they call a 'dominant design'—something that begins to set up the rules of the game. This can apply to products or processes; in both cases the key characteristics become stabilized and experimentation moves to getting the bugs out and refining the dominant design. For example, in the chemical industry we have moved from making soda ash (an essential ingredient in making soap, glass and a host of other products), from the earliest days, when it was produced by burning vegetable matter, through to a sophisticated chemical reaction, which was carried out on a batch process (the Leblanc process), to the current generation of continuous processes, which use electrolytic techniques and which originated in Belgium where they were developed by the Solvay brothers. Moving to the Leblanc process or the Solvay process did not happen overnight; it took decades of work to refine and improve the process, and to understand fully the chemistry and engineering required to get consistent high quality and output.

In product terms the original design for a camera is something that goes back to the early 19th century and—as a visit to any Science Museum will show—involved all sorts of ingenious solutions. The dominant design gradually emerged with an architecture that we would recognize—shutter and lens arrangement, focusing principles, backplate for film or plates, etc. But this design was then modified still further—for example, with different lenses, motorized drives, flash technology—and, in the case of George Eastman's work, to creating a simple and relatively 'idiot-proof' model camera (the Box Brownie), which opened up photography to a mass market. Innovation does not stop at the dominant design, but it moves from being big steps and radical experimentation to focusing more on improvement and refinement.

As the technology matures still further, so this incremental innovation becomes more significant and emphasis shifts to factors like cost—which means that efforts within the industries which grow up around these product areas tend to focus increasingly on rationalization, on scale economies and on process innovation to drive out cost and improve productivity.

Finally the stage is set for change—the scope for innovation becomes smaller and smaller, whilst outside—for example, in the laboratories and imaginations of research scientists—new possibilities are emerging. Eventually a new technology emerges, which has the potential to challenge all the by now well-established rules—and the game is disrupted. In the camera case, for example, this is happening with the advent of digital photography, which is having an impact on cameras and the overall service package around how you get, keep and share your photographs. In our chemical case, this is happening with biotechnology and the emergence of the possibility of no longer needing giant chemical plants but instead moving to small-scale operations using live organisms genetically engineered to produce what we need.

Abernathy and Utterback (1978) developed a helpful model of this innovation life cycle, which captures well the different characteristics associated with each stage and where emphasis in innovative activity is likely to be placed. Table 8.1 sets out the characteristics of each of these stages in the life cycle.

TABLE 8.1 Stages in the innovation life cycle (Abernathy and Utterback 1978).

Characteristic	Fluid pattern	Transitional phase	Specific phase
Competitive emphasis placed on:	Functional product performance	Product variation	Cost reduction
Innovation stimulated by:	Information on user needs, technical inputs	Opportunities created by expanding internal technical capability	Pressure to reduce cost, improve quality, etc.
Predominant type of innovation:	Frequent major changes in products	Major process innovations required by rising volume	Incremental product and process innovation
Product line:	Diverse, often including custom designs	Includes at least one stable or dominant design	Mostly undifferentiated standard products
Production processes:	Flexible and inefficient—the aim is to experiment and make frequent changes	Becoming more rigid and defined	Efficient, often capital intensive and relatively rigid

Effectively the pattern is one of complementary activity in breakthrough and improvement innovation. Organizations need the capability for both—the one style of innovation aimed at focused incremental problem finding and solving, the other looking for radical alternative opportunities. Unfortunately history suggests that the two do not always sit well alongside each other. When an existing technological framework is broken by a breakthrough, this often comes from outside the industry—perhaps bringing in a new way of looking at the problem or a new material or process hitherto not thought about in that context.

BOX 8.1 Innovation in the glass industry.

It is particularly important to understand that change does not come in standard-sized jumps. For much of the time it is essentially incremental, a process of gradual improvement over time on dimensions like price, quality, choice, etc. For long periods of time nothing much shifts in either product offering or the way in which this is delivered (product and process innovation is incremental). But sooner or later someone somewhere will come up with a radical change that upsets the apple cart.

For example, the glass window business has been around for at least 600 years and is — since most houses, offices, hotels and shops have plenty of windows — a very profitable business to be in. But for most of those 600 years the basic process for making window glass has not changed. Glass is made in approximately flat sheets, which are then ground down to a state where they are flat enough for people to see through them. The ways in which the grinding takes place have improved — what used to be a labour-intensive process became increasingly mechanized and even automated, and the tools and abrasives became progressively more sophisticated and effective. But underneath the same core process of grinding down to flatness was going on.

Then, in 1952, Alastair Pilkington in the UK firm of the same name began working on a process that revolutionized glass making for the next 50 years. He got the idea whilst washing up, when he noticed that the fat and grease from the plates floated on the top of the water — and he began thinking about producing glass in such a way that it could be cast to float on the surface of some other liquid and then allowed to set. If this could be accomplished, it might be possible to create a perfectly flat surface without the need for grinding and polishing.

Five years, millions of pounds and over 100 000 tonnes of scrapped glass later, the company achieved a working pilot plant and a further two years on began selling glass made by the float-glass process. The process advantages included around 80% labour and 50% energy savings plus those that came because of the lack of need for abrasives, grinding equipment, etc. Factories could be made smaller and the overall time to produce glass dramatically cut. So successful was the process that it became — and still is — the dominant method for making flat glass around the world.

When change of this kind happens, the rules change and there is a scramble for position — some people fall off and new ones come on board. Eventually things settle down until the next discontinuous shift. The message in this for strategic innovation management is that we have to watch both trends and be able to contribute to continuous incremental improvement, whilst also watching for and working on more radical and discontinuous shifts. Far from falling asleep, firms need to be wide awake and actively seeking the changes that will change the way their industry works. They should not sleep too soundly anyway because history tells us that this pattern is common — someone somewhere *will* come up with a new product or process that will render current experience and capabilities redundant.

8.3 Handling Different Innovation Types

Most organizations get very good at doing what they have always done and at continuously improving that—but this can set up a whole series of barriers, which filter out alternative ways of thinking or doing. For this reason, when major change comes along in an industry, the existing players often do rather badly in the transition and it is the new upstart small companies that reap the rewards—in part because they are not carrying any excess mental or cultural baggage (Tushman and Anderson 1987; Hamel 2000).

What does this mean in our context of high-involvement innovation? First, that organizations need, ideally, the capability to handle both 'do better' and 'do different' innovation; otherwise they will not be able to capitalize on new ideas. Both styles of innovation are needed—a kind of yin/yang relationship.

For example, within the literature on total quality two themes can be detected, the need to eliminate variation (through a variety of statistical measurement and monitoring techniques applied to the processes themselves) and the need to introduce controlled variation (via experiments designed to improve and extend process capability or performance) (Deming 1982; Garvin 1988; Atkinson 1990; Dale 1995). As Melcher *et al.* (1990) observe, eliminating variation and standard-maintaining are only half the battle—the complement of innovative experimentation is also required.

Second, the skills in breakthrough innovation—whilst sometimes involving specific technical knowledge—are mostly about looking in new and often radically different ways, asking unexpected or 'naïve' questions, challenging the status quo and being prepared to try out new possibilities with a high tolerance for failure. It is an area where having high fluency and flexibility in creative idea generation is a distinct asset—precisely the characteristics associated with high involvement.

8.4 R&D for All?

The scene is familiar—glancing through the glass door, we see a clean and shiny laboratory, glassware and ceramics containing reflected fluorescent light and the gentle hum of some seriously complex machinery working on arcane analysis of gas chromatography, nuclear magnetic resonance and other complex technologies. Around the room, clad in starched white, are the research staff, high priests of this ceremonial quest for knowledge and the denizens of this temple to which it is dedicated. We can all imagine the scene—or its equivalent, played out in rooms with the glow of computer-aided design screens as engineers wrestle with the complexities of finite element analysis and n-dimensional geometry to ensure that the new car they are planning really will slice through the air like a knife through butter. Or the scene is a pizza-strewn 3 am wasteland with rock music throbbing in the background as the dedicated programmers put the finishing touches to some seriously wicked code underpinning the latest generation of computer game.

These are all settings for the innovation-generating end of the business. Whether called research and development, or engineering or systems development or some other label, these are the places in which the great leaps forward are planned and created, and where the future of the company lies. If 'do better' innovation is what helps keep them in the race, 'do different' innovation gets them a head start in the next event.

But what do they do, and what actually goes on here? Stripped down to its essentials and moving beyond the jargon of specialist disciplines we have:

1. Professionally trained hunters after new knowledge, who use a structured and systematic approach to tackling problems—'scientific method' of some kind
2. Recognition that problems do not come fully formed at the front end; so much of the work is open-ended mapping—trying to give shape and definition to the problem. This involves a great deal of experimentation—playing hunches, testing intuition, following even rather odd leads. Essentially this is an experimental culture
3. An environment in which experiment is encouraged as a route to generating useful knowledge—even when a blind alley is found, it helps in the map by identifying where not to put resources in the next experiment. But the golden rule in experimenting is to capture knowledge and so each essay into the unknown is pinned down in laboratory notebooks and engineering journals, or increasingly in workgroup software
4. A climate of knowledge sharing, in which people talk frequently and share ideas in an open way—brainstorming of an informal nature is the common currency. People share because it helps others see where not to go and it

stimulates new insights about where to go. It can be supported by seminars, exhibitions, colloquia, etc., but it is mainly about display and sharing

5. A feature of such environments is that people are highly motivated—in large measure because their jobs are about deploying creativity—they have been licensed to play and to explore. Such motivation comes from having space and time to play, but it does not hurt to have financial packages that recognize that it is the ideas of these people which create the future business. Share options, bonus schemes and other mechanisms help, as do technological ladders and other forms of promotion that recognize that not everyone is a great manager and it is possible to develop alternative career paths

6. Space and time to think—and not to be 100% focused on producing outputs. The stories of 'do different' innovation repeatedly stress the role of serendipity and lucky accidents. After all, we should remember the famous edict of Louis Pasteur who said 'chance favours the prepared mind'. So we need the creation of an environment that allows the sense of 'bounded' slack/space to follow ideas, to play and to break rules

7. Research and development is always a balancing act between businesses with targets and limited resources, and the deployment of creativity in search of new ways of meeting those targets. So there is also a sense of structure and discipline, a sense of strategic purpose rather than just creating chaos

8. Balanced resource disposition—it is too simple to see the prescription being one of letting people loose and giving them unlimited resources. Indeed, there are some notable examples where limiting resource availability can actually enhance creativity. The impossible conditions that obtained in places like Colditz castle suggest that tight or even impossible conditions (confinement, the presence of guards, lack of time, technical impossibility, etc.) and minimal resources can sometimes bring out the most ingenious ideas. The story of the Lockheed skunk works—which generated some of the major advances in aeronautical technology of the 20th century—is characterized by a marked absence of available resources—indeed, it was impossible to procure certain resources for fear of drawing attention to top-secret programmes

Overall there is a clear sense of a strategy-driven process—the difference is that in such environments emphasis is placed on the end state (the *what*) and the boundaries within which that must fit—but the actual *how* is up to the players themselves.

8.5 High Involvement in High-Impact Innovation?

There is nothing in theory to stop organizations empowering their employees to work in this autonomous fashion. But 'licensing' a large number of people to work in this way represents a very advanced stage in the development of high-involvement innovation, where the organization is confident enough to 'let go' and allow people to experiment with their own ideas with a high degree of autonomy. It is attractive in that it opens up the possibility of radical innovation—doing something different—but it also carries risks since experimentation of this kind will inevitably involve making mistakes. In many ways, it is the kind of culture that one might expect to find in an R&D laboratory but not as a part of the general 'way we do things round here' in the organization as a whole.

Creating the conditions under which people can act autonomously is not easy and in many cases firms have solved this by creating separate units or even companies where a different operating culture can be developed. The problem with doing so—which we looked at briefly in Chapter 3—is that the organization loses out on the many synergies that come from creating new ideas and sharing them with others. Whilst such a set-up may help with breakthrough innovation—doing something totally new—it does not deal particularly well with the companion issues of then learning to do that new thing better. Instead, what is needed is some mechanism for transferring between the two—a capability that one commentator has christened 'ambidextrous'—an organization able to manage both 'do better' and 'do different' innovation under the same organizational roof (Tushman and O'Reilly 1996).

There are various ways of trying to achieve this and Figure 8.1 gives a diagrammatic view. One alternative, which is of interest here, is to try and create an innovation capability distributed across the organization to participate in *both* types of innovative activity.

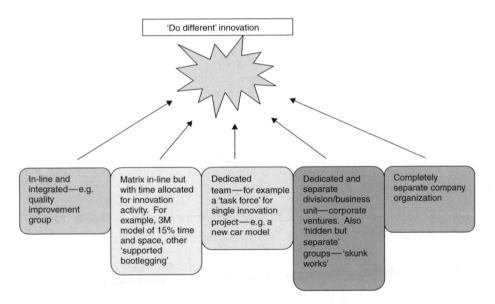

FIGURE 8.1   Options in organizing for 'do different' innovation.

8.6 Some Case Examples

Case 1. Dutton Engineering

This does not, at first sight, seem a likely candidate for world class. A small firm with 28 employees, specializing in steel cases for electronic equipment, it ought to be amongst the ranks of hand-to-mouth metal bashers of the kind that you can find all round the world. Yet Dutton has been doubling its turnover; sales per employee have doubled in an eight-year period; rejects are down from 10% to 0.7%; and over 99% of deliveries are made within 24 hours—compared to only 60% being achieved within one week a few years ago. This transformation has not come overnight—the process started in 1989—but it has clearly been successful and Dutton are now held up as an example to others of how typical small engineering firms can change.

At the heart of the transformation that Ken Lewis, the original founder and architect of the change, has set in train is a commitment to improvements through people. The workforce is organized into four teams who manage themselves, setting work schedules, dealing with their own customers, costing their own orders and even setting their own pay! The company has moved from traditional weekly pay to a system of 'annualized hours', where they contract to work for 1770 hours in a year—and tailor this flexibly to the needs of the business with its peaks and troughs of activity. There is a high level of contribution to problem solving, encouraged by a simple reward system, which pays £5–£15 for bright ideas, and by a bonus scheme whereby 20% of profits are shared (Lewis and Lytton 1994).

Case 2. Chaparral Steel

In her studies of Chaparral Steel, Dorothy Leonard-Barton characterizes the factory as a 'learning laboratory'—one where 'if it ain't being fixed, it's broke!' (Leonard-Barton 1992). Continuous and sometimes dramatic innovation takes place—for example, in the development of a novel process to cast 'near-net shape steel'—and it does so through high and active involvement of the entire workforce. She argues that this is not an accident, but rather that the company has put in place four key systems, each with its own underlying values, its own reinforcing system and typical activities. In other words, it has created and sustained a high-involvement culture.

These systems are:

1. *Owning the problem and solving it.* The underlying value here is that everyone can make a contribution, and there is a strong egalitarian emphasis (an important characteristic in a dangerous and highly physical environment like steelmaking where close co-operation is essential). The reinforcing system here is one of performance rewards—pay for skills, with all staff on salary, which helps minimize status differentials. A typical activity is active encouragement of experiment and use of problem-solving skills, linked to personal objectives and thus embedded in the system.

2. *Garnering and integrating internal knowledge.* The underlying value here is the importance of sharing what we know and making it available across the organization and building knowledge through teamwork. The reinforcing system is what Leonard-Barton terms 'apprenticeship', which is mentored learning on the job, backed up with extensive investment in formal education and training inputs that stress knowledge as a key resource to be valued in the organization. A typical activity through which this can be observed is the operation of a constant process of converting tacit knowledge to codified and share knowledge—a cycle similar to that described by Nonaka (1991).

3. *Creating a virtual research organization.* Here the core value is openness to new knowledge from diverse sources, avoiding the 'not invented here' effect. The reinforcing system is resourcing networking—internally and externally—by time and cash allocation. In providing the resource, the organization expresses a strong commitment to this kind of activity. Typical activities include internal and external networking and linking back—visits to others, benchmarking, etc.

4. *Challenge the status quo.* Here the core value is a positive attitude to risk—an attitude captured in phrases like 'it is riskier to do nothing', 'nothing ventured, nothing gained'. The reinforcing system is employee selection and development, where the organization seeks to find and encourage risk-taking and empowers people to stretch themselves through its training and development work. The resulting activity pattern is one of constant experiment—'If it ain't being fixed it's broke! If you have an idea, try it!'

Case 3. XYZ Systems

At first sight XYZ Systems does not appear to be anyone's idea of a 'world-class' manufacturing outfit. Set in a small town in the English Midlands with a predominantly agricultural industry, XYZ employs around 30 people producing gauges and other measuring devices for the forecourts of filling stations. Their products are used to monitor and measure levels and other parameters in the big fuel tanks underneath the stations and on the tankers which deliver to them. Despite their small size (although they are part of a larger but decentralized group), XYZ have managed to command around 80% of the European market. Their processes are competitive against even large manufacturers, their delivery and service level the envy of the industry. They have a fistful of awards for their quality and yet manage to do this across a wide range of products, some dating back 30 years, which still need service and repair. They use technologies from complex electronics and remote sensing right down to basics—they still make a wooden measuring stick, for example.

Their success can be gauged from profitability figures, but also from the many awards that they have received and continue to receive as one of the best factories in the UK.

Yet if you go through the doors of XYZ, you would have to look hard for the physical evidence of how they achieved this enviable position. This is not a highly automated business—it would not be appropriate. Nor is it laid out in modern facilities; instead they have clearly made much of their existing environment and organized it and themselves to best effect.

Where does the difference lie? Fundamentally, in the approach taken with the workforce. This is an organization where training matters—investment is well above the average and everyone receives over 100 hours per year, not only in their own particular skills area but across a wide range of tasks and skills. One consequence of this is that the workforce are very flexible; having been trained to carry out most of the operations, they can quickly move to where they are most needed. The payment system encourages such co-operation and teamworking, with its simple structure and emphasis on payment for skill, quality and teamworking. The strategic targets are clear and simple, and are discussed with everyone before being broken down into a series of small manageable improvement projects in a process of policy deployment. All around the works there are copies of the 'bowling chart', which sets out simply—like a tenpin bowling score sheet—the tasks to be worked on as improvement projects and how they could contribute to the overall strategic aims of the business. And, if they achieve or exceed those strategic targets, then everyone gains thorough a profit sharing and employee ownership scheme.

Being a small firm, there is little in the way of hierarchy, but the sense of teamworking is heightened by active leadership and encouragement to discuss and explore issues together—and it does not hurt that the Operations Director practises a form of MBWA, management by walking about!

Perhaps the real secret lies in the way in which people feel enabled to find and solve problems, often experimenting with different solutions and frequently failing—but at least learning and sharing that information for others to build on. Walking round the factory, it is clear that this place is not standing still—whilst major investment in new machines is not an everyday thing, little improvement projects—kaizens as they call them—are everywhere. More significant is the fact that the Operations Director is often surprised by what he finds people doing. It is clear that he has not got a detailed idea of which projects people are working on and what they are doing, but, if you ask him if this worries him, the answer is clear—and challenging. 'No, it doesn't bother me that I don't know in detail what's going on. They all know the strategy, they all have a clear idea of what we have to do (via the 'bowling charts'). They've all been trained, they know how to run improvement projects and they work as a team. And I trust them. . .'.

8.7 Characterizing Level 4 Innovation Capability

These are examples of companies clearly on the way to developing a high level of autonomous innovation amongst their workforces. The breakthroughs may still be within the overall envelope—they do not involve rocket science, but they do involve high levels of experimentation and tolerance of failure. People feel empowered to play around with ideas that they think will make a strategic difference without having to seek permission and without waiting to be told what to do. The outcomes are not always successful but there is usually a high degree of learning whatever the results. Table 8.2 gives some examples of indicators of the development of high-involvement capabilities at this level.

8.8 Barriers to Moving to Level 4

In many ways this level poses some of the most significant challenges to managing the development of high-involvement innovation. It is less about doing new things to shape and direct the organization than about letting go—allowing a higher level of autonomy to people who have hitherto been told what to do and how to do it. The loss of control that this implies is not easy to accept—and there are many situations where it will not be possible or desirable.

Another problem here is what we might term the 'kaizen fallacy'. One of the most influential models in the development of high-involvement innovation

TABLE 8.2 Developing Level 4 capability.

Key organizational abilities as they appear in the model	*Typical indicators of Level 4 capability development*
'Understanding'—the ability to articulate the basic values of high-involvement innovation	High levels of understanding and a sense of individual capability to make a difference Strong experimental culture, willingness to try things out knowing that blame will not be attached 'The only mistake is to make the same mistake twice!'
'Getting the habit'—the ability to generate sustained involvement in innovation	Problem finding and solving discipline is embedded and routine—people use it without thinking and there is a shared approach to this Measurement is seen as an enabler of innovation and is used both for corrective action and for identifying scope for innovation Training in and regular use of a range of tools, from simple quality aids through to more complex ones High priority placed on innovation so implementation is supported—either people are empowered to act by themselves or else resources can be mobilized for projects that they have identified and can 'sell' to others
'Focusing'—the ability to link high-involvement innovation activities to the strategic goals of the company	Clear sense of overall strategic direction and buy-in to the strategy Extensive use of policy deployment as an enabler of targeted action—both in improvement projects and in identifying areas for exploring more advanced innovation options Extensive use of monitoring and measurement as an aid to innovation, coupled with ownership of the measuring process
'Leading'—the ability to lead, direct and support the creation and sustaining of high-involvement innovation behaviours	Perceived sense of support, but key style here is apparent 'hands-off' approach by senior management—people feel empowered and supported Active involvement by managers, who replicate the values they are trying to promote—through support, recognition, encouraging blame-free experimentation, etc.
'Aligning'—the ability to create consistency between high-involvement innovation values and behaviour and the organizational context (structures, procedures, etc.)	Good fit between innovation routines and the way the organization works Supportive structures and systems—innovation is a way of life and considered an integral part of people's jobs Reward system links innovation results to individual and group recognition and reward—for example, through share ownership, bonus schemes, etc.
'Shared problem solving'—the ability to move innovative activity across organizational boundaries	Extensive cross-boundary working, and active use made of different perspectives on problems and their potential solutions Inter-firm activity
'Continuous improvement of the system'—the ability to strategically manage the development of high-involvement innovation	High-involvement innovation is a core strategic value and supported and enabled by senior management Keeping the system running and fine-tuned is often no longer a mainstream or full-time activity since so much has become embedded in the culture of the organization. However, use is made of reference frameworks and assessments—such as EFQM—to help with the fine-tuning process
'The learning organization'—generating the ability to enable learning to take place and be captured at all levels	High commitment to training and individual development Emphasis on sharing, displaying and capturing learning to avoid re-inventing wheels and to spread good practices

capability has been that of 'kaizen'—as discussed earlier, a Japanese concept that embraces the idea of everyone in the organization working together on a stream of incremental innovations. Eloquently set out and elaborated by Masaki Imai in his book of the same name, kaizen has found widespread acceptance and success around the world (Imai 1987; 1997). In our terms it represents a powerful framework for Level 2/3 capability development.

Implicit in the kaizen approach, however (and explicit in some presentations on the topic), is an 'either/or' view of the broader question of innovation. Kaizen is seen as enabling the 'do better' agenda, whilst more radical forms of innovation are the province of specialists.

The risk here is that we return to the kind of polarization of the workforce which we encountered in Chapter 3—the difference being that, whereas the old management model saw the split in terms of 'doers' and 'thinkers', here it becomes one separated by different levels of thinking about innovation. Although difficult, experience—such as that outlined here—suggests that higher levels of participation in more experimental and radical innovation are possible.

A further barrier to moving to Level 4 is the very success of Level 3—the argument being that, if you can get people on board and consistently chipping in their ideas, why go for more? If the systems appear to suit everyone—workers get bonuses and share in the benefits, companies get an engine to hook up to their strategic challenges—why bother to extend them further? If there is an effective policy deployment mechanism to link bottom-up problem-solving capability with top-down strategic challenges, why tinker with it. To coin a phrase, 'if it ain't broke, don't fix it!'.

To some extent this appears to be the emerging pattern with high-involvement innovation. Few large-sample studies exist, but those which have tried to explore this phenomenon (such as the CINET survey (Boer *et al.*, 1999)) indicate that most organizations are active at the Level 2/3 part of the model. Of more significance, perhaps, is that many long-term success stories of companies who manage to secure the benefits of high involvement are of organizations that appear to have chosen to retain and refine their Level 3 position.

Also acting as a 'glass ceiling' to higher levels of high-involvement innovation capability development is the traditional management model, which sees the need for boundaries to ensure they remain in control. The 'letting go' required in Level 4, with its implied tolerance for experimentation and making mistakes, can be perceived as a threat in some cases.

It is also important to acknowledge the concerns many organizations have about empowerment and the risk of loss of control or focus. Although there is an argument to suggest that innovating organizations 'thrive on chaos', this is a dangerous prescription without some form of underpinning to ensure strategic direction and operating discipline. Although letting people experiment and play around with ideas in a curiosity-driven environment is an attractive option, there are clearly cases and places where this may not be such a good idea. Whilst it might work for finding a new way to process sales orders or as a route to new product concepts, it could have disastrous consequences if applied to the formulation and preparation of medicines or the ways in which transport systems are operated.

What is needed is a clear understanding of and commitment to the overall goals of the organization and a recognition of the constraints that particular contexts impose. Ideally, we are looking to develop an 'internal control system' in which values and guiding principles operate to guide and limit the experimentation that an individual carries out—essentially what we would associate with the idea of a 'professional' (Mintzberg 1989).

8.9 Enablers for Developing Level 4 Capability

At Level 4 much of the groundwork has been done to establish a firm foundation for high-involvement innovation. People are trained, systems are in place, measurement frameworks exist for tracking progress on projects that have been identified and owned through a process of policy deployment. Vehicles and facilitation are available to ensure a high degree of involvement, and people re-encouraged to participate through the operation of an appropriate recognition and reward system, which shares the gains emerging from their ideas.

In order to move on from this, the organization needs two important shifts in its philosophy—a willingness to 'let go' and an orientation towards risk-taking. How can this be enabled in practice? Evidence suggests that training is particularly valuable—not just because it equips people with the skills to undertake increasingly sophisticated innovation behaviour, but also because it makes devolving autonomy more acceptable. If people are trained as professionals, then it becomes easier to let them operate as such.

Linked to this is the idea of pilot projects and managed risks—rather than committing to creating a risk-taking experimental culture overnight, many organizations choose to focus on a project-by-project approach, which allows exploration of autonomous working and the potential in this approach.

The case of 3M is widely reported as a company that has successfully managed to deliver both breakthrough and incremental innovation across its product range for over one hundred years. It has considerable faith in the extent to which it has built this high-involvement innovation capability to the extent that it sets itself the ambitious target of deriving up to 50% of its sales from products that it has developed during the past three years. But its achievement of this has come through a complex set of enabling structures and mechanisms rather than a single approach. These mechanisms include allowing people space to explore and be curious, seed funding for them to take their ideas forward, support structured to enable cross-department and inter-organizational contact and knowledge sharing, encouragement of 'bootlegging' activities, and a host of others (Mitchell 1991; Kanter 1997; Gundling 2000). In other words, they have managed to create the conditions for safely 'letting go' and allowing a high degree of autonomy to their staff.

Many other organizations are following similar paths—but each has to find its own version of the solutions (Pisano 1996; Tushman and O'Reilly 1996; Leifer et al. 2000; Graham and Shuldiner 2001). Simply letting people go off on their own is unlikely to be appropriate, any more than rigidly controlling their every movement. Putting all the emphasis on 'do different' innovation will risk the organization failing because it has no 'do better' products and services to keep it going until the radical breakthroughs can come on stream. Level 4 capability is an aspiration for most organizations—but one that is becoming increasingly important as the rate of catching up to 'world-class' benchmarks accelerates. Survival will depend on the capability to do better and to do different.

8.10 Summary

Level 4 represents a highly developed innovation capability and one to which most organizations would aspire. It involves risk-taking, but the potential advantages of combining 'do better' and 'do different' innovation modes are significant, particularly when this capability is distributed across the workforce. The challenge for firms that have reached this level is to spread and embed the process across all their activities and out into their inter-firm relationships. Above all, it involves mobilizing this 'ideas engine' as a resource to create the knowledge-based competitive advantage that will be critical for their survival in the long term. Building such learning organizations is the focus of the next chapter.

References

Abernathy, W. and J. Utterback (1978) 'Patterns of industrial innovation,' *Technology Review*, **80**, 40–47.

Atkinson, P. (1990) *Total Quality Management: Creating Culture Change*. IFS Publications, Kempston.

Boer, H., A. Berger, R. Chapman and F. Gertsen (1999) *CI Changes: From Suggestion Box to the Learning Organization*. Ashgate, Aldershot.

Dale, B. (1995) *Managing Quality*. Prentice Hall, London.

Deming, W. (1982) *Quality, Productivity and Competitive Position*. MIT Press, Cambridge, MA.

Garvin, D. (1988) *Managing Quality*. Free Press, New York.

Graham, M. and A. Shuldiner (2001) *Corning and the Craft of Innovation*. Oxford University Press, Oxford.

Gundling, E. (2000) *The 3M Way to Innovation: Balancing People and Profit*. Kodansha International, New York.

Hamel, G. (2000) *Leading the Revolution*. Harvard Business School Press, Boston, MA.

Imai, K. (1987) *Kaizen*. Random House, New York.

Imai, M. (1997) *Gemba Kaizen*. McGraw-Hill, New York.

Kanter, R. (ed.) (1997) *Innovation: Breakthrough Thinking at 3M, DuPont, GE, Pfizer and Rubbermaid*. Harper Business, New York.

Leifer, R., C. McDermott, G. O'Conner, L. Peters, M. Rice and R. Veryzer (2000) *Radical Innovation*. Harvard Business School Press, Boston, MA.

Leonard-Barton, D. (1992) 'The organization as learning laboratory,' *Sloan Management Review*, **34** (1), 23–38.

Lewis, K. and S. Lytton (1994) *How to Transform Your Company*. Management Books 2000, London.

Melcher, A., W. Acar, P. Dumont and M. Khouja (1990) 'Standard maintaining and continuous improvement systems; experiences and comparisons,' *Interfaces*, **20** (3), 24–40.

Mintzberg, H. (1989) *Mintzberg on Management*. Free Press, New York.

Mitchell, R. (1991) 'How 3M keeps the new products coming,' in Henry, J. and Walker, D. (ed.), *Managing Innovation*. Sage, London.

Nonaka, I. (1991) 'The knowledge-creating company,' *Harvard Business Review*, November/December, 96–104.

Pisano, G. (1996) *The Development Factory: Unlocking the Potential of Process Innovation*. Harvard Business School Press, Boston, MA.

Schumpeter, J. (1950) *Capitalism, Socialism and Democracy*, Harper and Row, New York.

Tushman, M. and P. Anderson (1987) 'Technological discontinuities and organizational environments,' *Administrative Science Quarterly*, **31** (3), 439–465.

Tushman, M. and C. O'Reilly (1996) *Winning Through Innovation*. Harvard Business School Press, Boston, MA.

Chapter 9

LEARNING ORGANIZATIONS

The phrase 'learning organizations' was fashionable in the late 20th century, but it has been superseded by other apparently more compelling prescriptions. However, the underlying theme—of mobilizing the full capability of the organization in creating, assimilating, capturing, sharing and using knowledge—remains of critical importance. This chapter looks at the mature high-involvement innovation organization in which innovation is a way of life and where there are multiple mechanisms in place that ensure high levels of involvement in the learning and knowledge management needed to become and remain competitive.

9.1 Learning Matters

To state the obvious, firms need to learn to survive. As de Geus (1996) points out (based on studies carried out by Shell), the average corporate survival rate for large companies is only about half as long as that of a human being. To put this into perspective, almost 40% of the names that made up the Fortune Top 500 ten years ago no longer exist, whilst of the top 12 companies that made up the Dow Jones index in 1900 only one—General Electric—survives today. Even apparently robust giants like IBM, GM or Kodak can suddenly display worrying signs of mortality, whilst for small firms the picture is often considerably worse since they lack the protection of a large resource base.

Behind these figures lies a challenge. Not all firms fail and some have undoubtedly thrived during this period; the key feature that they share is an ability to adapt and learn to deal with their rapidly changing and uncertain environments. Research suggests that there are two important components involved in such learning; the first involves the accumulation and development of a core knowledge base—the 'core competence'—which differentiates the firm from others and offers the potential for competitive advantage. Acquiring this is not simply a matter of purchasing or trading knowledge assets, but the systematic and purposive learning and construction of a knowledge base.

The second is the long-term development of a capability for learning and continuous improvement across the whole organization. Recognition of this need has led to growing emphasis on the concept of 'learning organizations' and on the mechanisms through which this capability can be developed. Beyond this lies the possibility of gaining traction and support for the learning process through working with others in what we term 'learning networks'.

The phrase 'learning organizations' was fashionable in the late 20th century but it has been superseded by other apparently more compelling prescriptions. But this underlying theme—of mobilizing the full capability of the organization in creating, assimilating, capturing, sharing and using knowledge—remains of critical importance. This chapter looks at the mature high-involvement innovation organization in which innovation is a way of life and where there are multiple mechanisms in place which ensure high levels of involvement in the learning and knowledge management needed to become and remain competitive.

9.2 Into the Stratosphere

In the firm Excellent Electronics innovation has become a way of life. Most of it is not rocket science, but it is making a difference to their ability to compete—and to stay ahead of much larger firms looking to push them out of the way through price, quality, speed or customer service. Despite their small size, their constant innovation approach has helped them punch above their weight and in the process secure accolades from customers, trade bodies and even their competitors.

Life in the factory is based on the principle that there is always scope for improving things, for doing them differently. Policy deployment of the overall strategy provides the framework within which this can happen, but how to deliver on the strategic targets is very much a mater of taking initiatives, trying things out—and sometimes failing. No one gets blamed for making mistakes—after all, you cannot make an omelette without breaking eggs. The only 'crime' is to make the same mistake a second time—because it means that an opportunity to learn and improve has been missed.

Look around the factory and one of the first things that strikes you is the 'home-made' quality of much of the equipment, fixtures and fittings. This is a place where, if people have an idea, they will beg, borrow or steal bits and pieces to help make it happen. Although some of the contraptions look unlikely, they all work, and help to add to the very high levels of quality and productivity that people consistently maintain.

Take the case of the printed circuit board assembly area. The task here is to insert and secure components onto boards—but to do so in a high-variety environment where the wide range of customer choices and product configurations available means that many of the boards are built on a one-off basis. Productivity was low and so a team of six operators decided to try and improve on it. They did some research and found that there were machines around that could do the job using wave soldering as a process—so they persuaded their manager to let them visit a large exhibition of such equipment to see what they could find. This quickly showed them that such machines were too expensive but that, in talking around, there were other, lower-cost alternatives. Even these looked pricy, but with a lot of cajoling and negotiating they managed to persuade one supplier to lend them a second-hand machine for some trials.

The next few weeks were filled with experiments on this borrowed machine—experiments carried out in lunch breaks and evenings because of the need to keep existing orders going out of the door. All sorts of adaptations were made—at one point an old filing cabinet and a hair dryer were pressed into service to create a very effective fume extraction system.

Eventually each operator had not only contributed to the emerging design but had adapted and shaped it to suit her particular style of working—a truly flexible production cell obtained for a fraction of the cost of a new machine. Did it work? Within two weeks of starting to use it in earnest, the team had exceeded their original productivity improvement target by 150%. The other benefits are also worth flagging: a high sense of motivation amongst the team—'it's our machine'—and a deep understanding of what makes it tick and how it can be further developed or repaired.

This is not an isolated case—throughout the factory small teams are constantly reconfiguring, adapting, extending or changing the equipment they work with. This is not seen as something special, but has simply become the way things happen. There was a time when people took specific times out to discuss improvements, and made use of a formal process in which they had been trained, but increasingly it has become second nature and happens without people thinking about it. They are still trained—indeed, the culture of the place is one in which learning is something highly valued. People enjoy visiting other firms or exhibitions to get new ideas, swap their own experiences with others and generally act as eyes and ears for new possibilities.

Why do people bother? Ask them and they will tell you how much they enjoy being in control of what they do and feeling that they are allowed to make changes—they recognize the limits and the need to ask before blindly jumping in, but they also acknowledge that almost all of the time the answer is 'yes' to a request to try something out. The company have never had a reward scheme specifically targeted at getting people to come forward with suggestions—'when we first started the reward was you kept your job!'. These days, as the company's performance has gone from strength to strength, the rewards come in the form of an annual bonus and recently through a share ownership scheme.

Nearly five thousand miles away across the Atlantic, the Chaparral Steel plant continues to thrive as one of the most efficient and innovative producers in what is a desperately competitive industry. Their success owes much to exactly the same kind of constant innovation as operates in Excellent Electronics—the factory has become, in Dorothy Leonard-Barton's phrase, a 'learning laboratory'. In her detailed account of how the workforce managed—against industry scepticism and enormous technological odds—to create and stabilize a process for casting near-net shape steel, she highlights exactly the same kinds of behaviour (Leonard-Barton 1995).

Not all examples are dramatic—one of the key features of the real learning organization is that the capacity for systematic finding and solving problems and capturing knowledge from the experience is deeply embedded—it has become 'the way we do things around here'. For example, in the north of the UK, Elmwood Sensors is a company producing heat sensors for the automotive and domestic market. In a brief report on experiences with high-involvement innovation, using a team-based approach, one of the cell team operators gave the description in

Box 9.1 of how her team reduced quality problems to zero defects over a 28-week period—and then maintained that level. Whilst some of the technical details may sound arcane, this extract demonstrates a high degree of awareness amongst the team operators about what they were working on, how that process worked and could be improved and what elements were relevant to capture and ratchet the knowledge gains.

BOX 9.1 Reducing quality problems at Elmwood Sensors.

We managed to keep our scrap rate down to less than 3%. This achievement is due to the fact that, when we hit a problem, we *stop*, and the *problem-solving* starts! We do NOT build scrap. ... The more we problem-solve, the more knowledge we gain. For example, creep rejects are constantly analysed. We started 'pin checking' every pin cycle some time ago and this has saved us a great deal of time. It is easier to re-pin a switch that reads more than three thou' out at the pin and gauge, rather than rejecting it at the creep, having to strip it, re-pin it, re-spin/crimp it and then re-creep it. Obviously the disc plays a major part in the switch, so we have eight discs checked out at the start of a batch, so if there is a problem it can be sorted out before too many completed thermostats are built.

Problems can occur with any job so the focus cell always keeps a job log sheet which contains all the information on the job, what problems have occurred, how we solved the problems, arm used, thou used, etc. so that if the job comes out again we have all the relevant information to refer to ...

Training has played a major part in Right First Time. All the members of the focus team can now use the computer, not only to move and complete batches out to go in and check how the job ran last time. This avoids hunting around for old pin cycles or paperwork if the job last ran on the shop floor...

(This example appeared in *CI News* (Spring 1988, p. 3), a networking publication for a group of organizations involved in trying to implement continuous improvement. More details of the Network can be found in Bessant (1995).)

These are all examples of organizations in which high-involvement innovation has become a way of life—and embedded at its heart is a learning process.

9.3 Why Knowledge Matters

To judge by the prevalence of the use of the term, knowledge management within organizations is becoming an issue of strategic concern in the early 21st century (Nonaka 1991; Blackler 1995; Quintas *et al.* 1997; Teece 1998; Sapsed *et al.* 2002). However we would not have to go back too far to find similar concerns being expressed about the need to develop 'learning organizations' (Senge 1990 a; b; Marquardt and Reynolds 1994; Senge 1999) and, before that, the focus on 'core competence' and the ways in which firms could accumulate and deploy their particular firm-specific knowledge to competitive advantage (Prahalad and Hamel 1990; Bogner *et al.* 1999).

If we can put aside the fashion statements and look for some underlying principles, it becomes clear that we are dealing with a very basic principle. Whilst the terminology varies and often confuses, the underlying message is that firms should seek to identify what they are distinctively good at and then develop and deploy this to gain a competitive advantage. And, because competence has to be accumulated gradually over time, it is hard for others to copy and thus the strategic advantage is more defensible (Kay 1993; Teece 1998).

The key message in this discussion is that competence has to be learned and accumulated over time—and thus there is growing interest in the mechanisms that firms utilize to enable this process. For example, Teece and colleagues look at the ways in which firms frame and reframe ('dynamic capability'), whilst Nonaka focuses on knowledge capture and sharing routines (Nonaka 1991; Teece and Pisano 1994; Krogh *et al.* 2000). Rush *et al.* (1997) and Kleiner and Roth (1997) look at ways of capturing learning from projects. Increasingly, companies are reporting on how they have approached the problem, whilst other writers—for example Senge, Leonard-Barton and Garvin—provide different integrated models of pro-active learning in organizations, indicating the set of capabilities required (Cohen and Levinthal 1990; Senge 1990 a; b; Adler 1992; Leonard-Barton 1995; Kim 1997; Senge 1999; Wenger 1999; Figueiredo 2002; Weick 2002).

It is clear from this that there is no generic solution, but rather that each firm has to work out its own approach; learning capabilities are as firm-specific as competencies. However, it is also clear that there is some commonality of experience—certain classes of approach to the learning problem are regularly used. Examples include R&D, benchmarking, collaboration, structured project review and staff development through training.

We should also take into account the key issue of tacit knowledge. Knowledge does not always exist in usable and written-down form. Codified knowledge—such as papers, instructions, blueprints, recipes, etc.—often represents only the tip of the iceberg in terms of what an organization actually knows about. One of the most influential writers on the subject, Polanyi, makes the distinction between knowledge that is codified and that which is known but not expressed—what he termed 'tacit' knowledge (Polanyi 1967). Tacit knowledge comes from experience and observation but may never be formally articulated or explained. For example, in controlling a chemical process to produce something, an operator may intuitively know just how much heat to give or how fast and for how long things should be stirred to make the product effectively. Yet, if you asked him or her, they would not necessarily be able to explain more than just that they 'know'. They may use simple rules of thumb (heuristics)—and they may well be deploying such tricks of the trade in the same form as they were shown when they first entered the job.

Such tacit knowledge is widespread throughout an organization and represents a significant source of potential advantage. It is knowledge that has been learned but is not available to others so is highly protected; the problem is of course that the organization itself may not know it has it or how to capture and make use of it.

BOX 9.2 Knowledge competition.

Knowledge advantage is not simply associated with product design and technology. In the car industry the major post-war impetus has come from Japanese producers who pioneered an alternative to the dominant mass production models which Henry Ford and colleagues first established in Detroit in the early twentieth century. The Japanese alternative — termed 'lean production' — has provided an alternative model which offers high productivity and quality and much greater flexibility in the face of fragmenting markets; it has become the dominant approach used around the world. Western producers began to notice the Japanese edge in the late 1970s and throughout the 1980s the gap widened until, in a famous study comparing automotive plants around the world, it emerged that Japanese plants were, on average, twice as good as their Western competitors on a wide range of production indicators. Inevitably this led to a flood of anxious managers visiting Japan to try and understand and absorb what it was that they were doing differently. They were extremely surprised to find firms like Toyota prepared to be quite open with their explanations and to allow their competitors to visit and see inside their factories. But the reason was clear — Toyota knew that the production system which they had developed (involving high levels of teamworking and practices like total quality management and just-in-time production) was simple to explain but very difficult to copy. It had taken them around thirty years to learn to make such a system work — and anyone copying it would have to invest heavily in time and money to catch up — by which time Toyota would have moved even further on!

Source: based on Womack *et al.* (1991)

9.4 How Learning Happens

All of these approaches can be mapped onto a basic model of the learning process. For example, Figure 9.1 shows the well-known experiential learning cycle originally put forward by David Kolb, who sees learning involving a cycle of experiment, experience, reflection and concept development (Kolb and Fry 1975). (We saw this earlier in Chapter 7.)

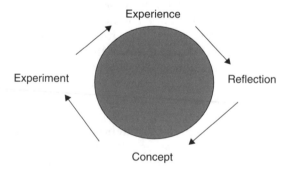

FIGURE 9.1   The learning cycle.

Where an individual or firm enters is not important (though there is evidence for different preferred styles of learning associated with particular entry points). What does matter is that the cycle is completed—and incomplete cycles do not enable learning. Viewed in this way, each of the modes in Table 9.1 can be linked to one or more stages in the learning cycle; this argues for a multiple approach.

TABLE 9.1   Learning mechanisms and their relationship to the learning cycle.

Learning approach	Position on learning cycle	Examples
Benchmarking—learning by comparison	Aids structured reflection	(Camp 1989; Zairi 1996; Massa and Testa 2002)
Collaboration—learning by working with others	Shared experience and experiment	(Dodgson 1993; Marsh and Shaw 2000)
Strategic challenge	Structured and challenging reflection	(Leonard 1992; Baden-Fuller and Pitt 1996; Tranfield *et al.* 1996; Kim 1997)
Training/developing the learners	New concepts Shared experience	Corporate universities (Garvin 1993; Gundling 2000; Graham and Shuldiner 2001)
Project capture—learning from reflection	Reflection	(Roussel *et al.* 1991; Rush *et al.* 1997; Gann and Salter 1998)
R&D and process development—learning from fast failure	Experiment and reflection	Rapid prototyping 'Development factories' 'Learning before doing' (Pisano 1996)

9.5 Learning and High-Involvement Innovation

To return to our core theme in this book, the biggest challenge facing the organization is not which of these mechanisms to choose or how best to implement them, but how to engage and involve a high proportion of the workforce in the process. Learning is the engine that creates innovations—new things and new ways of doing things do not appear by magic, but via the operation of this learning cycle. And, as we have seen, in developing a learning capability we are really concerned with clusters or patterns of behaviours that have become refined and rehearsed and that are increasingly and repeatedly used. A learning organization is one in which this cycle is embedded in the underlying mixture of values and beliefs that drive the 'way we do things around here' (Schein 1984).

The strength of high-involvement innovation is that it embeds a high-frequency learning cycle across much of the organization. For example, in producing their millions of suggestions per year, the employees of Toshiba, Toyota and others are involved in problem finding and solving on a daily basis, and the process they use links to all stages in the learning cycle. The underlying learning behaviours associated with innovation have become rehearsed and reinforced to the point where they really are 'the way we do things around here'.

In particular:

- High-involvement innovation mobilizes more learners across the organization in a formal sense. Instead of innovation being primarily the province of a specialist few, it now becomes the responsibility of the many
- It embodies a systematic (and often standardized) learning process, usually involving some form of explicit problem finding, solving and reviewing methodology, which can be shared and adapted
- It deals in easily digestible increments of learning, which can be absorbed—many and frequent small cycles rather than occasional disruptive big ones

- With its emphasis on display and on measurement (but also on understanding of those measures by users), it formalizes and makes available knowledge that hitherto was in the tacit domain—for example, about critical process variables
- Through involvement of non-specialists, it opens up the possibility for challenges to the accepted solutions; such naïve but often penetrating questions can enable 'unlearning' to take place

Typically, high-involvement innovation activities include systematic search, controlled experiment, structured reflection and capture and sharing of learning. In many cases this is enshrined in a simple problem-solving model such as that propounded by Deming (the Deming wheel of 'plan, do, check, act') or variations of it (Deming 1986). It can also be supported by a wide range of robust tools and techniques. Table 9.2 indicates some examples.

TABLE 9.2   Links between some high-involvement innovation tools and stages in the learning cycle.

Stage in learning cycle	Examples of high-involvement innovation enabling activities
Experiment	Design of experiments
	Brainstorming (Rickards 1988)
	Taguchi methods (Taguchi 1979)
Experience	Structured brainstorming (Cook 1999)
	Nominal group techniques
	Data collection and presentation via the simple seven tools of quality management (Shiba *et al.* 1993)
	Display and charting
	Statistical process control (Owen and Morgan 2000)
Reflection	Root cause analysis
	Flowcharting and process mapping tools (Davenport 1992)
	Video analysis
	CEDAC—cause and effect diagram with addition of cards (Fukada 1990)
Conceptualization	Capture into new procedures
	Statistical process control tools

There is growing empirical support for the view of organized high-involvement innovation programmes as a mechanism for embedding organizational learning. For example, Sirkin and Stalk (1990) in their description of the turnaround of a US paper mill identify four learning loops, whilst the Chaparral Steel case involves a similar process of building a deep understanding of the key process parameters and then extending that through a process of experimentation and consolidation (Leonard-Barton 1992). Sohal *et al.* (2000) explore in depth the links between TQM (as an integrated high-involvement approach) and learning organizations.

9.6 Enabling Learning in Organizations

Garvin (1993) describes a learning organization as 'an organization skilled at creating, acquiring, and transferring knowledge, and at modifying its behaviour to reflect new knowledge and insights' (p. 80). He continues by saying that learning organizations are adept at five activities:

TABLE 9.3   Learning organizations and high-involvement innovation practices.

Features of learning organizations	Explanation	Relevant high-involvement innovation practices
Training and development emphasis	By investing in training and development, organizations can develop not only operational capabilities but also the skills and approaches to learning itself—learning to learn	Formal development of problem-solving skills through tools and techniques. Also emphasizes the importance of individual thinking as well as doing, and seeks to develop this through formal skills training, background personal development, etc.
Establish a formal process	Central to effective organizational learning is the idea of a repeated cycle of action, experience and review	High-involvement innovation revolves around a shared and formalized model of problem finding and solving. These vary from Deming's PDCA to company-specific variants, but they have a common structure
Measurement	Learning depends on being able to evaluate the effect of what has been tried in the way of problem-solutions—and for this we need measurement systems. As Garvin puts it, '... if you can't measure it, you can't manage it...'	Most high-involvement innovation involves some component of measurement—from simple tally charts and data collection through to sophisticated statistical process control techniques
		Measurement also focuses attention on getting *information* about process activities, and in doing so, learning about them and what good performance means. Spreading this awareness across the whole workforce, rather than confining it to specialists, is important; for many people one of the blocks to effective participation in innovation is simply not knowing why improvements are important. Inevitably this moves measurement away from being an instrument for control and towards being a tool that people can use to guide improvement—and it poses major challenges for conventional measurement systems and targets
Document	Closely associated with measurement is the capture of information resulting from experiments in trying to solve	Organizations do not have memories as such, but they do have libraries, databases, procedures, drawings and

(continued overleaf)

TABLE 9.3   *(continued)*

Features of learning organizations	Explanation	Relevant high-involvement innovation practices
	problems. Whether successful or otherwise, there is a high risk of re-inventing the wheel unless information is captured and displayed for others to use	other storage mechanisms for information and knowledge. The challenge in effective innovation is to transfer the experience of individuals to some form in which it can be more easily shared and communicated to others. This process is particularly relevant in dealing with tacit knowledge (Nonaka 1991)
Experiment	A key feature of the learning organization is a climate that allows for extensive experimenting and which does not punish failures if those experiments go wrong. As one manager put it, 'if it ain't being fixed, it's broke', and this approach of continuing experimentation is essential to improving and developing new processes. Trying new things out can be encouraged, for example, by allocating a certain amount of time and resource to experiment—see the 3M example (Gundling 2000)	Core value in high-involvement innovation is a 'no blame' environment in which mistakes are seen as learning opportunities and experimentation is encouraged. Finding out the limits of processes, or possible new ways of managing them, is one of the tasks traditionally carried out in R&D and engineering departments. But mobilizing the resource to do this across the whole organization would take a great deal of effort if it were handled by specialists; high-involvement innovation offers an alternative by giving the responsibility and the authority to everyone to undertake experiments
Challenge	Learning organizations not only spend time documenting the results of problem finding and solving—they also display and communicate them. This serves several purposes: it provides a powerful motivator for the teams or individuals who have been responsible for them, and it also serves to carry over ideas that might find application elsewhere in the organization. Display via storyboard and other approaches may capture the dynamics as well, such that others can learn from the process that the groups went through as well as the results that they achieved	In order to maintain momentum, HII programmes often include not only stretching targets but also continually re-set them. A wide range of HII tools and techniques have been developed to assist this process of systematic challenge, from simple '5 why' approaches to complex analysis. Doing this requires a systematic approach to experiment and challenge and a refusal to accept that anything cannot be improved; as one commentator put it, '... best is the enemy of better...'. In his account of how Toyota reduced set-up times on presses, Shingo describes the relentless re-setting of targets

TABLE 9.3   *(continued)*

Features of learning organizations	Explanation	Relevant high-involvement innovation practices
		to drive the times down from several hours to, eventually, single minutes (Shingo 1983). A UK instrumentation company makes active use of what it terms 'stretch goals'—targets that are deliberately set as very challenging and almost unattainable. An example might be 'on-time delivery whenever the customer wants'; the point is that even if the targets are not reached, the efforts expended in aiming at them will probably have moved the organization a long way forward. In this particular case the stretch target became '90% delivery with a 2 week lead time to customers'—a significant leap from the initial situation of 55% within a 12 week lead time, but one which they have already come close to achieving
Reflect—learn from the past	The key message here is not to accept things at face value but keep challenging as a means of finding improvement possibilities and learning opportunities. Evidence suggests that learning often requires an element of stress in order to break away from traditional ways of looking at or doing things—and without it there is a big risk of doing what we have always done just because we have always done it that way. One example is the well-known Toyota Production System, which involves deliberately running inventory levels in the factory so low that problems emerge—in this way they are employing a powerful 'reveal' strategy to force learning (Monden 1983)	A common problem in establishing learning cycles within organizations is the absence of time, space and structure for reflection. HII programmes are often characterized by regular meetings at which progress is reviewed and new problems are identified for work. In many cases this cycle is daily—a brief 5–10 minute meeting before the shift starts—whilst in others it is a longer weekly session. In each case there is high-frequency reinforcement of HII and an institutionalized and structured approach to reflection and review. Again, many of the tools and techniques in HII are designed as structured aids to this process—from simple benchmarking, fishbone and other analytical tools through to more complex aids

(continued overleaf)

TABLE 9.3   *(continued)*

Features of learning organizations	Explanation	Relevant high-involvement innovation practices
Use multiple perspectives	Another powerful mechanism for enhancing and encouraging learning is to bring different perspectives to bear on a problem. This can be done in a number of ways, ranging from bringing different groups together in cross-functional teams through to broadening individual experience and outlook through training, rotation, secondment or visiting. It is also here that benchmarking plays an important role, providing an opportunity to review and explore how other organizations tackle particular issues and problems	Cross-boundary teams working on problems Tools for cross-boundary analysis—e.g. process mapping, value stream mapping There is a second reason for emphasizing movement of people and perspectives within the organization; such mobility helps to spread knowledge around the organization and builds up a shared 'organizational memory'. With traditional functional and departmental organization it is often possible to reach the situation where the left hand does not know what the right is doing. This can lead, in turn, to re-inventing the wheel, duplication of effort, failed attempts to solve problems because key skills or knowledge are missing, etc. By contrast, moving people around the organization and giving them a chance to see things in new ways or from different perspectives can be a powerful resource
Display	Much of what we learn comes from analysing and understanding mistakes and developing ways of avoiding them in the future. The same holds for organizations; as Maidique and Zirger (1985) put it in their extensive study of learning in new product development, '. . . failure is the ultimate teacher. . .'. By taking time out to review and explore why things went wrong—or right—it is possible to avoid future errors and improve performance on similar or related tasks	Closely linked to documenting the results of HII is the need to display and communicate them. This serves several purposes: it provides a powerful motivator for the teams or individuals who have been responsible for them, and it also serves to carry over ideas that might find application elsewhere in the organization. Display via storyboard and other approaches may capture the dynamics as well, such that others can learn from the process that the groups went through as well as the results that they achieved

- Problem solving
- Experimentation with new approaches
- Learning from their own experience and past history
- Learning from others
- Efficiently (and speedily) transferring this knowledge throughout the organization

Garvin lists several features common to 'learning organizations' and these can be mapped on to high-involvement innovation practices (Garvin 1993). Table 9.3 provides some examples.

9.7 Moving On – Extending the Learning Organization

Much of what would fit with Garvin's framework, or indeed with many other models of learning organizations, can be found in a firm with a good Level 3 capability. Systematic problem finding and solving, documentation and measurement, strategic targeting and deployment, cross-functional problem solving and sharing of perspectives—all of these are well illustrated in the cases in Chapter 7. Even if we accept that some of the other learning organization features like experimentation belong more in a Level 4 capability organization, we are still left with a big question. What is distinctive and challenging about Level 5 and why is it that very few firms can approach this level of capability development?

The difference lies not in moving further up some notional progression but rather in spreading out—ensuring that the high-level capabilities we saw in Chapter 8 are diffused throughout the organization and into its dealings with other organizations. High-involvement innovation becomes just that, something which is the culture—'the way we do things around here'—of the entire system in which the organization operates. Getting to this point will require dealing with a number of specific challenges, including the following:

- Moving beyond 'islands of learning in a sea of ignorance'—the organization may have extended participation beyond the limits of having specialist thinkers and the rest as doers, but is involvement as widespread as it could be? Or is successful involvement more patchy—by level or location in the organization?
- Extending to inter-firm level—this is not simply a matter of managing cross-boundary problem finding and solving (although this poses a significant challenge). What happens at the inter-firm level is that network effects begin to matter and the whole can perform as a system with emergent properties (Best 2001). Under the right conditions the whole can offer much more than the sum of the parts—but enabling this to happen requires development of an awareness of a system identity and the ability to manage in networks (Grandori and Soda 1995; DTI 2000; Dyer and Nobeoka 2000). For most organizations this level of development is still in its infancy, although some interesting experiments have been reported (AFFA 2000; Bessant 2003; Bessant *et al.* 2003).

- Managing learning modes—as we saw in the previous chapter, organizations need to develop the capability to manage both 'do better' and 'do different' modes of innovation. For most of the time, most of the people will be involved in the former—and, as we have seen, the kind of learning organization model propounded by Garvin and others is well suited to this task. Such models involve a cycle of continuous improvement mobilized across and beyond the organization and engaged in reflecting, challenging, rethinking, experimenting and ratcheting the knowledge gains acquired through the process. This process lends itself to the creation of supporting structures and mechanisms that manage to strike a balance between a degree of empowerment and autonomy and the need for control and targeting. It forms the basis for many formalized frameworks that have diffused across a wide range of public- and private-sector organizations—the Baldrige award in the USA, the Deming Prize in Japan, the European Foundation for Quality Management model, Investors in People and approaches based on the Balanced Scorecard are all examples (Garvin 1991; Kaplan and Norton 1996).

But these structures and mechanisms are essentially geared to creating a learning organization capable of dealing with the 'do better' challenge. The problem with 'do different' innovation is that it poses very different challenges. It is disruptive, destructive, hunch-based and uses different knowledge sets—and it is not only inherently much more experimental and risky, but it also may directly conflict with 'the way we do things around here' in the successful 'do better' innovation organization. Christensen (1997) highlights this 'innovator's dilemma', pointing out that sometimes doing the 'right' thing in terms of good practice for 'do better' innovation may actually be doing the wrong thing. His studies of product innovation and market leadership in the hard-disk-drive industry indicate that the prescription of getting close to and working with your best customers—whilst extremely effective in maintaining a stream of 'do better' innovations—actually militated against the breakthrough innovations emerging.

What is needed is a 'second order' learning capability—variously called 'double loop', 'generative learning' or meta-learning—which gives the organization the capability to challenge fundamentally the assumptions on which it has been built and operates (Argyris and Schon 1970; Hedberg 1981; Senge 1990 a; b; Dodgson 1991; Bessant and Buckingham 1993). Resetting the parameters occasionally may be essential to ensuring new growth possibilities through 'do different' innovation, but it also needs to be able to reconnect to the 'single loop' learning cycle to then exploit these innovations through 'do better' innovation activity. One solution to this challenge is to set up separate organizations or divisions to deal with 'do different' innovation, but, as we saw in the previous chapter, this raises the problem of not being able to re-integrate the new innovation stream. So a fundamental challenge to Level 5 organizations is to build 'ambidextrous' capability to handle both types of innovation, to know where and when to switch between them and to ensure close and synergistic links between the two (Tushman and O'Reilly 1996; Day and Schoemaker 2000; Leifer et al. 2000).

9.8 Summary

This chapter describes the Level 5 position in the model originally introduced in Chapter 4. It represents a high level of capability development, one in which there is high involvement in proactive learning behaviour, leading to both 'do better' and 'do different' forms of innovation. To some extent it represents an ideal state—few organizations can honestly claim to approach this level of practice, although there may be pockets where it can be approached. The challenge remains to extend the development of such capability across organizations and increasingly into the networks in which they operate.

References

Adler, P. (1992) 'The learning bureaucracy: NUMMI,' in Straw, B. and Cummings, L. (eds), *Research in Organizational Behaviour*. JAI Press, Greenwich CT.

AFFA (2000) *Supply Chain Learning: Chain Reversal and Shared Learning for Global Competitiveness*. Department of Agriculture, Fisheries and Forestry—Australia (AFFA), Canberra.

Argyris, C. and D. Schon (1970) *Organizational Learning*. Addison Wesley, Reading, MA.

Baden-Fuller, C. and M. Pitt (1996) *Strategic Innovation*. Routledge, London.

Bessant, J. (1995) 'Networking as a mechanism for technology transfer; the case of continuous improvement,' in Kaplinsky, R., den Hertog, F. and Coriat, B. (eds) *Europe's Next Step*. Frank Cass, London.

Bessant, J. (2003) 'Supply chain learning,' in Westbrook, R. and New, S. (eds), *Supply Chains: Concepts, Critiques, Futures*. Oxford University Press, Oxford.

Bessant, J. and J. Buckingham (1993) 'Organizational learning for effective use of CAPM,' *British Journal of Management*, **4** (4), 219–234.

Bessant, J., R. Kaplinsky and R. Lamming (2003) 'Putting supply chain learning into practice,' *International Journal of Operations and Production Management*, **23** (2).

Best, M. (2001) *The New Competitive Advantage*. Oxford University Press, Oxford.

Blackler, F. (1995) 'Knowledge, knowledge work and organizations,' *Organization Studies*, **16** (6), 1021–1046.

Bogner, W., H. Thomas and J. McGee (1999) 'Competence and competitive advantage: towards a dynamic model,' *British Journal of Management*, **10**, 275–290.

Camp, R. (1989) *Benchmarking—The Search for Industry Best Practices that Lead to Superior Performance*. Quality Press, Milwaukee, WI.

Christensen, C. (1997) *The Innovator's Dilemma*. Harvard Business School Press, Cambridge, MA.

Cohen, W. and D. Levinthal (1990) 'Absorptive capacity: a new perspective on learning and innovation,' *Administrative Science Quarterly*, **35** (1), 128–152.

Cook, P. (1999) *Best Practice Creativity*. Gower, Aldershot.

Davenport, T. (1992) *Process Innovation: Re-engineering Work through Information Technology*. Harvard University Press, Boston, MA.

Day, G. and P. Schoemaker (2000) *Wharton on Managing Emerging Technologies*. Wiley, New York.

De Geus, A. (1996) *The Living Company*, Harvard Business School Press, Boston, MA.

Deming, W.E. (1986) *Out of the Crisis*. MIT Press, Cambridge, MA.

Dodgson, M. (1991) *Technological Collaboration and Organizational Learning*. Science Policy Research Unit, University of Sussex, Brighton.

Dodgson, M. (1993) *Technological Collaboration in Industry*. Routledge, London.

DTI (2000) *Learning across Business Networks*. Department of Trade and Industry, London.

Dyer, J. and K. Nobeoka (2000) 'Creating and managing a high-performance knowledge-sharing network: the Toyota case,' *Strategic Management Journal*, **21** (3), 345–367.

Figueiredo, P. (2002) 'Does technological learning pay off? Inter-firm differences in technological capability-accumulation paths and operational performance improvement,' *Research Policy*, **31**, 73–94.

Fukada, R. (1990) *Cedac—A Tool for Continuous Systematic Improvement*. Productivity Press, Cambridge, MA.

Gann, D. and A. Salter (1998) 'Learning and innovation management in project-based, service enhanced firms,' *International Journal of Innovation Management*, **2** (4), 431–454.

Garvin, D. (1991) 'How the Baldrige award really works,' *Harvard Business Review*, November/December, 80–93.

Garvin, D. (1993) 'Building a learning organization,' *Harvard Business Review*, July/August, 78–91.

Graham, M. and A. Shuldiner (2001) *Corning and the Craft of Innovation*. Oxford University Press, Oxford.

Grandori, A. and G. Soda (1995) 'Inter-firm networks: antecedents, mechanisms and forms,' *Organization Studies*, **16** (2), 183–214.

Gundling, E. (2000) *The 3M Way to Innovation: Balancing People and Profit*. Kodansha International, New York.

Hedberg, B. (1981) 'How organizations learn and unlearn,' in Nystrom, H. and Starbuck, W. (eds), *Handbook of Organization Design*. Oxford University Press, Oxford.

Kaplan, R. and D. Norton (1996) 'Using the balanced scorecard as a strategic management system,' *Harvard Business Review*, January/February.

Kay, J. (1993) *Foundations of Corporate Success: How Business Strategies Add Value*. Oxford University Press, Oxford.

Kim, L. (1997) 'The dynamics of Samsung's technological learning in semiconductors,' *California Management Review*, **39** (3), 86–100.

Kleiner, A. and G. Roth (1997) 'How to make experience your company's best teacher,' *Harvard Business Review*, September/October, 172–177.

Kolb, D. and R. Fry (1975) 'Towards a theory of applied experiential learning,' in Cooper, C. (ed.), *Theories of Group Processes*. Wiley, Chichester.

Krogh, G., K. Ichijo and I. Nonaka (2000) *Enabling Knowledge Creation: How to Unlock the Mystery of Tacit Knowledge and Release the Power of Innovation*. Oxford University Press, Oxford.

Leifer, R., C. McDermott, G. O'Conner, L. Peters, M. Rice and R. Veryzer (2000) *Radical Innovation*. Harvard Business School Press, Boston, MA.

Leonard, D. (1992) 'Core capabilities and core rigidities; a paradox in new product development,' *Strategic Management Journal*, **13**, 111–125.

Leonard-Barton, D. (1992) 'The organization as learning laboratory,' *Sloan Management Review*, **34** (1), 23–38.

Leonard-Barton, D. (1995) *Wellsprings of Knowledge: Building and Sustaining the Sources of Innovation*. Harvard Business School Press, Boston, MA.

Maidique, M. and B. Zirger (1985) 'The new product learning cycle,' *Research Policy*, **14** (6), 299–309.

Marquardt, M. and A. Reynolds (1994) *The Global Learning Organization*. Irwin, New York.

Marsh, I. and B. Shaw (2000) 'Australia's wine industry. Collaboration and learning as causes of competitive success,' Working paper, Australian Graduate School of Management, Melbourne.

Massa, S. and S. Testa (2002) 'Benchmarking as a strategic tool to enable continuous innovation,' in Smeds, R. (ed.), *Continuous Innovation in Business Processes and Networks*. HUT Press, Helsinki University of Technology, Helsinki.

Monden, Y. (1983) *The Toyota Production System*. Productivity Press, Cambridge, MA.

Nonaka, I. (1991) 'The knowledge creating company,' *Harvard Business Review*, November/December, 96–104.

Owen, M. and J. Morgan (2000) *Statistical Process Control in the Office*. Greenfield Publishing, Kenilworth.

Pisano, G. (1996) *The Development Factory: Unlocking the Potential of Process Innovation*. Harvard Business School Press, Boston, MA.

Polanyi, M. (1967) *The Tacit Dimension*. Routledge and Kegan Paul, London.

Prahalad, C. and G. Hamel (1990) 'The core competence of the corporation,' *Harvard Business Review*, **68** (3), 79–91.

Quintas, P., P. Lefrere and G. Jones (1997) 'Knowledge management: A strategic agenda,' *Long Range Planning*, **13** (3), 387.

Rickards, T. (1988) *Creativity at Work*. Gower, Aldershot.

Roussel, P., K. Saad and T. Erickson (1991) *Third Generation R&D: Matching R&D Projects with Corporate Strategy*. Harvard Business School Press, Cambridge, MA.

Rush, H., T. Brady and M. Hobday (1997) *Learning between Projects in Complex Systems*. Centre for the Study of Complex Systems.

Sapsed, J., J. Bessant, D. Partington, D. Tranfield and M. Young (2002) 'Teamworking and knowledge management; a review of converging themes,' *International Journal of Management Reviews*, **4** (1).

Schein, E. (1984) 'Coming to a new awareness of organizational culture,' *Sloan Management Review*, Winter, 3–16.

Senge, P. (1990a) *The Fifth Discipline*. Doubleday, New York.

Senge, P. (1990b) 'The leader's new work: building learning organizations,' *Sloan Management Review*, **32** (1), 7–23.

Senge, P. (1999) *The Dance of Change: Mastering the Twelve Challenges to Change in a Learning Organization*. Doubleday, New York.

Shiba, S., A. Graham and G. Walden (1993) *A New American TQM: Four Practical Revolutions in Management*. Productivity Press, Portland, OR.

Shingo, S. (1983) *A Revolution in Manufacturing: The SMED System*. Productivity Press, Cambridge, MA.

Sirkin, H. and G. Stalk (1990) 'Fix the process, not the problem,' *Harvard Business Review*, July/August, 26–33.

Sohal, A., M. Terziovski, A. Howell and M. Morrison (2000) 'Establishing mutual dependence between TQM and the learning organization: a multiple case study analysis,' *The Learning Organization*, **7** (1), 23–31.

Taguchi, G. (1979) *Introduction to Off-Line Quality Control*. Central Japanese Quality Control Association, Magaya.

Teece, D. (1998) 'Capturing value from knowledge assets: the new economy, markets for know-how, and intangible assets,' *California Management Review*, **40** (3), 55–79.

Teece, D. and G. Pisano (1994) 'The dynamic capabilities of firms: an introduction,' *Industrial and Corporate Change*, **3** (3), 537–555.

Tranfield, D., S. Smith, S. Whittle and V. Martin (1996) 'Strategic regeneration of manufacturing through changing routines,' *International Journal of Operations and Production Management*.

Tushman, M. and C. O'Reilly (1996) *Winning through Innovation*. Harvard Business School Press, Boston, MA.

Weick, K. (2002) 'Puzzles in organizational learning,' *British Journal of Management*, **13**, September, S7–S16.

Wenger, E. (1999) *Communities of Practice: Learning, Meaning, and Identity*. Cambridge University Press, Cambridge.

Womack, J., D. Jones and D. Roos (1991) *The Machine that Changed the World*. Rawson Associates, New York.

Zairi, M. (1996) *Effective Benchmarking: Learning from the Best*. Chapman and Hall, London.

Chapter 10

DOING IT!

This chapter addresses the question of making the journey towards high-involvement innovation. It reports on the experiences of a number of organizations that have been wrestling with this challenge over many years and draws together an approach to such organizational development, which firms can use to maintain momentum in their quest for higher and sustainable levels of participation in innovation.

10.1 To Recap . . .

It may be worth beginning this chapter by taking stock of what we have covered so far. In the early part of the book a case was made for the importance not only of innovation to the survival of the organization, but also of developing a high-involvement capability to contribute to that process. Chapter 2 explored some of the significant body of evidence that underpins the case for high-involvement innovation. But, whilst there is considerable potential for engaging the natural creativity of people across the workforce, there are some significant barriers to making it happen—as Chapter 3 highlighted. If we are serious about wanting to do this, then we need to set about dismantling many of the beliefs and resulting behaviour patterns associated with the ways in which we used to operate and replacing them with new ones, which are reinforced until they become embedded and take root as the 'new way we do things around here'—the high-involvement innovation culture.

Chapter 4 provided a roadmap for that journey, and the following chapters explored the model in terms of five key stages on the journey towards effective high-involvement innovation. What we have not considered explicitly—although we have made repeated reference to it in the cases and other discussion—is the challenge of actually organizing and managing the change process towards high-involvement innovation.

Some of the pre-conditions for successful implementation of such a change include:

- Recognizing that it is likely to be an uphill struggle to try and rebuild organizations at the level of altering belief and behaviour systems. If anything, it is not even a matter of climbing uphill but rather of trying to climb a downward escalator—so many forces within the organization will be acting to try and restore the equilibrium of old patterns, which are deeply embedded. It is not surprising that many of the most successful cases of high involvement can trace their roots back to a significant crisis that threatened the survival of the organization. At this point old ways of thinking and working become useless—in some cases they were part of what got the organization into trouble—and so there is a break point that can be exploited to install new behaviour patterns. (Significantly the term 'crisis' derives from the Greek word for 'turning point')
- Putting in place structures and mechanisms that can 'fix' any changes made and the gains they bring, providing a 'ratchet' effect for the change process. Such 'fixing' elements will effectively articulate and clarify key beliefs and behaviour patterns and help reinforce and embed them
- Active management of the change process to try and steer and direct implementation and to make adjustments and improvements to both the content and delivery mechanisms. Given the number of people involved, the complexity of the behaviour changes required and the problems of an organization always trying to revert to its 'default' conditions, doing this requires skills on a par with fast jet formation flying!
- Making use of a measurement and reference framework to help this process. By assessing development of capability against such a framework, it is possible to get a diagnostic 'fix' on the organization's position on the journey—how far has it come, where and what else has to develop, etc.? A side benefit of this is that it may also help to make progress visible to others—key sponsors, participants and other stakeholders
- A structured organizational development process that links such diagnostic positioning to the design and implementation of change interventions, which are then reviewed and the cycle repeated

Experience of firms trying to implement change along the road to high involvement confirms this picture—as Box 10.1 highlights.

BOX 10.1 Typical barriers to moving forward in developing high-involvement innovation capability.

- *Narrow focus of CI initiative*—limiting the impact to local areas that do not offer the opportunity for people from other departments to get involved
- *Superficial implementation*—such as buying in expertise and technology, or giving glossy presentations or training programmes, without taking into account the underlying behaviours that need to be changed or developed
- *Copying programmes used by other organizations* without taking the local context into account, for example, company culture, educational level of workforce or the reason for CI implementation

- *Not changing emphasis of the CI programme* to rejuvenate enthusiasm, re-focus attention and sustain the momentum
- *Aligning CI to specific activities* in selected areas of the company, which can lead to very localized improvements that may have a limited impact on the overall aims of the company
- *Introducing an overly complex CI programme*, which incorporates a number of philosophies and projects, can prove difficult to co-ordinate and may quickly fizzle out as people start to suffer from initiative overload
- *Not using effective measurement* and feedback mechanisms to monitor and evaluate the success of the programme
- *Company culture* — lack of time, resistance to change and fear of the unknown. Or trying to enforce change on people at a pace that is too fast, or without first gaining their support and trust
- *Lack of management commitment* or active involvement, including little or no understanding of what the change process involves and what role they are expected to play in the process

Based on Gallagher and Austin (1997).

10.2 Some Journeys

The journey towards high-involvement innovation is long and difficult. This is not just a turn of phrase, but an apt description of the experience of many organizations. The attractions of involving people are clear and many far-sighted companies began trying to mobilize this potential back in the 1980s. Their progress since then is less a rapid scoot down a smooth tarmac-surfaced motorway than an uphill struggle over rocks, around potholes and with frequent dead ends where the only thing to do was to go back and find another way forward. Two examples follow.

Danfoss

This company is a major player in the engineering industry and widely regarded in its home country and internationally as a leader in its field and in its organization and management structures. It began in the early 1980s with a concerted campaign to introduce the principles of Total Quality Management. Despite an extensive awareness raising programme and a big investment in training in the basic concept, the idea never really took root—with hindsight because there was little middle-management commitment, no real attempt at measurement, no link to the real business drivers and no deployment of those into goals, etc. 'It was very much a vision thing—we were following a Juran-style prescription but somehow failed to get real involvement' (Juran 1951). By 1985 the programme had run aground and there was a fair degree of hostility towards the concept. (For more detail on this case see Vaag (2001).)

1991 saw a second large-scale attempt, which was reasonably successful in about a third of the company's plants. Much of the impetus behind the success stories came from a parallel initiative in Business Process Re-engineering, which involved a series of step-changes and which created a demand for follow-up continuous improvement. The success was mainly at the big-hit project level, though, and the difficulties of sustaining involvement remained.

Partly in response to this, a focused shop floor-oriented programme was launched in 1993 called 'Managing for success', which concentrated on simple, local-level improvements—essentially in line with what has now come to be labelled total productive maintenance (see Chapter 7). Things like cleaning up workplaces, simple machine improvements, etc. became the targets and a tradition of high-frequency incremental innovation began to emerge.

The company has continued to use various 'fashionable' themes to drive the involvement and improvement message—for example, lean production.

Complete Computers

This is a large manufacturer of IT systems and employs several thousand staff in a variety of locations in the UK and overseas. It has been active in the quality field for an extended period and has made several attempts to update and enhance its activities to enable higher levels of involvement. In this particular example, the problem of 'plateau' effects is discussed—a common experience amongst companies that manage to implement Level 2 capability and then find the pattern of involvement and activity beginning to level off or even decline; Westbrook and Barwise (1994) also mention this difficulty. In dealing with this issue the company shows the value of developing and implementing new and complementary enabling vehicles and of refocusing the programme.

The initial impetus for total quality originated in the mid 1980s and was based on the concept of conformance quality using the four principles of the Crosby (1977) approach:

- Conformance to requirements
- Prevention
- Zero defects
- Price of non-conformance (PONC) (cost of doing things wrong)

The programme was designed and implemented by external consultants, supported by a budget of around £2m and involved training literally thousands of people through a two-tier programme—the Quality Education System for managers and supervisors and the Quality Awareness Experience for other employees. This programme consisted of four half-day sessions on site. The training also introduced a Quality Improvement Process and a range of tools to support this process.

In conducting quality training across the whole organization, the aim was to develop a common understanding and language and to communicate that everyone at all levels in the organization had the ability to contribute toward quality improvement. Continued communication of quality improvement efforts was ensured through the creation of a hierarchy of steering committees and review boards. A secondary aim of the structure of quality committees was to spread ownership and responsibility for quality as widely as possible.

Managers were expected to actively demonstrate their quality commitment through teamwork, through the introduction of a vehicle for implementing improvement and through seeking opportunities to publicize the Quality Improvement Process. To help motivate employee involvement a corporate-wide recognition system was introduced. Under this scheme, any member of the organization could nominate somebody or be nominated themselves. It operated on four levels of recognition, each of which attracted a range of gifts, certificates and pins based on the assessment of a Recognition Council. Typically 3000–4000 awards were given each year, with the top winners receiving a significant prize such as a short holiday abroad.

Corrective Action Scheme   In order to operationalize the new philosophy and involve all employees in the Quality Improvement Process, the Corrective Action Scheme was introduced, which aimed to involve employees in identifying process-related problems. A practice of specifying and agreeing requirements between internal customers and suppliers was introduced, whereby any 'customer' could raise a Corrective Action (CA) on a 'supplier' who did not meet agreed outputs. Although the CA would be raised in relation to another person, the problem identified would relate to the process rather than that person. In operation it was based on the Crosby methodology, DEFICE (DEfine the problem, Fix the non-conformance, Identify the root cause, Correct the problem, Evaluate and follow up).

To support the operation of the scheme, there were 200 CA Co-ordinators, each co-ordinating around 100 people. The manner in which the CA was resolved varied according to the nature of the problem. If appropriate, a Corrective Action Team (CAT) could be set up to resolve the issue, either within a business or across businesses, and would disband having completed this task. However, in some case CATs continued to operate with a permanent review status. In this way, their role was more similar to the number of quality circles that were in operation around the organization, mainly in the UK manufacturing operations. In contrast to the CATs, these tended to be work-based improvement groups identifying local improvements on an ongoing basis.

One of the early problems with the scheme was the sentiment shared by many managers that the fewer CAs raised in their area the better, because CAs were seen by many as a sign that they had let people down. These negative feelings associated with the scheme meant that people were keen to complete the CA as soon as possible—in many cases after the short-term 'fix' phase, rather than proceeding to correcting the root cause and evaluation phases. Instead, the company wanted to create a climate in which high numbers of CAs were seen as a positive indicator of the extent of improvement activity.

Once established, around 10 000 CAs a year were being raised, and the majority of these were implemented. On the positive side, most people genuinely felt empowered to raise CAs. From this perspective, the scheme had some success in breaking down barriers between levels and promoting involvement on an organization-wide scale. There was, however, no measure of the numbers of employees who had actually been involved in raising or solving CAs. The scheme co-ordinator's view was that the 10 000 CAs a year probably came from no more than 10% of the employees, and could even be as little as 1%. Any success, therefore, was more likely to be attributable to pockets of high activity. For example, many CAs were raised by the customer service desk.

The existence of these pockets also highlighted that the nature of the scheme, based around the concept of internal customers and suppliers, was one in which there were natural raisers of CAs (e.g. sales divisions) and natural receivers (e.g. design and manufacturing units). In particular, many people in the sales divisions felt they were apart from the system and that their role was simply to 'raise CAs on other people'.

This attitude illustrates the strong personal connotations that became associated with the scheme. Whilst the intention was to highlight process faults, the fact that CAs were directed toward individuals led to a blame culture, where people receiving them felt they had let someone down. Effectively, the CA Scheme placed an emphasis on identifying other people's problems. Consequently, many people did not feel comfortable raising them. It was generally felt that the bureaucracy of the system discouraged people from using it in their local work area (raising a CA involved completing a four-part, double-sided, four-coloured form). The degree of bureaucracy and prioritization of the system also encouraged people to submit only 'big' issues—sometimes something had to go drastically wrong before any action was taken.

The use of the Crosby concept of the Price of Non-Conformance (PONC) exacerbated this bias toward bigger issues. The need to identify the PONC—the cost to the company of this process going wrong—created an emphasis on problems with clear tangible cost implications rather than other process problems with greater intangible costs, for example, customer-focused processes.

One final drawback of the system was that it was oriented toward problems rather than improvement opportunities. The scheme was effectively telling people they only had the right to improve things if they had previously gone wrong or were about to go wrong. As such, it did little to create a culture where 'everything can always be improved'.

Suggestion Scheme   Although the CA scheme provided the main focus for the quality improvement effort, a suggestion scheme was also introduced so that people could submit other ideas, which they felt fell outside the remit of the CA—for example, if the idea was not process-related or was not in response to something that had gone wrong. The suggestions were filled in on a form and placed in a suggestion box; they were then passed on to a Review Committee. However, the organization placed little emphasis on this scheme and the level of suggestions had been progressively declining.

Despite some of the problems experienced in the operation of the CA Scheme, the implementation of quality improvement, based on the Crosby principles, had been largely successful. Key achievements over the first three years included:

- Significant increases in on-time delivery and product reliability
- Reduction in rework and unnecessary paperwork
- 80% reduction in unresolved software bugs
- Annual saving of £10 million in administration systems development
- Planning cycle times reduced from 40 to 13 days
- Total inventory reduced from £220m to £138m
- Output per employee increased by 30%

Introducing a High-Involvement Continuous Improvement Scheme   Although many of the elements associated with continuous improvement (CI) had already been implemented as part of the other quality phases—in terms of both cultural and infrastructural change and in providing opportunities for employees to be involved in improvement activities—it was not until this stage that a specific focus on and commitment to CI was formally adopted and made an integral part of the strategy.

The impetus for the introduction of a new vehicle to promote CI emerged as a result of a visit to Japan by senior managers, who were impressed with the high levels of employee involvement in implementing change to improve processes through 'kaizen'. This was distinct from the involvement activities in the UK company in several ways. First, employees in the UK were engaged in identifying, rather than solving, problems. Second, their involvement was largely problem-, as opposed to improvement-, oriented. In comparing the different approaches of the two organizations, the board recognized the need to shift the emphasis of their improvement activities away from project-based improvements toward a system that promoted more 'ongoing' improvement—a large number of small improvements rather than a much smaller number of larger projects. The aim of such a shift would be to create a culture where improvement was seen as a way of life.

Building on earlier experiences with the CA scheme, the co-ordinator appointed to develop a new CI scheme wanted to ensure that the new process was unbureaucratic and easy to use, to facilitate high levels of participation and company-wide implementation. However, she realized that in doing so it was likely that people would prefer the new system and usage of the CA system and suggestion scheme would decline. Therefore it was important that the type of activities covered by these two schemes fell within the remit of the new vehicle so that the activities were not lost. There was also need to ensure that the vehicle was consistent with the culture throughout the company internationally and to avoid some of the problems experienced with the CA system where the culture in some countries, such as Scandinavia and Hong Kong, was not conducive to pointing the finger at an individual. Finally, the new vehicle had to be linked to the overall quality strategy of the business so that it was seen as a development not a replacement.

In order to reach these objectives, there were a number of underlying beliefs that would need to be communicated and integrated into the organizational culture, namely:

- Everything can always be improved
- The best ideas on how to improve the company's processes and systems, including the process of continuous improvement itself, come from the people using them
- We need to learn from other people, other ideas, other processes
- Our people are trusted to have the desire and commitment to improve their work
- Innovation requires a blame-free culture
- The role of the manager in this CI process is to enable people to express their ideas and to empower them to implement their proposed solutions

Originally, it was thought that the easiest way to develop a vehicle to meet these aims would be to look for examples being used by other companies and apply this learning—or possibly even buy their support system. With this aim, the co-ordinator embarked on a study mission looking at 20 companies over a six-month period. However, none of the examples observed in these companies was totally suited to Complete Computers' (CC)'s needs, because of the different environments in which they were operating:

- Some of the examples had been applied only in production areas, whereas CC wanted a vehicle capable of operating across the company in all functional areas
- Some of the successful vehicles were operating within relatively small companies with charismatic leadership. In contrast, CC had a dispersed workforce of around 25 000 people and therefore would need to operate via email rather than personally
- There were lots of successes in green-field, start-up companies, which had set up and selected staff with this in mind, but CC had a history of previous initiatives and would have to incorporate some of these into the new vehicle

Consequently, the co-ordinator put together a project team comprising people from different parts of the organization, whose task was to clarify the current problems and issues that would impact on the success of the new vehicle and then design it. In doing so, the team put together a simple draft process for the new vehicle in order to gauge people's initial reactions. They then conducted a survey, of both employees and managers, across a number of businesses to investigate attitudes to raising improvement ideas and how these were currently handled.

The results were very revealing. Whilst the responses from managers implied that all staff knew they had a responsibility to improve the process and that they themselves would be responsive to suggestions from their employees, many employees responded that they made few suggestions as they did not see it as part of their work role. They also felt that their managers would not be particularly open to such suggestions as it would mean additional work. Where employees did make suggestions, they used a range of mechanisms, such as the CA system, the suggestion scheme and talking directly to their manager.

Piloting the Scheme   Drawing on the survey results, a pilot scheme was launched in one of the European units with a staff of around 100 people. Within this scheme projects were run via the standard electronic mail system used by office workers. A message was sent to all employees in the selected areas saying that they were looking for ideas. Ideas were to be sent to their manager, who was obliged to respond. To support the activity, a co-ordinator was identified for each pilot site. The co-ordinators received copies of all ideas and were responsible for making sure that managers responded.

The pilots initially ran for six weeks. Encouragingly, many ideas were generated in each of the pilot areas, although some initial encouragement was needed. For example, in the initial pilot no ideas were submitted over the first eight days. However, once the local co-ordinator put in two very small ideas, 17 ideas were submitted the same day. It was found that initial reluctance was because people felt that their ideas were too small. The learning from this pilot, where co-ordinators were asked to launch the system by submitting some relatively trivial ideas, was incorporated into the final design of the scheme.

One of the main problems experienced in the pilots related to the levels of response from managers. In one case they found piles of suggestions on a manager's desk. On investigating this, it emerged that the manager did not know how to respond. It was then realized that training was needed to support the management role in the process, rather than assuming that managers knew how to respond. Because of the poor response levels from managers, once the system had collected around 150 ideas, the co-ordinators were overloaded since they found themselves having to chase about half of them. It was also difficult to measure the success of the pilot since the standard mail system was not designed to generate the type of management information required to monitor progress (such as the number of people using the system, number of usable ideas, response rates, etc.).

The main learning that came out of these first pilots was the need for more co-ordinator support, so that the management of the system took up less of their time, and the need for a measurement system. To deal with the issue of measurement, a localized extension to the office mail system was developed, which provided an electronic form for people to send to their manager. Each form had a number so that they could be identified and managed more easily by the co-ordinators, who stored all completed forms in a database. Employees were also able to access the local database and it was hoped that, by doing so, more employees would be encouraged to submit ideas by seeing that no idea was too trivial.

With these amendments, a second wave of pilots was launched and two of the original pilots were continued. These ran for six weeks and, once again, there were no problems in encouraging employees to submit ideas. The co-ordinators found the management of the system a little easier than in the first pilots, since the system now generated some of the information they had previously had to chase. However, there was little improvement in the need to chase managers who did not respond (or responded in the wrong way) and, therefore, they were still unable to cope when the number of ideas on the system exceeded 150. Some co-ordinators found that they were spending between one and one and a half days a week on the scheme, mainly chasing responses. Extrapolating this on an organization-wide scale, 250 co-ordinators would be needed to support the total workforce of 25 000 and, if each was spending, on average, one day a week on the scheme, this would be equivalent to 50 new full-time jobs to support the process. This demand on resources was clearly too high, yet many of the tasks the co-ordinators were doing were so important that without them the process would not work.

As a result of the combined effects of the range of problems that had emerged from the pilots, it was decided that full-scale implementation could not go ahead without significant changes to the system. Consequently, work was begun on developing a system based on a database. The main advantage of the new system was that it automatically did the chasing that the co-ordinators had previously done manually. The system was set up to take different courses of action depending on the content of certain fields. For example, it was able to remail those who had not responded (co-ordinators could set their up their own parameters on the system, for example, how many days to wait before the system should send a reminder). It could also keep a history of a particular idea—who had seen it and when. One field indicated whether the suggestion was a Corrective Action or an idea for improvement and the system could be set up to take different actions accordingly.

Full Launch of the CI Scheme   Initially, the full-scale introduction of the scheme was through a gradual, largely voluntary process. Rather than telling businesses they had to adopt it, efforts were made to 'sell' it to business managers. If the managers themselves decided that they wanted to introduce the system, levels of commitment were likely to be considerably higher. However, as the implementation proceeded, the approach shifted toward making the CI scheme a mandated, rather than recommended, system.

Before it was launched in a particular area, a period of six to eight weeks was spent in preparation. Managers and co-ordinators worked together in devising an introduction plan. The pre-launch period was also spent customizing the scheme to the local situation. This flexible approach was an important aspect of the implementation since it ensured that ownership was transferred from the corporate centre to the local business.

To support the operation of the scheme, a Help Desk and a support mail box were introduced. In addition to providing a help line, the staff on the Help Desk were also responsible for running co-ordinator training, giving presentations, producing a newsletter and preparing management reports and statistics related to the operation of the scheme. This help-line service was intended for anyone who required help, although it was largely the co-ordinators who utilized the service. In recognition of this, a Workbench for co-ordinators was set up along side the Help Desk, where they could try out the system and access a library of books and articles and useful improvement-related tools. The co-ordinators were also encouraged to network with other co-ordinators, which was supported by a co-ordinators' newsletter every two weeks.

To encourage people to submit ideas, a range of recognition items was introduced with a triangular theme, symbolizing the scheme's logo. Initially, a supply of triangular-shaped boxes of chocolates and a triangular mouse pad with the scheme's logo were made available, which businesses could use to thank people for their first idea, or on reaching a particular number of ideas. Other businesses have since supplied their own triangular gifts. A range of options in the rewards available and the need for these to be chosen by the local manager was one lesson learnt from the pilots, particularly in view of the international dimension.

Later a lottery was introduced to encourage people to submit ideas, whereby an idea was picked at random and the winner received £2000 to donate to a charity chosen by their business. The press office worked with that business to publicize the outcomes of the lottery.

Success of the CI Scheme   In the first six months of operation, 7500 people raised 5500 ideas, an average of 73 ideas per 100 people (although on average, these ideas were actually coming from 20% of those on the system). After a year of operation, around 60% of the workforce was connected to the scheme, a total of approximately 15 000 ideas had been raised, 58% of which had been implemented.

10.3 A Generic Organizational Development (OD) Model

The value of reference models like that presented in Chapter 4 is that they provide a basic 'road map' for the journey towards development of high-involvement innovation capability. By reviewing the experience of many different organizations travelling on the same road and through the same stages, we can begin to detect patterns in the likely obstacles and pitfalls that they might encounter, and in the strategies that they use to deal with them. In this way it becomes possible to build an organizational development process to support firms in their implementation and development of high-involvement innovation capability.

The process follows the typical organizational development cycle of diagnosis, identification of relevant changes, intervention and review (French and Bell 1995); see Table 10.1. Diagnosis involves positioning a firm on the model and from this identifying which behaviours need introducing, which need reinforcing, which need further development, etc. At this stage knowledge about common blocks and barriers can be used to help identify likely problem areas and knowledge of enabling mechanisms used elsewhere to deal with these can be used to design intervention strategies.

TABLE 10.1 Outline organizational development methodology for developing CI.

Basic stages in OD	CI stages	Support tools
Audit—survey and feedback	Position against reference model	An assessment tool, a diagnostic instrument based on the reference model
Target areas for action	Identify next stages in development with respect to reference model Identify potential blocks and enablers	Strategic review of progress drawing on: • Reference model and description • Blocks and enablers 'catalogue' • Archetypes of 'firms like us' to provide guidelines
Implement		'Toolbox' of resources—enablers Action-learning network
Review and repeat cycle		

10.4 The Role of Framework Approaches

As organizations develop in their high-involvement capability, so they need more focused ways of monitoring and measuring their progress. Instead of trying to instill some very basic behaviour patterns in *ad hoc* fashion (Level 1) they begin to look for areas for particular effort or locations within the organization that require focused attention. This diagnostic process can be assisted by the use of structured reference frameworks—of the kind we have been using in this book. There are a number of such tools available, some of which have diffused widely—for example, in the USA the Malcolm Baldrige National Quality Award has become a widely used template for assessment and organizational development of total quality capabilities (Garvin 1991). Similarly, in Europe the European Foundation for Quality Management (EFQM) offers a framework which is widely used and which has been the subject of a number of national level campaigns promoted by government. (Details of the EFQM and its various support programmes including the European Quality Award framework can be found on its website: http://www.efqm.org.) Both of these models and the principle of structured frameworks for assessment can be traced back to the Deming Prize and other awards in Japan.

Although nominally intended to help make a judgement around awarding a prize or recognition, the real value of these frameworks and their emergent purpose has been in helping firms monitor and measure their progress towards higher levels of capability. They share several key elements:

- A structured framework describing high levels of capability ('excellence' is a term often used), which is rooted in both research and experience
- Within this framework a disaggregated view of the components of success or excellence—it is not a case of doing a single thing well, but of all-round performance in a number of areas
- A measurement framework that awards some kind of score for levels of achievement in different areas of the model
- External/independent assessment via trained facilitators or the development of in-house certificated assessors who can perform this role using the reference model framework
- Mechanisms for development and improvement of the model over time

---

BOX 10.2 The Business Excellence Model.

One of the most widely used frameworks in Europe has been that developed by the European Foundation for Quality Management, which can be used either as a self-assessment tool or as a framework within which trained external assessors can provide an audit of a firm's progress towards improved performance. It is regularly updated to take account of new developments in both business concerns and the availability of new tools and approaches. Research has been carried out on the model to assess its relevance and validity and there appears to be a strong correlation between award winners and business success (Hendricks and Singhal 2002).

The basic framework model is as below:

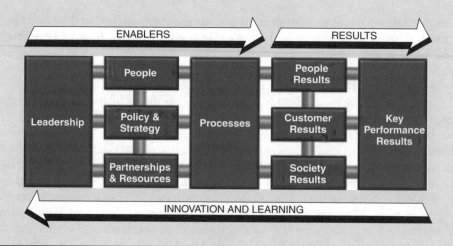

Another source of frameworks for assessment is in national, international or company-based standards. There is no doubt that the increasing importance attached to ISO 9000 as a 'badge' to indicate some guarantee of quality-enhancing processes helped to give focus to efforts amongst firms to develop high-involvement capability around the total-quality theme. Similarly many companies make extensive use of quality and performance assessment schemes to look at their suppliers, not only in terms of what they deliver and when, but also in the processes that they use to create and deliver their offerings. Achieving certification in standards of this type—such as Ford's Q101—is often perceived as more difficult than national standards, and the targets for year-on-year continuous improvement are often more stretching (Bessant *et al.* 2001a).

Frameworks vary widely in their focus, from those that are somewhat high-level exhortations to improved organizational culture through to more specific and focused assessment and development frameworks. Table 10.2 gives some examples, from which it can be seen that there is broad overlap between many of them and a high degree of variation in focus. They form part of a wider trend towards the use of 'benchmarking' auditing as an enabler of organizational development and also as a way of highlighting where and how good practice can be observed and from which learning can take place.

TABLE 10.2 Audit frameworks as an aid to organizational development for high-involvement innovation.

Assessment framework	Key focal points
Baldrige Award, Deming Prize, EFQM, Business Excellence Model	Total quality (Garvin 1991; Hendricks and Singhal 2002)
TPM prize	Total productive maintenance (Japan)
Investors in People, Partnerships with People	HR practices (DTI 1997; IIP 2002)
Balanced Scorecard	Financial and non-financial measures of performance (Kaplan and Norton 1996)
Six Sigma	Quality processes applied across all activities
ISO 9000 and derivatives	Quality assurance processes
Living innovation, Innovation—your move, Innovation audits	Innovation processes and culture (Chiesa *et al.* 1996; Francis 2001)
CIRCA model (see Chapter 4)	High-involvement innovation (Bessant *et al.* 2001a)
Capability-maturity model	Software development innovation (Paulk *et al.* 1993)
Q101 and company based schemes	Supplier quality assurance
Probe, Microscope, UKBMI, etc.	General manufacturing performance indices

10.5 The High-Involvement Innovation Model

Within this context the model that we have been working with is relatively specific. It focuses in on the key sets of behavioural routines that enable effective involvement in the innovation process and can help organizations to explore and develop these. In this respect, it fits within some of the broader assessment frameworks outlined in Table 10.1—for example, within EFQM there is a section on employee involvement, whilst the IIP framework is focused strongly on HR practices with a strong emphasis on high involvement.

The high-involvement innovation reference model is offered as a generic model and can be configured and adapted to suit specific situations that build on such high-involvement innovation behaviours. For example, it has been developed further by the Confederation of Danish Industries for use with small and medium-sized enterprises as part of an organizational development programme (Jorgensen and Boer 2002). Enabling continuous improvement innovation within the product development process has been another fertile area of application and development and research describing survey and case study work using this approach is described in Caffyn (1998) and Corso *et al.* (2001).

The Appendix describes the model in more detail and highlights the contribution of the different behavioural components. A simplified version suitable for an initial self-assessment by an organization of its high-involvement innovation capability is available on the website accompanying this book: http://www.wiley.co.uk/innovation/.

10.6 Implementation in Practice

The above section describes and illustrates the diagnostic stage of the organizational development process, but on its own this is not enough—organizations need not only to know where they are on the journey, but also what they could or should do to move further along. This requires the design and testing of a range of enabling mechanisms and resources—structures, procedures, training, tools, etc.

Whilst each organization involves a unique configuration of existing culture, operating contingencies and prior experiences, there is some degree of convergence around the journey that they are trying to make. In particular, it is becoming clear that progress in implementing high involvement is inhibited by a set of commonly experienced and typical problems—for example, losing momentum and focus because of a lack of measurement capability or ineffective connection between idea generation and implementation. By the same token, there is a broad set of 'enablers'—interventions such as training, tools, structures, procedures, etc.—which can be deployed to help deal with specific blocks. Each organization needs to adapt and shape these enablers to their own particular circumstances, but there are significant opportunities for learning through experience-sharing.

Table 10.3 gives some examples of typical blocks and enablers that emerged in the research.

Experience with making the journey tends to have been concentrated around the first three levels in the model—and the resulting knowledge base has been well populated in terms of useful and proven enabling resources. As we have seen in the detailed discussion of these levels, a series of structures, tools, vehicles, etc. can help embed and reinforce key behaviours and help reduce the likelihood of reverting to older behavioral patterns. The availability of a well-documented toolkit and a series of case studies makes it possible for organizations to access and configure enabling resources in a number of ways.

For example, there is a growing number of 'packaged' intervention programmes available from consultancies, which offer a structured, step-by-step approach to developing capabilities at least up to Level 3. Many of these build on a mixture of 'standard' enablers linked to a diagnostic framework (such as the

TABLE 10.3 Example enablers for organizational development.

Behaviour/routines	Blockage	Enablers
'Getting the CI habit'	No formal process for finding and solving problems	Basic problem finding/solving model—for example, Deming's 'plan, do, check, act' (PDCA) or similar structural model plus training
	Ideas are not responded to	Simple idea management system, based on rapid response
	Lack of skills in problem solving	Training in simple tools—brainstorming, fishbone techniques, etc.
	Lack of motivation	Recognition system
	No structure for enabling activities to happen	Simple vehicles, based on groups
	Lack of group process skills	Facilitator training
'Focusing CI'	No strategic impact	Focus problem solving on strategic targets/policy deployment
Spreading the word	Lack of co-operation across divisions	Cross-functional teams
	Lack of process orientation	Process modelling tools and training
Leading CI	Conflict between espoused and practised values	Articulation and review
The learning organization	No capture of learning	Post-project reviews Storyboard techniques Encapsulation in procedures
Continuous improvement of continuous improvement	Lack of direction	Formal steering group and strategic framework
	Running out of steam	Regular review and relaunch of high-involvement innovation activities

EFQM model or the Balanced Scorecard) or to systematic capability-enhancing approaches such as Six Sigma. There is also considerable scope from sharing experiences about the implementation issues and from reviewing cases, exchanging ideas about enablers, inter-organizational visits and other forms of networked learning.

The challenge in these remains twofold. First, there is a risk that they will offer a standard, 'one size fits all' approach. Although the behavioural abilities that we wish to see installed are generic in nature, we have seen that each organization has its own highly contingent set of conditions under which it operates. So creating and implementing interventions designed to enable high involvement must, of necessity, involve a high degree of configuration and adaptation to suit local circumstance.

Second, the knowledge base around high-involvement resources is much less well populated as we move to the higher levels of the model, and the nature of the organizational development challenge makes it less likely that Level 4 and above would be susceptible to the same kinds of standardized approaches. There is undoubtedly a role for external and independent agents but this is increasingly likely to be one of process facilitation rather than expert consultancy.

10.7 Roads to Rome

As Rijnders and colleagues point out, implementation is much less widely reported on than other dimensions of high-involvement innovation (Rijnders *et al.* 2000). Most reports are descriptions of tools, or before and after case studies or descriptions of blocks and barriers and how they can be avoided. Whilst a helpful base on which to draw, this does not help with the key question facing organizations—how to introduce the changes and manage and sustain the change process?

Evidence on programmes in this direction is worrying. For example, data on TQM implementation suggests that a significant proportion of such efforts fail—either to deliver the expected benefits or to sustain the levels of involvement originally achieved (EIU 1992; Krishnan *et al.* 1993; Lu and Sohal 1993; Bennett and Kerr 1996; Kanji 1996; Knights and McCabe 1996; Liu 1998). In part this is likely to be linked to the ways in which such programmes are implemented and particularly in the (unrealistic) belief that there is 'one best way' to carry this out (Hackman and Wageman 1995; Beyer and Ashmos 1997).

Research by Smith, Tranfield and colleagues on TQM implementation identified three generic clusters of approaches to the implementation question (Tranfield *et al.* 1992). '*Visionary TQ*' describes those programmes that emphasize senior-management enthusiasm for a major cultural change in their organizations. Triggered by the experience of others, or by presentations from evangelical consultants, such an approach begins with the articulation of a new vision, which is then shared and elaborated throughout the organization. Enabling this vision comes down to a specialist group, who have to convert enthusiasm and passion into a workable system. The strengths of such an approach are in the top-level commitment and the resourcing which follows that—but these are also its weaknesses. Such commitment is often not sustained—the attention of senior management is taken by something else and support wavers. As a result, people think that this is another initiative or following current fashions and there is little persistence—something that is not helped by the fact that structures and enabling mechanisms may not have had a chance to take root in the organization.

'*Planned TQ*' by contrast represents an approach that is driven by systems and procedures—typified by the response many organizations made to the challenge of ISO 9000 and its variations. In this model the strengths lie in systems and mechanisms supported by tools and training. Although implementation of this kind is often successful in achieving short-term goals such as ISO certification, its weakness often lies in the lack of perceived strategic importance and the lack of active involvement and participation from amongst the workforce. It is seen as the province of specialists and middle managers and long-term support from other stakeholders may be hard to sustain.

'*Learning TQ*' relates to those programmes with a strong human-resource development emphasis, often aiming to equip people with a broader set of skills and to create a more supportive kind of organization. Emphasis on training, teamwork, empowerment and other features means that a high level of employee 'buy-in' can often be achieved in such programmes—but their weakness may lie in the lack of system and structure to provide focus for the long term. Strategic advantage may not emerge and benefits may be concentrated on improved morale and motivation rather than business-level benefits—with the result that the return on heavy training investment is questioned.

The point the authors make about this analysis is that there are at least three coherent approaches to implementation, each with its own strengths and weaknesses. None is 'right' or 'wrong', but rather each is suited to particular circumstances at a particular time. The key to long-term sustainability and effective implementation is, in their view, the need for a fourth 'meta-level' approach, which rings the changes between these three options. 'Transformational TQ' takes into account the need to use all three (and possibly other) approaches to sustain momentum and to address the components needed to ensure high involvement, strategic support and direction and underlying system and structure.

This pattern—of constantly reviewing where and how the system is developing and then making appropriate changes—is central to the implementation issue. As the case studies we highlighted at the beginning of the chapter show, developing high-involvement innovation is a long-term journey, not a short-term excursion. Having the behavioural abilities to monitor progress and to either fine-tune and adapt (single loop) or move to a different level or approach (double loop) is of critical importance in managing the implementation process.

10.8 Summary

This chapter has looked at the question of implementation—how organizations might approach the challenge of building high-involvement innovation capability. Throughout the book we have stressed that this is not something that can be switched on or plugged in at will but is a living culture—a shared pattern of behaviours which define 'the way we do things around here'. Implementing such a culture requires an extended learning and development process.

References

Bennett, D. and M. Kerr (1996) 'A systems approach to the implementation of total quality management,' *Total Quality Management*, **7**, 631–665.

Bessant, J., S. Caffyn and M. Gallagher (2001a) 'An evolutionary model of continuous improvement behaviour,' *Technovation*, **21** (3), 67–77.

Bessant, J., R. Kaplinsky and R. Lamming (2001b) 'Enabling learning in supply chains,' in *What Really Matters in Operations Management—8th Annual Conference of European Operations Management Association*. University of Bath, Bath.

Beyer, J. and D. Ashmos (1997) 'Contrasts in enacting TQM: mechanistic vs. organic ideology and implementation,' *Journal of Quality Management*, **2**, 3–37.

Caffyn, S. (1998) *Continuous Improvement in the New Product Development Process*. Centre for Research in Innovation Management, University of Brighton, Brighton.

Chiesa, V., P. Coughlanu and C. Voss (1996) 'Development of a technical innovation audit,' *Journal of Product Innovation Management*, **13** (2), 105–136.

Corso, M., A. Martini, E. Paolucci and E. Pellegrini (2001) 'The role of ICT in fostering continuous product innovation in SMEs,' in Gertsen, F. (ed.), *CI2001: From Improvement to Innovation*. Aalborg University Press, Aalborg, Denmark.

Crosby, P. (1977) *Quality is Free*. McGraw-Hill, New York.

DTI (1997) *Competitiveness through Partnerships with People*. Department of Trade and Industry, London.

EIU (1992) *Making Quality Work: Lessons from Europe's Leading Companies*. The Economist Intelligence Unit, London.

Francis, D. (2001) *Developing Innovative Capability*. University of Brighton, Brighton.

French, W. and C. Bell (1995) *Organizational Development: Behavioural Science Interventions for Organization Improvement*. Prentice Hall, Englewood Cliffs, NJ.

Gallagher, M. and S. Austin (1997) *Continuous Improvement Casebook*. Kogan Page, London.

Garvin, D. (1991) 'How the Baldrige award really works,' *Harvard Business Review*, November/December, 80–93.

Hackman, J. and R. Wageman (1995) 'Total quality management; empirical, conceptual and practical issues,' *Administrative Science Quarterly*, **40**, 309–342.

Hendricks, K. and V. Singhal (2002) *The Impact of Total Quality Management on Financial Performance: Evidence from Quality Award Winners*. European Foundation for Quality Management, Brussels.

Jorgensen, F.G.F. and H. Boer (2002) 'Development of a team-based framework for conducting self-assessment of continuous improvement,' in Smeds, R. (ed.), *Continuous Innovation in Business Processes and Network*. HUT University Press, Helsinki University of Technology, Helsinki.

Juran, J. (1951) *Quality Control Handbook*. McGraw-Hill, New York.

Kanji, G. (1996) 'Implementation and pitfalls of total quality management,' *Total Quality Management*, **7**, 331–343.

Kaplan, R. and D. Norton (1996) 'Using the balanced scorecard as a strategic management system,' *Harvard Business Review*, January/February.

Knights, D. and D. McCabe (1996) 'Do quality initiatives need management?,' *The TQM Magazine*, **8**, 24–26.

Krishnan, R., A. Shani, R. Grant and R. Baer (1993) 'In search of quality improvement: problems of design and implementation,' *Academy of Management Executive*, **7**, 7–20.

Liu, C. (1998) 'Pitfalls of total quality management in Hong Kong,' *Total Quality Management*, **9**, 585–598.

Lu, E. and A. Sohal (1993) 'Success factors, weaknesses and myths concerning TQM implementation in Australia,' *Total Quality Management*, **4**, 245–255.

Paulk, M., B. Curtis, M. Chrissis and M. Bush (1993) *Capability Maturity Model for Software*. Software Engineering Institute, Carnegie-Mellon University, Pittsburgh, PA.

IIP (2002) *Investors in People*. Investors in People, London.

Rijnders, S., H. Boer and R. Schuring (2000) 'Developing a process typology of CI implementation,' in *CI 2000 from Improvement to Innovation*. Aalborg University, Aalborg, Denmark.

Tranfield, D., S. Whittle, S. Smith and M. Foster (1992) 'Total quality and change management: integrating approaches for organization design,' in *Factory 2000*. Institution of Electrical and Electronic Engineers, London.

Vaag, M. (2001) 'The introduction of CI through TPM,' in Gertsen, F. (ed.), *CI2000: From Improvement to Innovation*. Aalborg University Press, Aalborg, Denmark.

Westbrook, R. and P. Barwise (1994) *Continuous Improvement in Leading FMCG Companies*. London Business School, London.

Chapter 11

FURTHER CHALLENGES

This final chapter looks at new and emerging challenges in the field of high-involvement innovation. In particular, it looks at the changing innovation agenda, where new strategic challenges such as concern for environmental sustainability are coming to the forefront. It also looks at the challenge of building and sustaining high-involvement innovation at the inter-firm level. With an increasing emphasis on networks comes the need to think about and learn to manage beyond the individual organization—and this poses significant questions about how to develop and sustain an innovation culture at network level.

11.1 Introduction

In many ways this chapter is about what is *not* in the book. We have looked in some detail at experiences on the road to building and sustaining competitive advantage through high-involvement innovation, and we have explored some of the key issues involved at various stages of this journey. Making the journey poses plenty of challenges for organizational development, but we should also take into account that we are dealing with a moving target. As more and more organizations learn and develop high-involvement innovation capability at the early levels on our model, so our attention shifts to a new set of challenges associated with moving further forward. What we will do here is to look—briefly—at five of these emerging challenges, which set up an agenda for research and experimentation over the coming years.

11.2 Challenge 1. Further on up the Road

Interest in high-involvement innovation has always been around, but there is no doubt that the last part of the 20th century brought the subject onto centre stage. In part this was triggered by an increasingly demanding environment in which organizations required massive improvements in flexibility, quality, speed and other key performance dimensions, as well as offering low costs.

And in part it came from a realization—led by experience in Japan—that significant traction on these problems could be gained by moving to higher levels of employee involvement. The result has been an acceleration of diffusion of the concept and—as far as we have data on diffusion—a considerable increase in the number and type of organizations trying to engage in high-involvement innovation.

Whereas the question that dominated in the 1980s was 'what?', the 1990s saw it shift to 'how?'. Many organizations have now placed themselves on Level 2—trying systematically to put high involvement in place—and a significant number are connecting it to their strategic plans through various forms of policy deployment and other Level 3 enablers. Chapter 2 provided an overview of some of the research that has led to this shift in thinking.

The difficulties of getting this far are not to be underestimated but—as we saw in Chapter 8—there is a risk that firms will consolidate at Level 3 and not try for further progress. In part, this comes because powerful driving frameworks like total quality management and lean thinking emphasize the 'do better' part of the innovation agenda. Error correction, quality improvement, waste reduction, set-up time reduction and other activities have proved highly valuable targets for high-involvement innovation, but all of these are essentially working within an existing envelope. It becomes difficult to push the boundaries of the envelope, especially when there is so much slack to take up and where the organization is able to obtain a regular 'dividend' of performance improvement in what it already does.

The challenge here is to stretch development of high-involvement innovation into more widespread autonomous innovative activity of the Level 4 variety.

11.3 Challenge 2. Developing 'Do Different' Innovation Routines

Associated with developing higher-level innovation capability is the challenge of creating new routines to support more radical 'do different' innovation. Much of what constitutes 'good practice' in innovation management is built on experience of 'do better' work and it is possible for organizations to develop a sophisticated portfolio of structures and procedures to deal with it. But when it comes to 'do different' innovation, there is much less clarity about what organizations should do and how they should carry this out. In part this is because 'do different' innovation happens less frequently (so there is less opportunity to 'routinize' useful behaviours) and in part it is because of the higher levels of uncertainty involved. At the limit, looking for new products, processes and markets simultaneously involves groping around in some very dark space.

Research on this issue is still in its infancy (Boisot 1995; Day and Schoemaker 2000; Leifer *et al.* 2000; Bessant *et al.* 2003a), but a number of themes emerge:

- Need for different routines—for example, in searching and in picking up weak signals, often from unexpected places
- Conflict between 'do better' and 'do different' routines—sometimes the very things that support 'do better' innovation may act against 'do different' innovation. For example, staying close to good customers and co-developing

incremental improvements with them is an excellent prescription for 'do better' innovation, but may act to exclude linkages with others who may form the embryonic network of 'do different' innovation
• Need for unexpected linkages and connections
• Need for looser controls and structures

These routines need articulating and clarifying, but they will only emerge through experimentation—something that many firms are reluctant to undertake because of the high risks which can be involved. If they do try to experiment, they will often do so in a controlled environment—a separate division or operation, a skunk works, etc. Potentially a Level 4 high-involvement organization could offer an extended laboratory not only for developing innovations themselves but also for learning about how to produce them—but, as we have seen, it requires a brave organization prepared to 'let go' at this level.

11.4 Challenge 3. Inter-Organizational Innovation

No firm is an island—and, increasingly, competitive advantage is a function of various forms of inter-organizational networking. It is difficult enough to manage within an organization, but as we move to inter-organizational relationships so we realize how limited our knowledge base and practical experience are. There is a need to develop new routines but—as experience in supply management shows, for example—simply articulating a 'good practice' model of how it could happen is a long way from enabling it to happen in reality (Lamming 1993; Cox and Hines 1997; Hines *et al.* 1999).

A significant aspect of this is the potential for inter-firm innovation—whether of the 'do better' variety, driving out waste and resolving problem issues at the interface between players in chains and networks, or of the 'do different' variety, working together to combine experiences and knowledge sets to create new products or processes. There has been growing exploration of mechanisms and structures that can support or facilitate inter-firm shared learning (Bessant and Tsekouras 2001). The potential benefits of such learning include mutual support, risk reduction through shared experimentation, exposure to different perspectives and challenging reflection on progress (Dent 2001).

A number of different configurations of inter-firm learning can be identified and loosely grouped under the heading of 'learning networks'. Essentially these address the problems that firms have in innovation, both within their own activities and later in the interfaces that they share with other organizations. Learning is not easy and, at the organizational level, many factors act to minimize the chances of its occurring—as Table 11.1 shows.

The potential benefits of *shared* learning include the following:

• In shared learning there is the potential for challenge and structured critical reflection from different perspectives
• Different perspectives can bring in new concepts (or old concepts that are new to the learner)
• Shared experimentation can reduce perceived and actual costs risks in trying new things

TABLE 11.1 Key blocks to learning.

Learning block	*Underlying problem*
Lack of entry to the learning cycle	Perceived stimulus for change is too weak Firm is isolated or insulated from stimulus Stimulus is misinterpreted or underrated Denial
Incomplete learning cycle	Motivation to learn is present but process of learning is flawed Emphasis given to some aspects—e.g. experimentation—but not to all stages and to sequence
Weak links in the cycle	Reflection process is unstructured or unchallenging Lack of access to or awareness of relevant new concepts Risk avoidance leads to lack of experimentation Lack of sharing or exchange of relevant experiences—parochial search for new ideas 'Not invented here' effect
Lack of learning skills or structure	Lack of supporting and enabling structures and procedures
Knowledge remains in tacit form	Lack of mechanisms for capturing and codifying learning
Repeated learning	Lack of mechanisms for capturing and codifying learning leads to repetition of same learning content
Learning is infrequent, sporadic and not sustained	Mechanisms for enabling learning are not embedded or are absent

- Shared experiences can provide support and open new lines of inquiry or exploration
- Shared learning helps explicate the systems principles, seeing the patterns—separating 'the wood from the trees'
- Shared learning provides an environment for surfacing assumptions and exploring mental models outside of the normal experience of individual organizations—helps prevent 'not invented here' and other effects

Arguably this approach has much to offer inter-organizational learning and the experience of regional clusters of small firms provides one important piece of evidence in support of this. The ability of textile or ceramic producers to share knowledge about product and process technology and to extend the capabilities of the sector as a whole is recognized as central to their abilities to achieve export competitiveness. In the case of Italian furniture, for example, a dominant position in world trade has been achieved and sustained over 15 years—yet the average firm size is less than 20 employees (Piore and Sabel 1982; Best 2001).

If we accept that there is potential in the concept of learning in networks or clusters, two questions are raised. The first is the extent to which we can consciously build in this concept in the design and operation of 'managed networks'—such as supply chains or technological collaborations. The second is the extent to which it can be used as an alternative or complementary model for enabling learning around a specific theme—for example, technology transfer, upgrading and competence development amongst small firms.

Learning networks can take many forms—Table 11.2 lists some examples. Although there is wide variety, the primary feature of such learning networks is

TABLE 11.2   Outline typology of learning networks, based on Holti and Whittle (1998) and Bessant and Francis (1999).

Type	Learning target	Examples
Professional	Increased 'professional knowledge and skill' = better practice	Professional institution
Sector-based—association of firms with common interests in the development of a sector	Improved competence in some aspect of competitive performance—e.g. technical knowledge	Trade association Sector-based research organization
Topic-based	Improved awareness/knowledge of a particular field—e.g. a new technology or technique in which many firms have an interest	'Best practice' clubs
Region-based	Improved knowledge around themes of regional interest—for example, SMEs learning together about how to export, diffuse technology, etc.	'Clusters' and local learning co-operatives
Supplier or value-stream based	Learning to achieve standards of 'best practice' in quality, delivery, cost reduction, etc.	Particular firms supplying to a major customer or members of a shared-value stream
Government-promoted networks	National or regional initiatives to provide upgrades in capacity—knowledge about technology, exporting, marketing, etc.	Regional development agencies, extension services, etc.
Task support networks	Similar to professional networks, aimed at sharing and developing knowledge about how to do a particular—especially novel—task	Practitioner networks

that they all use the principle of shared learning to enable innovation—whether (as in most cases) in the form of 'do better' improvements or (occasionally) to support radical 'do different' developments. However, experience with such models suggests that, even at the basic 'do better' level, the difficulties of putting it into place mean that progress will be slow (AFFA 2000; DTI/CBI 2001; Bessant et al., 2003b). As a recent UK government report indicates, 'learning is not a natural feature of business networks'. It is unlikely to thrive unless it is part of the emergent new models for inter-company collaboration which stress trust, co-operation and mutual dependence' (DTI 2000).

Once again the challenge is one of developing new routines through experimentation rather than trying to absorb and embed those that are well proven. Obtaining the benefits from such inter-organizational innovation is, again, going to depend on learning and deploying new routines to deal with working within networks. Experience suggests that many of the basic principles in our model, and suitably adapted and configured enabling mechanisms, can be applied.

11.5 Challenge 4. Focus of Innovation

Much of the early reported experience of high-involvement innovation was from manufacturing, and within that sector from what were mainly 'shop floor' activities. There has been an expansion of effort in other areas, recognizing the ubiquitous demand for innovation across all kinds of organizations and also the generic potential of high-involvement innovation. For example, much work has been carried out in service sectors, looking at how principles of high-involvement innovation can be applied even where the 'product' is intangible (Owen and Morgan 2000). Although R&D has traditionally been the province of innovation specialists, there is growing recognition that many of the tools and disciplines we associate with enabling higher involvement can usefully be applied in a broader context (Endres 1997; Dilani and Pearson 2000).

Whilst much early work was focused on stabilizing and improving the processes within organizations to create and deliver products and services to satisfy existing customers, an increasing amount of emphasis has been given to looking at the new product/service creation process as a target for high-involvement innovation (Caffyn 1998; Cooper 2003). And, although the driver for innovation has always been strong in businesses that compete directly for customers, the scope for improvements in non-profit and public-service activities—such as health care, education, police work, etc.—is just as high and therefore the potential application of high-involvement principles is just as great (Kaplinsky et al. 1995).

So there is still considerable scope for elaborating the basic model of high-involvement innovation and particularly for looking at ways in which enabling mechanisms can be developed and configured to suit particular local conditions and sector contingencies.

Beyond this there is clearly a need to explore further and emerging targets for innovation. Much high-involvement innovation has been hitherto concerned with meeting the challenges of becoming and remaining competitive—dealing with issues like cost reduction, quality enhancement, waste elimination, time compression, etc. But new drivers are emerging, which will also represent important targets for future innovation and require adaptation and configurations of mechanisms and resources to enable high-involvement innovation. One clear example is the growing concern with the sustainability agenda, with organizations and organizational networks trying to develop 'greener' approaches to what they offer and how they deliver it.

11.6 Challenge 5. Inter-Cultural Learning

High-involvement innovation is not a new concept, and it is one that relates to a basic human capability—to find and solve problems creatively. Whilst there have been particular periods when it has been exploited to good effect and where a range of enabling resources—tools, techniques, structures, etc.—have emerged, there is no particular geographical source for it. The case of Japan is often cited, but although post-war conditions were favourable for its development and diffusion there, the 'Japanese model' derived from experience in the USA and was transferred via programmes to help economic reconstruction. (In turn some of the American model drew on earlier European ideas.)

Development in Japan tended to overshadow experience being accumulated elsewhere—for example the strong socio-technical and group work tradition in Scandinavia and various activities within the 'humanization of work' programmes in Germany. In fact, what we have is a global laboratory, in which many different countries are the sites of experiments and experiences in putting high-involvement innovation in place (Boer *et al.* 1999; Gertsen 2000; De Jager *et al.* 2002; Smeds 2002).

Whilst we should be very clear that simply copying what works in one country is a recipe for failure, such diversity offers enormous learning opportunities. Mimicking the quality-circles approach of Japan led many American and European firms into difficulties during the 1970s, because the idea was transplanted with no thought for the underlying cultural context—strong group-work norms etc. But taking the basic idea and adapting it to suit local circumstances in various problem-solving teams, workgroups etc. has proved enormously valuable.

What is needed are mechanisms to capture and share country-specific experiences and tailor and adapt ideas emerging from them to suit different national cultural contingencies. Such international networking is an analogue of the firm-level groupings where traction is gained on the journey towards high-involvement innovation through the inter-change of experience, ideas and enablers.

11.7 Conclusions

In a book that has the idea of continuous innovation at its heart it becomes difficult to draw a line and make some form of closure. This chapter has tried to identify where and how the high-involvement innovation field is moving and some of the emerging and challenging directions for the future.

Innovation is, as we noted at the start of this book, not a luxury or optional item on an organization's agenda, but a survival imperative. Put simply, without continuous and well-directed change, the prospects of being able to maintain a position, never mind grow, in an increasingly hostile environment are not promising. So every organization needs to give this topic a high priority—and, to judge from the increasing use of the word in mission statements, annual reports and other public announcements, this is the case for many of them. The question is whether or not they can deliver on the expressed commitment to innovation.

We can think, a little fancifully, in terms of organizations having a kind of 'IQ'—an 'innovation quotient'. Have they got sufficient innovation capacity to meet the challenges they are facing? This IQ is a complex mixture of an all-round capability, targeted at innovation in product/service offerings, processes that deliver those, the contexts into which they place their offerings and the overall ways in which they frame what they do. It also needs to take account of short-term 'steady state', 'do what we do better' innovation and longer-term, 'breakthrough', 'do different' innovation, and to strike an effective balance between the two. Above all, it depends on the ability to organize and manage the process of translating often weak signals about possible changes into successfully adopted and implemented innovations.

Like all open-ended problems, this one has no single 'right' answer, but rather a set of potential and complementary solutions. Much undoubtedly depends on things like strategic targeting of innovation, energizing leadership, access to adequate resources, which fuel the knowledge base for innovation, development and maintenance of different competencies, etc. 'High involvement' in this context is a significant theme, in the sense that innovation is a co-operative, knowledge-based process. Organizations need to learn to work across organizational and knowledge boundaries, to develop and manage networks and partnerships beyond their own confines, to link different perspectives on needs and means, to foster communities of practice, and so on. These themes form part of the emerging and significant agenda for research and experimental practice around innovation in the 21st century.

One component of this compound prescription is the ability to mobilize and involve more people in the process. Since every human being is capable of creative behaviour, at a minimum the IQ of an organization is likely to be enhanced by the sheer volume of effort if attempts are made to bring more people into the process. But the potential goes much deeper—innovation is particularly about creative and new combinations of needs and means and the development of those combinations into effective and implemented solutions. Bringing different knowledge sets to bear (including formal qualifications, personal and professional experience, tacit knowledge, emotional intelligence and interpersonal skills) offers much greater traction on the innovation problem. The whole can be significantly greater than the sum of its parts, and in surprising and exciting ways.

Enabling this to happen—and, more importantly, to happen regularly such that it represents the 'normal' pattern of behaviour in the organization—is not easy. This book sets out a crude road map for the journey towards such a goal—and, even though the map is still only a basic sketch, it does indicate that the road is less a four-lane highway than a relatively lightly trodden path. Whether organizations decide to embark on the journey or not is a matter of choice, but, with the destination being something that can make a significant contribution to survival and growth in an increasingly hostile environment, it may well be worth while taking a few steps in that direction.

References

AFFA (2000) *Supply Chain Learning: Chain Reversal and Shared Learning for Global Competitiveness.* Department of Agriculture, Fisheries and Forestry—Australia (AFFA), Canberra.

Bessant, J. and D. Francis (1999) 'Using learning networks to help improve manufacturing competitiveness,' *Technovation*, 19 (6/7), 373–381.

Bessant, J. and D. Francis (2003a) 'Managing radical organizational transformation', *Management Decision*, forthcoming.

Bessant, J., R. Kaplinsky and R. Lamming (2003b) 'Putting supply chain learning into practice,' *International Journal of Operations and Production Management*, 23 (2).

Bessant, J. and G. Tsekouras (2001) 'Developing learning networks,' *A.I. and Society*, 15 (2), 82–98.

Best, M. (2001) *The New Competitive Advantage.* Oxford University Press, Oxford.

Boer, H., A. Berger, R. Chapman and F. Gertsen (1999) *CI Changes: From Suggestion Box to the Learning Organization.* Ashgate, Aldershot.

Boisot, M. (1995) 'Is your firm a creative destroyer? Competitive learning and knowledge flows in the technological strategies of firms,' *Research Policy*, **24**, 489–506.

Caffyn, S. (1998) *Continuous Improvement in the New Product Development Process*. Centre for Research in Innovation Management. University of Brighton, Brighton.

Cooper, R. (2003) 'Profitable product innovation,' in Shavinina, L. (ed.), *International Handbook of Innovation*. Elsevier, New York.

Cox, A. and P. Hines (eds) (1997) *Advanced Supply Management: The Best Practice Debate*. Earlsgate Press, Boston, UK.

Day, G. and P. Schoemaker (2000) *Wharton on Managing Emerging Technologies*. Wiley, New York.

De Jager, B., M. Welgemoed, C. De Jager, C. Minnie, J. Bessant and D. Francis (2002) 'Enabling continuous improvement—an implementation case study,' in R. Smeds (ed.), *Continuous Innovation in Business Processes and Networks*. HUT University Press, Helsinki.

Dent, R. (2001) *Collective Knowledge Development, Organizational Learning and Learning Networks: An Integrated Framework*. Economic and Social Research Council, Swindon.

Dilani, J. and A. Pearson (2000) 'Continuous improvement within the scope of an integrated quality management system. R&D experience,' in F. Gertsen (ed.), *From Improvement to Innovation*. Aalborg University Press, Aalborg, Denmark.

DTI (2000) *Learning Across Business Networks*. Department of Trade and Industry, London.

DTI/CBI (2001) *Supply Chain Learning—A Resource for Management*. 'Fit for the future', DTI/CBI, London.

Endres, A. (1997) *Improving R&D Performance the Juran Way*. Wiley, New York.

Gertsen, F. (ed.) (2000) *From Improvement to Innovation*. Aalborg University Press, Aalborg, Denmark.

Hines, P., P. Cousins, R. Lamming, D. Jones and N. Rich (1999) *Value Stream Management: The Development of Lean Supply Chains*. Financial Times Management, London.

Holti, R. and S. Whittle (1998) 'Guide to developing effective learning networks in construction,' Report IP/26, CIRIA/Tavistock Institute of Human Relations, London.

Kaplinsky, R., F. den Hertog and B. Coriat (1995) *Europe's Next Step*. Frank Cass, London.

Lamming, R. (1993) *Beyond Partnership*. Prentice Hall, London.

Leifer, R., C. McDermott, G. O'Conner, L. Peters, M. Rice and R. Veryzer (2000) *Radical Innovation*. Harvard Business School Press, Boston, MA.

Owen, M. and J. Morgan (2000) *Statistical Process Control in the Office*. Greenfield Publishing, Kenilworth.

Piore, M. and C. Sabel (1982) *The Second Industrial Divide*. Basic Books, New York.

Smeds, R. (ed.) (2002) *Continuous Innovation in Business Processes and Networks*. Helsinki University of Technology Press, Helsinki.

DETAILS ON
THE HIGH-INVOLVEMENT
INNOVATION REFERENCE MODEL

A.1 Research Base and Problem Statement

A key theme in the literature surrounding employee involvement in innovation is the difficulty of translating the simple concept into a sustainable set of organizational practices. Case studies and interviews with practitioners regularly highlight the difficulties in implementation and there are a number of reports of failures in programmes aimed at engendering high levels of employee involvement in what is often termed 'continuous improvement' (CI). The problem of implementation is not simple and the solutions clearly involve more than simple inputs of training or the application of proven tools and techniques.

Concern with these problems of implementation led to the establishment of a major research programme in the UK in the 1990s. The CIRCA programme has been working with a range of industrial organizations over a sustained period in what might be termed 'action research', aimed at understanding the problems in establishing and sustaining CI and in developing a methodology to support this.

A.2 Key Findings

The main conclusion from the CIRCA research is that CI can best be understood and managed if it is seen as being about behavioural routines in the organization. Introducing and sustaining CI is about creating and embedding a set of routines around systematic, focused problem finding and solving, and doing so with a wide group of people rather than just within the context of R&D or other specialist groups.

Capability—such as high-involvement innovation—can be seen as a hierarchical concept, made up of abilities, which in turn depend upon behavioural routines. For example, a virtuoso musician has the overall capability of entertaining and captivating an audience. This derives from a set of constituent abilities—for example, the ability to play the instrument technically, to interpret compositions in an emotionally rich way, to 'read' the audience and react to their responses, to entertain through gestures and on-stage behaviour, etc. Below this are some basic (but nonetheless learned) behaviours that function in relatively autonomous fashion—reading the notes on the page, making the mechanical movements to play the instrument, getting dressed for and appearing on time for the concert, etc. An important mechanism whereby these behaviours become automatic is that of practice, rehearsing every day until they become second nature.

Table A.1 lists the key abilities (sets of behavioural routines) associated with CI and their constituent behaviours.

A.3 Towards a 'Reference Model' for Continuous Improvement

Our case-study research indicated that different firms had developed these abilities to a greater or lesser extent, and this development of practice had some bearing on the likely performance improvements that they could expect. From this experience it seems that the development of CI is essentially an evolutionary process involving gradual learning and embedding of an increasing number of behavioural abilities.

This led us to postulate a staged development model which identifies particular levels of evolution of these behaviours and tries to connect them with likely performance impacts. These levels are:

Level 1. Pre-CI ('natural' or background improvement, *ad hoc* and short-term)
Level 2. Structured CI (formal attempts to create and sustain CI)
Level 3. Goal-oriented CI (CI directed at company goals and objectives)
Level 4. Proactive CI (CI largely self-driven by individuals and groups)
Level 5. CI capability (CI is the dominant culture—'the way we do things around here')

Organizations move through the levels as the CI behaviours (identified in Tables A.3 to A.10) are adopted and reinforced, and as the form a behaviour takes becomes more highly evolved. For example, at Levels 2 and 3 staff may work effectively at solving problems allocated to them by management, but at Level 4 employees would take responsibility for discovering and prioritizing, as well as solving, problems for themselves. The model is evolutionary, as opposed to additive—all the key behaviours would be present at Level 2, although in a relatively immature form; for a firm to advance to a higher level the behaviours need to evolve further.

Classifying CI evolution in these terms can help firms understand where they stand in relation to other companies and how they can develop a plan to expand their own CI abilities. Table A.2 provides an overview of the expected patterns at each stage in the model.

It is important to recognize that these represent generic 'archetypes'. Each organization's experience will be specific to it, but its development of CI capability will have to pass through these common stages. Progression from one stage to the next involves both maturing of particular routines (and their constituent behaviours) and also adding new routines to the core set.

TABLE A.1 The key abilities associated with CI.

Ability	Constituent behaviours
'Understanding CI'—the ability to articulate the basic values of CI	People at all levels demonstrate a shared belief in the value of small steps and that everyone can contribute, by themselves being actively involved in making and recognizing incremental improvements When something goes wrong, the natural reaction of people at all levels is to look for reasons why etc., rather than to blame individual(s)
'Getting the CI habit'—the ability to generate sustained involvement in CI	People make use of some formal problem finding and solving cycle People use appropriate tools and techniques to support CI People use measurement to shape the improvement process People (as individuals and/or groups) initiate and carry through CI activities—they participate in the process Closing the loop—ideas are responded to in a clearly defined and timely fashion, either implemented or otherwise dealt with
'Focusing CI'—the ability to link CI activities to the strategic goals of the company	Individuals and groups use the organization's strategic goals and objectives to focus and prioritize improvements Everyone understands (i.e. is able to explain) what the company's or department's strategy, goals and objectives are Individuals and groups (e.g. departments, CI teams) assess their proposed changes (before embarking on initial investigation and before implementing a solution) against departmental or company objectives to ensure that they are consistent with them Individuals and groups monitor/measure the results of their improvement activity and the impact it has on strategic or departmental objectives CI activities are an integral part of the individual or group's work, not a parallel activity
'Leading CI'—the ability to lead, direct and support the creation and sustaining of CI behaviours	Managers support the CI process through allocation of time, money, space and other resources Managers recognize in formal (but not necessarily financial) ways the contribution of employees to CI Managers lead by example, becoming actively involved in design and implementation of CI Managers support experiment by not punishing mistakes but by encouraging learning from them
'Aligning CI'—the ability to create consistency between CI values and behaviour and the organizational context (structures, procedures, etc.)	Ongoing assessment ensures that the organization's structure and infrastructure and the CI system consistently support and reinforce each other The individual/group responsible for designing the CI system designs it to fit within the current structure and infrastructure

(continued overleaf)

TABLE A.1 (*continued*)

Ability	Constituent behaviours
'Shared problem solving'—the ability to move CI activity across organizational boundaries	Individuals with responsibility for particular company processes/systems hold ongoing reviews to assess whether these processes/systems and the CI system remain compatible
	People with responsibility for the CI system ensure that, when a major organizational change is planned, its potential impact on the CI system is assessed and adjustments are made as necessary
	People co-operate across internal divisions (e.g. cross-functional groups) in CI as well as working in their own areas
	People understand and share a holistic view (process understanding and ownership)
	People are oriented towards internal and external customers in their CI activity
	Specific CI projects with outside agencies—customers, suppliers, etc.—are taking place
	Relevant CI activities involve representatives from different organizational levels
'Continuous improvement of continuous improvement'—the ability to strategically manage the development of CI	The CI system is continually monitored and developed; a designated individual or group monitors the CI system and measures the incidence (i.e. frequency and location) of CI activity and the results of CI activity
	There is a cyclical planning process whereby the CI system is regularly reviewed and, if necessary, amended (single-loop learning)
	There is periodic review of the CI system in relation to the organization as a whole, which may lead to a major regeneration (double-loop learning)
	Senior management make available sufficient resources (time, money, personnel) to support the ongoing development of the CI system
'The learning organization'—generating the ability to enable learning to take place and be captured at all levels	People learn from their experiences, both positive and negative
	Individuals seek out opportunities for learning/personal development (e.g. actively experiment, set their own learning objectives)
	Individuals and groups at all levels share (make available) their learning from *all* work experiences
	The organization articulates and consolidates (captures and shares) the learning of individuals and groups
	Managers accept and, where necessary, act on all the learning that takes place
	People and teams ensure that their learning is captured by making use of the mechanisms provided for doing so
	Designated individual(s) use organizational mechanisms to deploy the learning that is captured across the organization

TABLE A.2   Stages in the evolution of CI.

CI level	Characteristic behaviour patterns
Level 1—Pre-CI Interest in the concept has been triggered—by a crisis, by attendance at a seminar, by a visit to another organization, etc.—but implementation is on an *ad hoc* basis	Problems are solved randomly No formal efforts or structure for improving the organization Occasional bursts of improvement punctuated by inactivity and non-participation Solutions tend to realize short-term benefits No strategic impact on human resources, finance or other measurable targets Staff and management are unaware of CI as a process
Level 2—Structured CI There is formal commitment to building a system that will develop CI across the organization	CI or an equivalent organization improvement initiative has been introduced Staff use structured problem-solving processes A high proportion of staff participate in CI activities Staff has been trained in basic CI tools Structured idea-management system is in place Recognition system has been introduced CI activities have not been integrated into day-to-day operations
Level 3—Goal-Oriented CI There is a commitment to linking CI behaviour, established at 'local' level, to the wider strategic concerns of the organization	All the above plus: Formal deployment of strategic goals Monitoring and measuring of CI against these goals CI activities are part of main business activities Focus includes cross-boundary and even cross-enterprise problem solving
Level 4—Proactive CI There is an attempt to devolve autonomy and to empower individuals and groups to manage and direct their own processes	All the above plus: CI responsibilities devolved to problem-solving unit High levels of experimentation
Level 5—Full CI Capability Approximates to a model 'learning organization'	All the above plus: Extensive and widely distributed learning behaviour Systematic finding and solving problems and capture and sharing of learning Widespread, autonomous but controlled experimentation

A.4 Detailed Behaviour/Capability Analysis

The underpinning behaviours contributing to the key abilities and an indication of differentiating levels of performance are given in Tables A.3 to A.10.

Key Ability 1. Understanding CI

This cluster of behaviours (Table A.3) refers to how well the organization understands and shares the underlying values and beliefs about CI.

TABLE A.3   Key behaviours in understanding CI.

Key behaviours	Trigger questions	Level 1	Level 2	Level 3	Level 4	Level 5
1a. People 'live' the CI values— 'workplace innovation matters to this business', 'I can make a difference', the value of small steps, etc.	What do you think of CI? How frequently do people think about and come up with proposals for change?	Only when facilitated	From time to time on specific issues	Goal-oriented and against targets (internal)	Proactive improving	Integral part of operations = work + improvement
1b. The 'management style' reflects commitment to CI values (e.g. the belief that everyone can make a contribution) Examples might include: • Adopting a facilitating rather than directive approach • Their reaction to individuals when things go wrong • Attaching importance to smaller achievements • Not letting go of CI principles when under a lot of pressure • Providing recognition for small improvements	Are you allowed to recommend/suggest changes? Do you feel you can make a difference? Does management also contribute to improvement?	Yes, but …	Share ideas on a structured basis	Is it part of performance appraisal of managers?	It is expected—and widespread across levels and functions	It is the way we do things around here
1c. When something goes wrong the natural reaction of people at all levels is to look for reasons why etc., rather than to blame individual(s)	What is the reaction around here when something goes wrong?	Who made the mistake?	'Let's talk about it'	What is the source of the problem? Problems are formally analysed	Mistakes are seen as improvement opportunities and experiments encouraged even if they lead to problems	No-blame culture/mistakes are opportunities

Key Ability 2. Strategy Deployment

This cluster of behaviours (Table A.4) refers to how well the organization links its CI activities to the strategic mission and key performance drivers of the business.

Key Ability 3. Leading CI

This cluster of behaviours (Table A.5) refers to how well leadership at different levels in the organization supports the values and practice of CI.

Key Ability 4. Participation in CI

This cluster of behaviours (Table A.6) refers to how well people are enabled to participate proactively in CI within the organization.

Key Ability 5. Consistency in CI

This cluster of behaviours (Table A.7) refers to how good a fit there is between CI and the rest of the organization.

Key Ability 6. Cross-boundary CI

This cluster of behaviours (Table A.8) refers to how well the organization is able to extend CI activity across organizational boundaries.

Key Ability 7. Sharing and Capturing Learning

This cluster of behaviours (Table A.9) refers to how well the organization shares and captures the learning coming from CI activities.

Key Ability 8. Continuous Improvement of CI

This cluster of behaviours (Table A.10) refers to how well the organization monitors and develops its CI processes, structures and activities.

TABLE A.4   Key behaviours in strategy deployment.

Key behaviours	Trigger questions	Level 1	Level 2	Level 3	Level 4	Level 5
2a. Individuals and groups use the organization's strategic goals and objectives to focus and prioritize improvement in their activities. CI is 'in-line' rather than 'off-line'	How do you prioritize? If you have problems, how do you decide which to work on? How far do you use the company strategy to help choose which problems to work on?	No role	Some alignment but not fixed Loose view of strategy	Strategy is transformed into targets and standards which are used in prioritizing—policy deployment	Strategy integrated in all priorities	Priority process is a benchmark and a way of life
2b. Everyone understands (i.e. is able to explain) what the company's or department's strategy, goals and objectives are	Are targets for problem solving linked to the bottom line? Are they linked to daily activities? Is there a link between department activities and higher level strategy? Ownership?	Limited understanding of strategy	Understanding of strategy but not implemented continuously—'flavour of the month'	Understanding is reflected in results—people know what the strategy is and how they fit into it	People know what the strategy is and have an awareness of why these targets matter for the business	People know what and why and participate in helping to set/make strategy
2c. Individuals and groups monitor/measure the results of their improvement activity and the impact it has on strategic or departmental objectives	Visible monitoring system? How do you measure activities and their results? Impact of results on strategy?	No measurement	Measuring takes place occasionally but no interpretation or action. May be carried out by outsiders	Measurement and feedback used to drive improvements and corrective initiatives	Part of daily activities and people carry out their own measurement	Measurement culture, used as a benchmark for others

TABLE A.5   Key behaviours in leading CI.

Key behaviours	Trigger questions	Level 1*	Level 2*	Level 3*	Level 4*	Level 5*
3a. Managers at all levels display active commitment to, and leadership of, CI	Do they (management) visit your section or talk about it? Do they trigger you to think about new ways of doing things? Do they give you feedback on your CI activities?	Sometimes/ rarely	On formal occasions but not often. Not all managers do this	Frequently and most managers do it—it is part of their job.	As 3 but proactively—they are 'champions of CI'	It is the way we do things round here—all managers, all levels believe in and promote CI
3b. Managers give their time to CI-related activities (e.g. as members of an improvement team, delivery of CI training, incorporating CI into business plans, leading local initiatives, recognizing and acknowledging people's contribution, etc.)	Are they involved in problem solving or part of focus groups? Does CI form part of their formal budgeting process—do they set targets and allocate resources to it?	Sometimes	On formal occasions but not all of them—pockets of support	All of them, most of the time—it is part of their job and they are judged on it	Actively support CI, formally and informally	Managers seen as part of the group and participate and help others to participate in CI
3c. Managers encourage their people to take part in CI activities (e.g. as facilitators, CI team members), for example by allowing them time to do so, recognizing people's involvement (ongoing, at appraisals).	Do they lead by example, by getting involved in CI? Do they take time off or allow others to do so to carry out CI activities?	Occasionally	Some of them, regularly (once a month)	Most of them, most of the time	Everybody in company, formally and informally	People act automatically on CI and do not wait for management formal backing

*All of these scales refer to how many managers do these things and how frequently.

TABLE A.6 Key behaviours in participation in CI.

Key behaviours	Trigger questions	Level 1	Level 2	Level 3	Level 4	Level 5
4a. Individuals and groups use a problem-solving/improvement opportunity-finding cycle	How do you solve problems round here?	No formal cycle but people may use problem lists and informal approaches	Problem-solving cycle exists and people have been trained in using it	Problem-solving cycle used regularly to work on problems focused on key drivers	People automatically use the cycle to tackle problems—it is the way we do things round here. Closing the loop in terms of measurement and implementation	Problem-solving approaches adapted to suit different problems and circumstances—flexible problem solving
4b. Individuals and groups draw on a wide range of appropriate tools and techniques including process measurement to assist with CI activity	Do you use problem-solving tools? Can you list/tell us about the ones you use?	People are aware of tools but not trained in their use	People are trained in basic cycle and tools	People use a cycle and a toolbox of different aids to help them	As 3 but people do not need facilitation—can support themselves	Anyone in the team can coach/train others in problem solving
4c. There are 'vehicles'—problem-solving teams, idea schemes, etc., which enable individuals and groups, at all levels, to initiate CI activities and carry them through to completion	If you want to change/improve something what do you do?	No formal approaches or mechanisms	Use of formal approach based on one major approach—e.g. teams	Use of teams working on strategic problems, which may go beyond section to department or mine level. May use multiple approaches—e.g. teams plus individual mechanisms	Skilled teams and other mechanisms involved—for example, *ad hoc* project teams for bigger problems	*Ad hoc* teams and other mechanisms used to extend range of CI capability—'horses for courses'

TABLE A.7 Key behaviours in consistency in CI.

Key behaviours	Trigger questions	Level 1	Level 2	Level 3	Level 4	Level 5
5a. The CI system fits within the current structure and infrastructure of the organization (e.g. in selecting the type of CI vehicle that is most appropriate to the work organization)	How well does CI fit into the day-to-day operations and structures of the company? Is CI a special extra thing or part of the overall way the company works?	No fit—CI is an add-on extra	Some fit at local level but still seen as something different	Formally linked—CI is in line with the day-to-day work of the business People are expected to do it, time and resources are allocated for it, benefits which come from it are shared, etc.	As 3, and people are enabled and encouraged to change their ways of working to allow for development of CI	CI is at the heart of our way of doing things around here
5b. Individuals with responsibility for particular company processes/systems (e.g. the reward system, the personal development process, the production process) hold ongoing reviews to assess whether these processes/systems and the CI system remain compatible, and take action as necessary.	Do the systems in the company make it easy for you to carry out CI as part of your daily working life? If so, where? If not, where and why not?	No links, systems often conflict with CI	Some links but also some conflicts—e.g. reward system	Formally linked—CI is in line with the day-to-day work of the business People are expected to do it, time and resources are allocated for it, benefits which come from it are shared	As 3, and people are enabled and encouraged to change their ways of working to allow for development of CI	CI is at the heart of our way of doing things around here
5c. Person(s) with responsibility for the CI system ensure that, when a major organizational change is planned, its potential impact on the CI system is assessed and adjustments are made as necessary.	When big changes happen, is the CI system changed as well or is it something which is set in stone and does not change?	No links	Sometimes considered, usually as an afterthought	Formal links in process of change planning and implementation	Designed in at the outset as a way of making changes happen and develop	CI is a way of ensuring constant change capability

TABLE A.8 Key behaviours in cross-boundary CI.

Key behaviours	Trigger questions	Level 1	Level 2	Level 3	Level 4	Level 5
6a. People at all levels carry out CI activities—e.g. joint problem-solving teams—effectively across internal (vertical and lateral) and external divisions (e.g. with customers or suppliers)	Who does CI? Is any of it done across departments? Who takes ownership? Is CI done over external borders—e.g. with suppliers?	No cross-boundary working	Informal network	Formal structure/cross-boundary teams	Active CI across multiple boundaries	No boundaries—CI extends across the real and 'virtual/extended' organization
6b. Everyone shares a holistic view of the organization (common goals) and has a good understanding of what other departments/functions do	Do you know what other departments are doing? Do you know how you impact on their performance? Do you trust other departments?	Unhealthy competition No focus on shared concerns	Understand impact on others, but still work in silos	Co-operation is enforced through formal structures	Co-operation is natural—people see the value of improved effectiveness through working together on common problems	Shared goals more important than competition
6c. People at all levels co-operate and work effectively across internal boundaries (e.g. between departments, functions, divisions)	Do you work with other departments?	No cross-boundary working	Informal participation	Formal participation—action teams, problem-solving teams, etc.	Natural phenomenon—formal and informal co-operation	Significant ability to work across boundaries

TABLE A.9   Key behaviours in sharing and capturing learning.

Key behaviours	Trigger questions	Level 1	Level 2	Level 3	Level 4	Level 5
7a. Everyone learns from their experiences, both positive and negative (i.e. they do not repeat actions that gave rise to a negative experience; they build on/repeat actions that resulted in positive outcomes)	Are you frequently involved in reviews of completed task/projects (post-mortems) to identify problems and corrective actions/learning points?	Only on an *ad hoc* basis	Frequently, but informal discussions only	Formal forums with action plans which lead to changes—e.g. in standard operating procedures and performance indicators etc. and generate post-project reports	Happens automatically and leads to implementation of changes in process and standards	Consistent learning
7b. Individuals and groups at all levels share their learning from CI activities, both positive and negative (They do this formally and informally—e.g. participate openly in development project reviews, feed into the organization learning/insights acquired from outside the organization, do not try to hide negative experiences, talk to colleagues)	Do you discuss your problems and solutions with other: • People • Departments • Centres	*Ad hoc* or by accident Some use of different reporting/sharing mechanisms—e.g. reports, presentations, storyboards	Section or mine—internally and formally Use of multiple mechanisms	Company-wide focused interest groups Use of multiple mechanisms	Best-practice forums over hierarchical boundaries	Internet Intranet Setting new standards Distance learning
7c. Individuals are enabled to seek out opportunities for learning/personal development (e.g. actively experiment, set their own learning objectives)	Does the company give you opportunities to develop yourself and your skills? How? How else could they do it?	No formal training/development opportunities	Limited to task-related skills	Training and development to enable strategic problem solving	High commitment to training and development Individual training needs assessment and individuals contribute to identifying their needs	Everyone in the organization is encouraged and enabled to be an active learner

TABLE A.10 Key behaviours in continuous improvement of CI.

Key behaviours	Trigger questions	Level 1	Level 2	Level 3	Level 4	Level 5
8a. Designated individual or group monitors the CI system and measures the incidence (i.e. frequency and location) of CI activity and the results of CI activity	Does anyone look after CI in this company—reviewing it and trying to improve the way it works? Who and how? Does anyone monitor the CI activities you do and the results they bring?	No-one responsible, CI not monitored or measured	Someone is responsible and monitoring takes place of activity but not necessarily of impact	Someone responsible and monitoring how well the systems works and the ways in which CI affects the business drivers/bottom line	Work teams monitor and measure their own CI activities and link to a site or company CI steering/support team	Self management of CI—everyone involved in developing CI systems
8b. Designated individual or group follows a cyclical planning process whereby (a) the CI system is regularly reviewed and, if necessary, amended (single-loop learning) and (b) there is periodic review of the CI system in relation to the organization as a whole, which may lead to a major regeneration (double-loop learning)	Has the way you solve problems or carry out other kinds of CI activity ever changed? Do you think the way you do CI is the 'best way'?	No review of CI process or system	Review process takes place regularly but *ad hoc* framework	Review takes place regularly using consistent framework and results are used to improve aspects of CI system—e.g. further inputs of training	CI improved continuously not only by CI support team (looking to manage and develop on a company/site-wide basis) but also by individual CI teams themselves outside of formal review process	CI improved on a do-better basis but also occasionally the whole system is reset to a higher level of maturity
8c. Senior management make available sufficient resources (time, money, personnel) to support the ongoing development of the CI system	What changes have been made to CI systems in the company lately? Who and what helped you do CI better?	No changes to the way we do CI	Limited resources provided to review CI—time, money, people	Senior management allow changes to CI and support regular internal and external reviews	People are trusted to develop and change their CI process—'unlimited resources'	Continuous improvement of CI by everyone involved in the CI system

INDEX